POWER AT PLAY

MEN AND MASCULINITY
Series Editor: Michael S. Kimmel

BEACON PRESS · BOSTON

POWER AT PLAY

Sports and the Problem of
Masculinity

Michael A. Messner

Beacon Press
25 Beacon Street
Boston, Massachusetts 02108-2892

Beacon Press books
are published under the auspices of
the Unitarian Universalist Association of Congregations.

99 98 97 96 95 94   8 7 6 5 4 3 2

Text design by Dan Ochsner

Library of Congress Cataloging-in-Publication Data

Messner, Michael A.
    Power at play : sports and the problem of masculinity / Michael A.
Messner.
        p. cm.—(Men and masculinity)
    Includes bibliographical references (p.   ) and index.
    ISBN 0-8070-4104-1 (cloth)
    ISBN 0-8070-4105-X (paper)
    1. Sports—Psychological aspects.   2. Sports—Social aspects.
3. Masculinity (Psychology)   4. Identity (Psychology)   5. Sex role.
I. Title.   II. Series
GV706.4.M47   1992
796´.0194—dc20   91-28600

For my father and my coach,
Russell John Messner, Jr.
1920–1977

Contents

Acknowledgments

Over the years that I worked on this book, I was encouraged and supported by a number of people. First and foremost, I would like to acknowledge the thirty men who took the time to tell me their stories. I am very grateful for their willingness to share their thoughts and feelings about their boyhoods, their athletic careers, their fears, defeats, and victories, their friendships and family relationships, and their future hopes and dreams. This book would not have been possible without their generous contributions. Though I have no doubt that some of these men will disagree with some of my sociological interpretations of their lives, I have done my best to portray their words and their lives to the reader accurately and respectfully.

In its earliest stage, this research formed the basis of my doctoral dissertation in the Department of Sociology at the University of California, Berkeley. I am grateful to my Ph.D. Committee members John Hurst and Harry Edwards for the help they gave me. I would especially like to thank Bob Blauner for his intellectual contributions to my understanding of masculinity, and for his moral support as I researched and wrote the dissertation. I was also aided in the early stages of the research by David Meggyesy of the NFL Players Association and by Tom Cordova of the Oakland A's. Bob Dunn, Stan Eitzen, Michael Kimmel, Don Sabo, and Pierrette Hondagneu-Sotelo all provided helpful feedback on early versions of the work. Terry Messner, Muffy, Anita Messner-Voth, Melinda Rios, and Bill Solomon provided friendship and support.

As I began to shape the dissertation into a book, I benefited from the helpful comments and criticisms of Maxine Baca Zinn, Lois Banner, Harry Brod, Bob Dunn, Mary Duquin, Stan Eitzen, Juan Gonzales, Carol Jacklin, Jon Miller, Ed Ransford, Barrie Thorne, Charles Varni, Carol Warren, and Walter Williams. The final version of the manuscript was greatly enhanced by comments and suggestions from Bob Connell, Nancy Theberge, and from my editor at Beacon Press, Lauren Bryant.

During the earlier stages of this project, I worked as a lecturer in the Department of Sociology and Social Services at California State University, Hayward. Since 1987, I have been assistant professor of Sociology and the Study of Women and Men in Society at the University of Southern California. I am grateful to colleagues and students at these two institutions for their encouragement and intellectual stimulation.

I would especially like to thank Michael Kimmel, who has seen this project through from start to finish and has always offered supportive criticisms, useful advice, and warm friendship. Don Sabo has also been an extremely helpful intellectual guide over the years. Don is the pioneer in applying feminist perspectives to the study of masculinity and sport. His work has inspired me, his friendship has nurtured me, and his comments and suggestions, at various stages of my work, have guided me.

More than anyone else, Pierrette Hondagneu-Sotelo has lived with this project. Though she does not like sports, she has always been a "good sport" about my work. I am ever grateful for her intellectual and editorial contributions, her willingness to listen to my seemingly endless monologues about "the book," and especially for her loving support. Our son, Miles Hondagneu-Messner was born in time to contribute immeasurable joy (and a bit of stress) during the final revisions of this work. The completion of this project would be far less fulfilling if I did not have Pierrette and Miles to share it with.

Finally, this book is dedicated to my father, who was also my high school basketball coach. Measured by conventional standards of wins, losses, and championships, he was a "successful" coach. But toward the end of his coaching career, in the late 1960s and into the 1970s, he was increasingly disturbed at how the "winning is everything" ethic was permeating sport from the professional levels down to Little League baseball. He continued to insist that winning *isn't* everything, that what's most important is "how you play the game," what kind of a person you are, and how you treat other people. My father was a conservative, both in terms of his general political philosophy, and in terms of his conceptions of men's and women's "proper roles" in society. Thus I suspect that were my father still alive, he would, like some of the men I interviewed for this project, disagree with some of the critical and feminist perspectives on sport which I develop in this book. Ironically though, it was his highly principled coaching philosophy—indeed, his stubborn integrity in the face of what he saw to be the deterioration of sport—that first led me to think critically about the dominant value system of U.S. sport. I will be forever grateful to him for that, and for much more.

Michael A. Messner
May 1991

Introduction

I turned ten in 1962. Willie Mays and my Giants won the National League Pennant and I was developing a pretty deadly shot in basketball, though I was troubled by my inability to hit the fastball in Little League. Already, sport was *everything* to me. I was virtually being raised in the fraternal environs of the locker room. My heroes, the basketball players at Salinas (California) High School, where my father was the coach, seemed larger than life to me. During games or practices, in the locker room or in the bus, I observed and scrutinized my idols (and my father) carefully, and I attempted to mimic more than just their bounce passes and jump shots.

But throughout grammar school, the best athlete in my classes never got to play with us. She was a girl. Somehow we boys all knew that she was the fastest runner, could hit a baseball further than any of us, yet we never had to confront that reality directly. Our teachers, by enforcing strict sex segregation on the playground, protected our fragile male egos from the humiliation that presumably would result from losing to a girl. In that prefeminist era, insulated within the all-male world of athletics, our attitudes and values about the "natural" differences between males and females developed and solidified virtually unchallenged. Athletic girls such as our talented classmate were rare: at best, they were marginalized and ignored; at worst, they were ridiculed and dismissed as "sex deviants."

As a result, for my male peers and for me, athletic competition was an unambiguously male world. It was this world of athletic competition that provided us with the major social context in which we developed relationships with each other, and in which we shaped our own identities and self-images. Things like school and dinner and sleeping seemed only to get in the way of what we all really wanted to do, which was to play sports—football, basketball, baseball, and back to football again. The rhythms and contours of our activities together were governed as much by the changing athletic seasons as by anything else.

And we dreamed . . . dreamed of becoming professional athletes with the San Francisco Giants, Warriors, or Forty-Niners. My dream-

1

ing—of being the hero, always modest in the face of the overwhelming adoration of millions of fans—was largely a private affair. I spent untold hours alone, on weekends and after school, shooting baskets on the driveway and imagining, *planning,* my future stardom. Always, in my imagination, I made the crucial winning shot. Always I did the impossible, coming through in the clutch, to be mobbed afterward by frenzied teammates, fans, and of course, girls.

The reality was somewhat different. I did play high school basketball on my father's team, and I did have my fleeting moment of heroism: One night I sank a long, pressure-packed shot to win the game in the final seconds. My years of practice and visualization had paid off in that single zenlike moment: I can still feel the perfection of that shot—ball, hand, and basket all one. But my moment in the limelight was all too brief. I was not the great player I had planned on being. I was too small to be a good forward, too slow to be a good guard. But I was adequate: I was the starting point guard and I scored about ten points a game on a .500 team. Given my dreams and expectations, though, I considered this a miserable failure.

My first year of college, 1971, I sat the bench on a good community college team and faced up to a grim reality: No call was forthcoming from the Warriors. Indeed, I wasn't even going to make it as a college athlete. I took a bit of a tumble over that. I had always been "Mike Messner-the-basketball-player," at least in my own mind. Now, at the age of twenty, who was I?

By the early 1980s, the athletic success and failure and disengagement from sport that had been, for me, intensely personal experiences became fascinating sociological questions. Why was it that I, and so many thousands of other boys and young men, became so intensely committed to athletic careers? How and why did our developing identities become so closely intertwined with our successes—or failures—as athletes? How had our athletic careers shaped, expanded, or constrained our relationships with other boys and men, and with girls and women? What effect had our athletic careers had on our personalities, our health (both emotional and physical), and on the ways that we relate to others as competitors in public life, as friends, as lovers, as family?

Increasingly, I saw "the social construction of masculinity" as being the most interesting and useful lens through which to examine these questions. What led me to reconceptualize the athletic experience of

myself and of other males in terms of masculinity? I might explain my
shift in conceptual orientation by way of analogy: After graduating
from high school, I took a summer car trip with a friend. This was
1970, a year that followed several years of intense racial politics and
strife in the United States, so when we found ourselves talking with an
elderly white man in a small town in Oregon, we asked him if there had
been any racial problems there recently. He replied instantly: "Oh, we
had a couple Indians here a few years back, but we ran them off. Nope.
No racial problems in this town." Until very recently, a question asked
about the existence of "gender problems" in sport would likely have
been answered similarly. Men have been so thoroughly dominant, so
much in the foreground of organized sport, that their experiences in
sport *as men* have been obscured. So why look at sport in terms of gender, and why now? The major reason is that girls' and women's recent
movement into sport has created a new standpoint through which to
view males' experiences in this traditionally masculine institution. Just
as the old man was insulated from thinking that his town (indeed, *he*)
had a "racial problem" so long as his town consisted entirely of white
people, so, too, men in organized sport have ignored gender issues so
long as sport has remained essentially a homosocial institution.

Ignoring "the gender issue" in sport is no longer possible. Along
with women's steady movement into the labor force after World War II,
what had been from the 1930s through the 1960s a quiet undercurrent
of female athleticism suddenly swelled into a torrent of female athletic
participation and demands for equity. In the United States, the 1972
passage of Title IX gave women a legal basis from which to push for
greater equity in high school and college athletics. As a result, athletic
participation of school-age girls increased dramatically. In 1971, only
294,015 girls participated in high school sport, compared with
3,666,917 boys. By the 1989–90 academic year, there were 1,858,659
girls participating in high school sport, compared with 3,398,192
boys.[1] Increased numerical participation by girls has been accompanied
by changing attitudes as well. A recent national survey found large ma-
jorities of parents and children agreeing that "sports are no longer for
boys only."[2]

With increases in opportunities for female athletes, including expanded youth programs, better and earlier coaching, and increases in
scholarships for college women athletes, some dramatic improvements
in female athletic performance have resulted. In fact, a number of com-

mentators have noted that the "muscle gap"—the degree of difference between male and female athletic performance in "measurable" sports like swimming and track and field—has closed considerably in recent years.[3]

These increases in participation, improvements in athletic performance, and changing attitudes concerning females and sport do not, however, signal an unambiguously progressive movement forward for women's athletics. Ironically, as women attempted to move out of the athletic ghetto and into the mainstream of U.S. sport in the 1970s and 1980s, actual control of women's athletic teams and organizations rapidly shifted from female to male hands.[4] And the Reagan administration all but gutted the enforcement mechanisms of Title IX, leading to considerable backsliding in movements toward equity in women's sport in the 1980s. As a result, gross inequities persist: Only one dollar in five of financial aid based on athletic ability is awarded to a woman; only 31 percent of 1985–86 NCAA participants were female; salaries for female coaches and athletic directors (who are declining in number) are well below salaries of their male counterparts.[5]

Despite these persistent institutional inequities, increasing female athleticism has challenged the assumption that sport is and should be a male world. Organized sport, though still dominated by men at nearly all levels, has in the past two decades become a contested terrain in terms of gender relations: an eleven-year-old girl goes to court for the right to play Little League baseball; a high school girl and her family fight coaches and school boards for her right to try out for quarterback of the football team; groups such as the National Organization for Women and the Women's Sports Foundation lobby public officials for enforcement of Title IX; professional women athletes break sex barriers in race car driving, jockeying, and even with the famed Harlem Globetrotters; women journalists fight for the right to work on the sports desk and to enter the locker room.

Women's movement into the world of sport has also inspired a new feminist scholarship on sport. Since women's athletics had been so thoroughly ignored by social scientists and historians of sport, the first feminist sport scholars in the 1970s and early 1980s put the majority of their efforts into uncovering and illuminating these realities. But this corrective approach tended to leave men's relationship to sport unexamined, as the unquestioned norm, while women and sport became "the gender issue." As a result, in the rapidly growing sociology of sport literature—both feminist and nonfeminist—masculinity was largely taken for granted and ignored.[6] Even radical critics of sport, such as Paul Hoch and Harry Edwards, tended to ignore gender or at best to ghettoize it as a "women's issue" that was generally subordinated to class or race analysis. It could be said that while women athletes were obscured by being too far in the background, men athletes could not be seen clearly for being too much in the foreground.[7]

In roughly the same time period that sport sociology was developing, a separate literature on men and masculinity, inspired by feminist scholarship, was emerging. This early "men's studies" literature, for the most part, ignored sport as a focus of inquiry.[8] The early 1980s saw the first attempts by researchers to focus on the masculinity/sport relationship. Most notable among these early works was Sabo and Runfola's groundbreaking anthology *Jock: Sports and Male Identity,* which represented an important departure from the analyses presented both by the radical critics, who tended to collapse gender issues into a race or class dynamic, and by the men's liberationists, who tended to focus on the "costs" of narrow definitions of masculinity *to men*, while downplaying or ignoring how sport fit into the construction and legitimation of male privilege.

These early attempts to develop a feminist analysis of masculinity and sport were impeded by the lack of any sophisticated theoretical conceptualization of masculinity. But by the late 1980s, there existed a critical mass of theory and research on men and masculinity.[9] Soon, the development of feminist scholarship on men was reflected in a small, but growing genre of feminist studies on men, sport, and masculinity.[10] This book seeks to contribute to this emergent genre by exploring the development and changes in masculine identity in the lives of thirty male former athletes whom I interviewed.

My own experiences as a former athlete and as a coach and referee of youth and adult sport serve as a valuable point of departure for this analysis. These experiences gave me a privileged entrée to the masculine world of sport. As a former athlete, I carry an enduring love for the beauty of sport, as well as the knowledge of the pressures, pain, and frustrations that athletes often endure. This knowledge helped me in interviewing men who are former athletes, and aided me in interpreting the meanings of what these men say about their lives.

But though my experiences in sport can be seen as a necessary basis for this study, they clearly are not sufficient for the kind of analysis of masculinity and sport that I develop here. The idea to analyze the social construction of masculinity in sport did not come through personal experience; rather, I am able to view my own experience of masculinity and sport (and the interviews with male athletes that make up the empirical basis of this book) in new (and I think, ultimately, more accurate) ways only through the theoretical standpoints of sport studies scholars who have come before me. In particular, if it were not for the intellectual and political terrain opened up by feminist scholars of the past fifteen years or so, I am convinced that I would not be writing a book concerned with illuminating the relationship between masculinity and sport. In fact, the subject would probably never have crossed my mind.

1 : Sport, Men, and Gender

> *Perhaps we give athletics too much prominence, but it is the fault of the age. The end of the century is an era of rampant athleticism. But these contests play their part in making sturdy citizens, and training men in the invaluable qualities of loyalty, self-sacrifice, obedience and temperance.*
>
> —EDITORIAL IN *WESLEYAN UNIVERSITY BULLETIN*, November 1895

As I began my research for this book, I explained to one of my first interviewees that I was "pursuing an understanding of the lives of ex-athletes." He winced. When I inquired about his reaction, he replied, "I'm *not* an *ex*-athlete. Just because my career is over, doesn't mean I'm no longer an athlete." His statement only begins to give us an appreciation of the depth of identification that many men develop with their roles as athletes; it's almost as though by calling him an "ex-athlete," I had called him an "ex-man."

How do we explain such intense commitment among boys and young men to their roles as athletes? Ray Raphael has argued that modern societies lack the masculine initiation rituals which so often characterize tribal societies. As a result, he argues, today's men are confused about what it means to be a man, and they find in athletics an inadequate, but nevertheless extremely salient, substitute for such initiation rituals. On the surface, Raphael's thesis is compelling. Clearly, the question of masculinity must be central to understanding American men's relationships to sport. Sport participation does offer young males a way into a world of masculine values, rituals, and relationships. But Raphael assumes that all young males "need" to be separated from females and introduced by adult males into a masculine world. If this does not happen, he argues, men become confused. Thus, in modern societies, institutions such as sport, fraternities, and even the military become important to men because they offer "reasonable facsimiles" of ancient initiation rituals.[1]

My approach to the lives of male athletes differs from Raphael's. I begin with two assumptions. First, sport is not an expression of some biological human need; it is a social institution.[2] Like other institutions, such as the economy, politics, and the family, the structure and values of sport emerge and change historically, largely as a result of struggles for power between groups of people. Second, rather than defining masculinity as some buried biological "essence of manhood," I maintain that it too is socially constructed, and thus that masculine identity tends to vary historically and cross-culturally. As over two decades of feminist social-scientific research has shown, one's sex may be male or female, but one's gender identity is developed through a complex process of interaction with culture.[3] My aim in this book is to develop an understanding of the relationship between the development of masculine identities and the structure of sport as a social institution. Thus, rather than comparing men's current involvements in sport with idealized masculine initiation rites in tribal societies, I examine the lives of male athletes in terms of what C. Wright Mills called the relationship between "biography and history," between "personality and social structure," with the aim of exploring and interpreting the meanings that males themselves attribute to their participation in athletic careers.[4]

Between 1983 and 1985, I conducted interviews with thirty male former athletes. Most of the men I interviewed had been involved in the U.S. "major sports"—football, basketball, baseball, track. All had at some time in their lives based their identities largely on their roles as athletes and could therefore be said to have had "athletic careers." Twelve had played organized sport through high school, eleven through college, and seven had been professional athletes. At the time of the interviews, most had been retired from playing organized sport for at least five years. Their ages ranged from twenty-one to forty-eight, with the median, thirty-three. (For more detailed information on the individuals I interviewed, see appendix 1.)

In collecting what amounted to life histories of these men, my purpose was to discover how masculine gender identities develop and change as boys and men interact with the socially constructed world of organized sport.[5] During our interviews, which were semistructured and took from one and one-half to six hours to conduct, I asked each man to talk about four broad eras in his life: his earliest experiences with sport in boyhood, his athletic career, retirement or disengagement from his athletic career, and life after his athletic career. I focused on the meanings of "success and failure," and on the man's relationships with family, with other males, with women, and with his own body. (For more information on how I selected my sample, and for a discussion of the process of interviewing these men, see appendix 2.)

I had two aims in collecting and analyzing the interview data. First, I wanted to be able to draw some generalizations about the relationship between masculinity and sport, about the motivations, experiences, feelings, and problems that male athletes share. But I was also concerned with sorting out some of the variations among boys and men, based on class and racial inequalities, that led them to relate differently to athletic careers. I divided the athletes into two comparison groups based on social class of origin. The first group comprised ten men from middle-class backgrounds (nine of whom were white, one black). The second group, which I refer to as lower class, comprised twenty men from poor and working-class backgrounds (thirteen of whom were black, two Latino, and five white). (See appendix 3 for group data on class and race, as well as a more in-depth discussion of my decision to utilize a class analysis in this book.)

SPORT AS A SOCIAL INSTITUTION

For most people, "the sportsworld" is an escape from the pressures and problems of everyday life. For decades, this perspective led to a dearth of social scientific studies of sport, which in turn reinforced the perception of sport as the realm of the "natural," separate from society. But research over the past two decades has shown convincingly that sport is indeed a social institution.[6] As sociologists began to argue in the 1970s, the perception that sport is separate from the rest of society masks the

fact that the values and structure of sport have always been closely intertwined with dominant social values, power relations, and conflicts
between groups and between nations.[7]

Historical analyses of sport reveal that ruling groups have shaped and
utilized sport to maintain control, but subordinate groups at times have
also used sport to contest that control. For instance, historian J. A.
Mangan has demonstrated that in the late nineteenth and early twentieth centuries, the British consciously developed sport in their public
schools as a means of preparing boys to one day administer the Empire.[8] Team sports, based as they were on the twin values of dominance
over others and deference to the authority of leaders, were valued as a
means to inculcate "initiative and self-reliance," along with "loyalty and
obedience." In short, the British promoted, developed, and used sport
to socialize boys to a certain kind of "manliness" whose raison d'etre
was the administration of domination over (mostly nonwhite) colonized
peoples. A leading advocate of the virtues and merits of sport was the
Reverend J. E. C. Welldon, headmaster of Harrow school from 1881
to 1895:

> The pluck, the energy, the perseverance, the good temper, the self con-
> trol, the discipline, the co-operation, the espirit de corps, which merit
> success in cricket or football, are the very qualities which win the day
> in peace or war. The men who possessed these qualities, not sedate or
> faultless citizens, but men of will, spirit, and chivalry, are the men who
> conquered at Plassey and Quebec. In the history of the British Empire
> it is written that England has owed her sovereignty to her sports.[9]

The British upper classes did not create sport from thin air. Organized play, folk games, and community-organized sporting events had
existed for centuries. Rather, the upper classes appropriated existing
sports and then shaped the structure, rules, values, and meanings of
sport in ways that supported and furthered their own interests. As
Mangan points out, the British eventually extended their schooling system, along with sports such as cricket, to the middle classes of the colonized nations in hopes that these middle classes would adopt British
morality, ethics, and values and thus help to solidify colonial control.
But despite the intentions of the British elite, sport did not always function in ways that unambiguously supported colonial domination. Historian and social analyst C. L. R. James, in his brilliant book on
cricket in the colonial West Indies of the 1920s and 1930s, shows that

the British sporting ethic tended to cut both ways. On the one hand, public schools—and especially cricket—taught middle-class mulatto (mixed race) West Indian boys and young men the values of "Puritanism" and "moral restraint," as well as the "general superiority of British culture." As a result, many West Indian males, like James, had "British tradition soaked deep into [them]."[10] But since teams were strictly segregated by race as well as by nationality (British vs. colonized), the game provided a context in which the contradictions of racism and colonial domination were revealed for all to see. As James wrote of his experience as a cricket player and a sport journalist in the 1930s, "My Puritan soul burnt with indignation at the injustice in the sphere of sport. . . . Cricket had plunged me into politics long before I was aware of it."[11] With the contradictions of colonial domination laid bare, the cricket field often became "a stage on which selected individuals played representative roles which were charged with social significance."[12] In effect, cricket matches became important arenas for symbolic resistance against racism and against British domination.

As in Britain, sport in the United States (as we now know it) originated in the nineteenth century mostly with upper- and middle-class whites who were concerned with "building character" in an expanding entrepreneurial environment. Blue-collar workers and people of color were largely denied access to major sporting institutions. By the turn of the century, historians have argued, the expansion of organized sport into widespread "recreation for the masses" was seen by the upper classes as a means of integrating immigrants and the growing industrial working class into an expanding capitalist order where work was becoming routinized and leisure time was increasing.[13] Though the extension of sport to workers and blacks was viewed by elites as a means of control, underprivileged and oppressed groups eventually learned to utilize sport for self-expression, and—especially for blacks in the twentieth century—as a means to attain status and mobility in an otherwise limited structure of opportunity.

With sport participation extended to the lower classes and to people of color in the twentieth century, the sporting arena often became a contested terrain of social meanings. For instance, when Jack Johnson, a black man, defeated Jim Jeffries, a white man, for the world heavyweight boxing championship in 1910, many blacks saw this as a symbolic victory against racism. Some whites responded to this threat by rioting and attacking blacks in many towns and cities. Newspaper reporters, who had predicted that Johnson would lose because blacks were so "obviously inferior" to whites, scrambled to put a new, but equally racist, spin on the story. As one writer put it, "[Johnson] has demonstrated that his race has acquired full stature as men. Whether they will ever breed brains to match his muscle is yet to be proven."[14]

When Paul Robeson became the first black football player at Rutgers University in 1915, and the first black to win football All America honors, he was physically abused on the field by white players, verbally abused from the stands, and constantly subjected to racist diatribes in the press. When Jackie Robinson and others broke the color bar in major league baseball in the 1940s, similar antagonisms emerged. Still today, many whites await the "Great White Hope" who will win the heavyweight boxing crown, while many blacks take pride in the accomplishment of blacks in basketball and other sports. Meanwhile, the U.S. media still appear to be preoccupied with interpreting the meaning of "black domination" of certain sports.[15] Clearly, sport continues to provide an institutional context in which racial and class antagonisms are played out. One former athlete I interviewed spoke of an experience he had in the mid-1970s in his small, Midwest town:

> Our town had two high schools. Ours was mostly the poor and blue-collar workers, and the rich kids all went to Northside. They always beat us in sports, but my senior year we had a good basketball team and we hoped we could beat Northside. Well, by the middle of the first half, our team was just totally dominating them—it was amazing—and the crowd on our side did this cheer: "IN YOUR FACE, NORTHSIDE!" After a couple of minutes, the Northside crowd yelled back: "THAT'S ALRIGHT, THAT'S OKAY, YOU'LL BE WORKING FOR US SOME DAY!"

These examples from Britain and the United States illustrate an important point about sport as a social institution: The structure and values of sport are largely shaped by, and in the interests of, those who hold power. But as Canadian sociologist Richard Gruneau has pointed out, the control and domination of ruling groups is never total, never a finished product.[16] Power is not simply a top-down, one-way process in which dominant groups assert and enforce their rules, values, and beliefs over dominated groups. Rather, power is a process in which dominated groups may partially accept, but also attempt to redefine, negotiate, or even reject, the ruling group's rules, values, and meanings.

People have the ability to recognize injustice and to use sport as a means to resist (at least symbolically) the domination imposed upon them. Sport must thus be viewed as an institution through which domination is not only imposed, but also contested; an institution within which power is constantly at play.

SPORT, POWER, AND GENDER RELATIONS

The recognition that sport is an institution in which colonial, class, and racial power relations are played out is important. But feminist historians and sociologists of the 1970s and 1980s pointed to another fact that, in its apparent obviousness, had been largely ignored: The struggles over power and meanings within sport have been struggles fought almost exclusively between men. The divide between men and women in sport is much wider, much more fundamental and sharply defined, than the divide between men of different nationalities, social classes, and races.

Feminist scholars such as Helen Lenskyj and Stephanie Twin have argued that although class and racial dynamics are important, we cannot fully understand why and how the modern institution of sport developed without an analysis of the changing relations between women and men.[17] Sociologist R. W. Connell has written that at times, gender relations in society are relatively stable, their dominant meanings more "naturalized," and thus less subject to question. At other times, especially when socioeconomic changes undermine existing definitions of gender, and particularly if these changes are accompanied by organized feminist movements, the dominant structures and ideologies of gender relations are more subject to contest, crisis, and change.[18] As historian Peter Filene has pointed out, the late nineteenth and early twentieth century was one such period in the United States, when the forces of modernization, urbanization, and an active women's movement combined to bring about what Filene calls a "crisis of masculinity."[19]

Crisis in Gender Relations and the Rise of Sport

The transformation of the United States from a largely farm and small business economy to urban, industrial capitalism both bolstered and undermined the social basis of men's power over women. On the one hand, the creation of separate (public/domestic) and unequal spheres of life for men and women created a new foundation for masculine power and privilege, especially to the extent that men increasingly came to control the family wage.[20] But the separation of wage labor from the home also brought about a dramatic decline in the amount of time that most men spent with their families. As a result, boys were more and more often raised and socialized by women in the home and in public schools. As historian E. A. Rotundo has written, by the late nineteenth century, "motherhood was advancing, fatherhood was in retreat . . . women were teaching boys to be men."[21] Moreover, in an era of wage labor and increasingly concentrated ownership of productive property, fewer males owned their own businesses and farms or controlled their own labor. Sociologist Andrew Tolson argues that since wage earners are always subject to being fired or laid off, the breadwinner role provided a less secure foundation upon which to base masculine privilege than the preindustrial system of property ownership passed on from father to son.[22]

With no frontier to conquer, with physical strength becoming less relevant in work, and with urban boys being raised and taught by women, it was feared that males were becoming "soft," that society itself was becoming "feminized." Many men responded to these fears with a defensive insecurity which manifested itself in the creation of new organizations such as the Boy Scouts of America (founded in 1910) as a separate cultural sphere of life where "true manliness" could be instilled in boys by men. The rapid rise and expansion of organized sport during this same era can similarly be interpreted as the creation of a homosocial institution which served to counter men's fears of feminization in the new industrial society.[23]

But it was more than simply modernization and changes in the organization of men's work that led to a crisis in gender relations. The late nineteenth and early twentieth centuries were also characterized by dramatic cultural and political changes among American women. An active and vibrant women's movement began to challenge men's institutional power. As historian Carroll Smith-Rosenberg has documented, by the 1880s, the United States had seen the rise of a new phenomenon: "the single, highly educated, economically autonomous New Woman," who repudiated the Cult of True Womanhood and "threatened men in ways her mother never did."[24] As Smith-Rosenberg demonstrates, "for the next half a century, American women and men bitterly debated the social and sexual legitimacy of the New Woman. Through her, they argued about the naturalness of gender and legitimacy of the bourgeois order. They agreed on one point: The New Woman challenged existing gender relations and the distribution of power." [25]

That the modern institution of sport was shaped during the time when women were challenging existing gender relations helps to explain the particular forms that sport eventually took. A number of feminist analyses have suggested that one of the key elements in maintaining men's overall power over women is the elevation of the male-body-as-superior through the use (or threat) of violence. Susan Brownmiller, for instance, argues that although various forms of control (psychological, ideological, etc.) are utilized, ultimately men's control of women rests on violence. [26] According to sociologist Eric Dunning, historical and cross-cultural evidence shows that the balance of power tips more strongly toward men when violence and fighting are endemic parts of social life. With industrialization and modernization, social life became more rule-governed and "civilized," more controls were placed on the interpersonal use of violence, and the balance of power thus shifted more toward women. British men responded to this threat to their power by instituting "combat sports" such as boxing and rugby: "Such games were justified ideologically, partly as training grounds for war, partly in terms of their use in the education of military and administrative leaders in Britain's expanding empire, and partly as vehicles for the inculcation and expression of 'manliness.' " [27]

Similarly, historian E. J. Gorn has interpreted the rapid rise in popularity of bare-knuckle prize fighting in late nineteenth-century America as, in large part, a masculine backlash against feminism. [28] Sport, especially in its more violent forms, supported male dominance not simply through the exclusion or marginalization of females, but also, according to sociologist Lois Bryson, "through the association of males and maleness with valued skills and the sanctioned use of aggression, force, and violence." [29] In promoting dominance and submission, in equating force and aggression with physical strength, modern sport naturalized the equation of maleness with power, thus legitimizing a challenged and faltering system of masculine domination. [30]

An important aspect of the threat to men's power was a shift in sexual relations. Women's quest for control of their bodies (their sexuality, their reproductive capacities) constituted a challenge to male-dominant forms of sexuality. In addition, the increasingly public existence of urban enclaves of gay men represented a challenge to a masculinity that was defined largely through heterosexuality. One of the most salient features in the rise of organized sport was the elevation of the male body, and of male sexuality, as superior to female sexuality. Within the homosocial world of sport, the denial of any homoerotic impulse was a key element of this elevation of male (hetero)sexual superiority.[31]

We can say, then, that modern sport is a "gendered institution." That is, it is a social institution constructed by men, largely as a response to a crisis of gender relations in the late nineteenth and early twentieth centuries. The dominant structures and values of sport came to reflect the fears and needs of a threatened masculinity. Sport was constructed as a homosocial world, with a male-dominant division of labor which excluded women. Indeed, sport came to symbolize the masculine structure of power over women. Finally, sport constituted and legitimized a heterosexist social organization of sexuality. As a result, the institution of sport in the twentieth century has played a key role in the construction and stabilization of a male-dominant, heterosexist system of gender relations.

Yet it is crucial to recognize that sport's role in constructing and legitimizing a male homosocial world, masculine power, and masculine heterosexuality has continually been contested.[32] Turn-of-the-century feminism was accompanied by what Stephanie Twin has called a "wave of athletic feminism." Women's athletics blossomed in the first two decades of the twentieth century, especially in women's colleges. But by the 1920s, virulent opposition to female athleticism had emerged. A 1923 survey of physical education instructors revealed that 93 percent were opposed to intercollegiate play for women. The Women's Division of the National Amateur Athletic Foundation, led by Mrs. Herbert Hoover, opposed women's participation in the 1928 Olympics. By the 1930s, according to Helen Lenskyj, medical experts in the United States and Canada were claiming that sport was dangerously unhealthy for girls and women.[33] A 1935 article in an American Medical Association publication stated that "in some cases, basketball can make too heavy a demand on the organic vitality of a growing girl."[34] What did medical experts fear was being deprived when this "organic vitality" was "used up" in athletic participation? As doctor Donald Laird wrote in the *Scientific American* in 1936, "Feminine muscular development interferes with motherhood. What a woman needs—and has—is a good system of involuntary muscles . . . she has plenty of muscle and oxygen-carrying power for simple household tasks which take plenty of oxygen. She has ample development for a multitude of light office and factory work. But men should keep her away from the heavier tasks, both out of chivalry and good sense.[35]

The message in the 1930s was clear: Women are biologically destined to tend to the business of housework, childbearing, and childrearing. Athletic participation undermines their ability to do these important tasks. Increasingly, athletic women were stereotyped as unwomanly, as unfeminine, and were labeled "mannish lesbians," no matter what their actual sexual orientations. As a result of this backlash against the New Woman and female athleticism, the 1930s saw a "phasing out of inter-school and intercollegiate competition for girls and young women throughout most of the American states and in some parts of Canada."[36] At a much reduced and less visible level, women's athletics persisted throughout the middle of the twentieth century. But women's sport was so marginalized and the female athlete so stigmatized, they represented no real challenge to male-dominant gender relations. The equation of sport participation with manliness had been successfully reaffirmed.

Sport, Masculinities, and the Gender Order

It is now widely accepted among feminist sport scholars that the institution of sport is, in its dominant forms, "a fundamentally sexist institution that is male dominated and masculine in orientation."[37] Yet a cursory glance at men's historical and contemporary experiences in athletics suggests that it is overly simplistic to view sport simply as a patriarchal institution that reinforces men's power over women. As we have seen, the rise of sport as a social institution in the late nineteenth and early twentieth centuries had at least as much to do with men's class and racial relationships with other men as it did with men's relations with women.

On the surface, then, there appears to be a contradiction between the feminist view of sport as an institution that unites men in the domination of women and historians' analysis of sport as a site of contested colonial, class, and racial relations among men. But this dual reality is only contradictory if we insist on viewing one form of domination as fundamental. Recently, feminist theorists such as Sandra Harding have argued that a more accurate picture of social reality can be created by an "inclusive" understanding of the intersections of race, class, gender, and sexual systems of power.[38] R. W. Connell's conception of "the gender order" is a good starting point for the development of such a theory. Connell argues that men do benefit from the oppression of women, but at any given historical moment, there are also competing masculinities—some hegemonic, some marginalized (e.g., black or lower class), some stigmatized (e.g., gay). Hegemonic masculinity, the form dominant today, is defined in relation to various subordinated masculinities as well as in relation to femininities. The gender order is thus a social system that is constantly being created, contested, and changed, both in the relationships and power struggles between men and women, and in the relationships and power struggles between men.[39]

Employing the concept of the gender order, we can see that the turn-of-the-century "crisis of masculinity" was, in actuality, a crisis of legitimation for *hegemonic* masculinity. In other words, upper- and middle-class, white, urban, heterosexual men were the most threatened by modernization, by changes in the social organization of work, by the New Woman's movement into public life, by feminism, and by working-class, ethnic minority, immigrant, and gay men. These were the men who formed the Boys Scouts of America, and these were the men who initially created sport as a refuge, as a bastion of masculinity.[40] Helen Lefkowitz-Horowitz argues in her history of U.S. "campus life" that fraternities and organized sport arose on college campuses in the nineteenth century first and foremost as a "revolt" by upper-class male students against adult male authority. The emphasis on fun and on physical competition was an expression of anti-intellectual masculinity that at once bonded them against their (feminized, bookish) professors and administrators and provided a clear distinction between upper-class "college men" and the lower-middle-class "grinds" who were destined for the ministry. It was only later, when colleges became coeducational, that fraternities and sport became directly meaningful in terms of college men's relations with women. As Horowitz put it, "Coeducational schools forced their male students to sit beside females in class, but they allowed the men to dominate the all-important life outside the classroom."[41]

Fraternities and organized sport, then, within the context of the turn-of-the-century U.S. university, served to define the gender order by differentiating men from women and higher-status men from lower-status men. As an institution, sport developed a structure and a system of values that supported the values and world view of upper-class white males. In the words of sociologist Bruce Kidd, organized sport in this era was "characterized by rules, a bureaucratic structure, the privileging of 'records' and the concepts of 'fair play'—by middle- and upper-class males in the increasingly elitist institutions of the public school, the university, and the private club."[42] More specifically, a culturally dominant conception of masculinity was being forged and legitimated within and through sport. The social Darwinist belief that a natural hierarchy emerges out of a competitive, meritocratic system ("may the best man win") provided ideological support for the existing class and gender privilege of upper- and middle-class white males.[43]

In the twentieth century, as colonized, racial and ethnic minority, poor and working-class men participated in sport in increasing numbers, they learned to play largely by the rules set up by the dominant group of men. Subordinated groups of men often used sport to resist racist, colonial, and class domination, and their resistance most often took the form of a claim to "manhood." Struggles to achieve a public masculine status through sport became a key locus around and through which men of different backgrounds competed with each other. In the twentieth century, gender has thus become the central organizing principle of the institution of U.S. sport. Sport is a domain of contested national, class, and racial relations, but the hegemonic conception of masculinity in sport also bonds men, at least symbolically, as a separate and superior group to women. It is this simultaneous expression of difference and bonding among men that defines the role that modern sport plays in the contemporary gender order.

I begin my examination of the lives of male athletes, then, with the assumption that as young boys come to their first experiences with organized sport, they approach an institution that is by no means "gender neutral." In its structure, values, and ideology, sport is deeply gendered, thus boys' experiences in sport constitute a "gendering process." That is, through participation in sport, boys and men learn the dominant cultural conceptions of what it means to be male. In order to examine this process, we need to examine some social-psychological theories of the development of masculine identity.

GENDER IDENTITY AND SPORT

Through the late 1960s, the belief that "sport builds men" was widely accepted. Politicians and military leaders praised sport for instilling in boys and young men the courage and strength necessary to defend the nation. Coaches and school administrators touted the "character-building" effects of athletic participation, pointing to the large number of corporate and civic leaders, even U.S. presidents, who were former athletes. But by the early 1970s, feminists had begun to criticize the exclusion of girls and young women from this socially valued process. Sociologist Janet Lever, for instance, argued that since sport teaches boys skills and attitudes that prepare them to compete successfully in public life, the exclusion of girls from sport unfairly blocks their ability to compete with men.[44] By 1980, feminist analyses of sport stretched beyond simply criticizing the exlusion of girls and women. According to sociologists Donald Sabo and Ross Runfola, sport socialized boys and young men to a destructive "male sex role": "A primary function of sports is the dissemination and reinforcement of such traditional values as male superiority, competition, work, and success. . . . Through sports, boys are trained to be men, to reflect all the societal expectations and attitudes surrounding such a rigid role definition. Sports act as a mirror of the dominant culture and a link between sexist institutions."[45]

Sabo and Runfola agreed that sport socializes boys to many of the values, attitudes, and skills that are so important in the adult world of men. But they were critical of these values and skills for their perpetuation of the domination of women. Moreover, they argued that this narrowly defined male sex role was emotionally limiting and often physically unhealthy for men.[46] Despite their groundbreaking contributions, these early studies were limited by their tendency to view boys essentially as "blank slates" who came to their athletic experiences to be socialized into male roles.[47] By the late 1970s, sociologist Nancy Chodorow and others argued that sex role theory had inadvertently simplified the complexities of gender. Boys and girls do not passively await socialization by institutions such as sport. Early developmental differences, grounded in the social structure of the family—the fact that women "mother" infants—lead to deeply rooted (unconscious) differences between girls and boys, and these differences persist into adulthood.[48] In short, Chodorow's psychoanalytic perspective identified categorical differences between the sexes. Because females and males have different experiences of separation from and attachment to the mother, males tend to develop more "positional" identities (with fears of intimacy), while females tend to develop more "relational" identities (with fears of separation).[49]

Feminist psychoanalytic theory has been criticized by some for overgeneralizing differences between women and men, and for ignoring race, class, cultural, sexual, and other differences within gender categories.[50] Indeed, feminist psychoanalytic perspectives on gender have often viewed "core gender identity" as relatively fixed early in life. In this view, masculine and feminine personality structures are like an onion, the core of which is created in the first three years of life, retaining causal significance throughout life, no matter how many "layers" are added through subsequent socialization processes. The effects of social structure and power relations can all but disappear within this framework.

Feminist psychoanalytic theory can, however, be an important component of a social constructionist theory of gender.[51] Social structure does not simply shape personality, nor is gender identity simply created and internally fixed in the first three years of life. Instead, as sociologist Ian Craib has argued, social structure and personality exist in a dynamic relationship with each other: "The 'normal' structure and operation of institutions, as they have developed in modern capitalist society, makes use of, and perhaps routinely (though not necessarily) confirm the routine structure and processes of the male personality."[52] In other words, there is an affinity between masculine gender identity, as psychoanalytic theorists see it, and the present structure of social institutions. This theoretical perspective best illuminates the relationship between developing masculine personalities and the institution of organized sport. Instead of viewing the personality as an onion, with gender identity as the fixed and causal core, it is more accurate to view the personality as a never-completed tapestry, and gender identity as a thread running through the entire weave.[53] Pieces of the tapestry are added as the person interacts with other people within social institutions (families, education, sport, etc.). The ways in which the pieces are added and arranged are, in part, shaped by the thread. Yet the thread itself is flexible: it is woven, moved, stretched, rewoven, as new pieces of the tapestry are added. Rather than viewing gender identity as a "thing" people "have," I conceptualize it as a process of construction that develops, comes into crisis, and changes as a person interacts with the (always changing) social world. It thus becomes possible to speak of "gendering" identities, rather than of "masculinity" or "femininity" as relatively fixed identities or social roles.

There is agency in this process; people are not passively shaped by their social environment. As recent feminist analyses have pointed out, girls and women are implicated in the creation of their own identities and personalities, both in terms of how they participate in their own subordination and how they resist.[54] Yet this self-construction is not a fully conscious process. There are also deeply-seated, unconscious motivations, fears, and anxieties at work. So, too, in the development of masculinity. Psychoanalytic theory suggests that young males are predisposed to define their masculinity through their achievements, rather than through intimate relationships with others.[55] As sociologist Christine Williams argued in her study of male nurses and female Marines, "Psychoanalytic theory . . . recognizes that socialization is not a one-way street. Individuals bring to every social interaction a particular set of motives, interests, and desires not entirely reducible to contemporary social forces. . . . Individuals do not simply conform to preset 'roles'; they bring their own interests and desires to bear upon their social activities, often redefining them in the process."[56]

My examination of the lives of male athletes proceeds from an analysis of the dynamic interaction between the "internal" (conscious values and beliefs as well as the less conscious separation-attachment dynamic) and the "external" (social institutions). In short, masculine identity is neither fully formed by the social context nor caused by some personal dynamic put into place during infancy. Instead, it comes to be in the interaction between the internal and the social. The internal gender identity of a person may set developmental "tasks," may create thresholds of anxiety and ambivalence, yet it is only through a concrete examination of people's relations with others within social institutions that we can begin to understand both the similarities and the differences in the construction of gender identities.[57]

Specifically, this conception of gender invites us not simply to examine how social institutions "socialize" boys, but also to explore the ways that boys' developing gender identities interact with social institutions (which are themselves the product of gender relations). Since men of different social classes, races, and sexual orientations often have substantially different interactions with the world, we can expect that their definitions of masculinity will reflect their varied backgrounds.

Though most of the men I interviewed (26 of the 30) gave me verbal permission to use their real names in this book, I decided to use pseudonyms and at times to change key biographical facts which might lead to the identification of the interviewees. My aim is not so much to tell individual stories, as a journalist might, but to come to some more general understandings about masculinity and sport. Throughout the book, I trace the construction of masculine identities, with particular focus on how boys and men weave the psychological thread of separation/unity within the institution of sport (as well as within the institutions of family, education, and economy). While identifying commonalities in the experiences of male athletes, I also point to the ways in which men's motivations and experiences with athletic careers differ along the lines of social class, race, and (to a certain extent) sexuality.

Subsequent chapters of this book follow a "lifecourse" format. Chapter 2 explores the early motivations and experiences of athletes during boyhood. Chapters 3, 4, and 5 examine various aspects of athletic careers: the realities of success, failure, and masculine identity; male athletes' relationships with their bodies, with special attention to violence, injuries, and health; the athletes' relationships with women and with other men during the athletic career. I examine disengagement from athletic careers as a period of "crisis" in the lifecourse in chapter 6, and in chapter 7 I explore the kinds of lives, relationships, and self-images that these former athletes develop. Finally, in chapter 8, I return to some of the broader sociological and theoretical questions discussed in this opening chapter.

2 : Boyhood: The Promise of Sport

> *When I was eleven, in 1958, we won the state champion-*
> *ship All Star game in Little League baseball—went to*
> *Louisville, Kentucky, to play. And really from that point*
> *on, I was in the limelight, even though the light wasn't*
> *glowing that brightly in a small town—you were a big*
> *fish in a little pond. But fortunately I had some athletic*
> *ability, and quite naturally, once you start doing well in*
> *whatever it is—I don't care if it's jacks—if you're doing*
> *well in it, you enjoy playing, and you try, you show off*
> *what you do. That's your ability, that's your blessing, so*
> *you show it off as much as you can.*
>
> —GENE H.,
> **Retired professional football player**

Zane Grey once said, "All boys love baseball. If they don't, they're not real boys."[1] This is, of course, an ideological statement: Some boys do not love baseball, or any other sports, for that matter. There are millions of males who at an early age are rejected by, become alienated from, or lose interest in organized sport. Yet, studies in the 1970s and the 1980s consistently showed that sport remains the single most important element of the peer-status system of U.S. adolescent males.[2] The fact is, boys are, to a greater or lesser extent, judged according to their ability, or lack of ability, in competitive sport.

How and why did organized sport come to play such a central role in the lives of the men I interviewed? When asked to recall how and why they initially got into sport, many of these men seemed a bit puzzled: after all, sport was "just the thing to do." Calvin H. explained, "It was

24

just what you did. It's kind of like, you went to school, you played athletics, and if you didn't, there was something wrong with you. It was just like brushing your teeth: it's just what you did. It's part of your existence."

Spending one's time playing competitively with other boys appeared as natural as the cycle of the seasons: baseball in the spring and summer, football in the fall, basketball in the winter—and then it was time to get out the old baseball glove and begin again. As former professional football player Nathan C. put it, "I'd say when I wasn't in school, 95 percent of the time was spent in the park playing. It was the only thing to do. It just came as natural."

"It just came as natural." "It was natural instinct." Several athletes used words such as these to explain their early attraction to sport. But surely there is nothing "natural" about throwing a ball through a hoop, hitting a ball with a bat, or jumping over hurdles. A boy may have amazing hand-eye coordination, but this does not predispose him to a career of hitting baseballs any more than it predisposes him to a life as a brain surgeon. Indeed, when one listens more closely to what these men said about their early experiences in sport, it becomes clear that their adoption of the self-definition of "natural athlete" is the result of what R. W. Connell calls "a collective practice" that constructs masculinity.[3] For example, notice how Chris H., who eventually became a professional basketball player, explained his early experiences in sport: "My principal and teachers said, 'Now if you work at this you might be pretty damned good.' So it was more or less a community thing—everybody in the community said, 'Boy, if you work hard and keep your nose clean, you're gonna be *good*.' 'Cause it was *natural instinct*."

Clearly, the boy's self-definition as "natural athlete" results from interaction with people and social institutions. Many of these men eventually came to see themselves as "naturals," but when they discussed their earliest experiences and motivations in sport, they all spoke of the importance of relationships with family members, with peers, and with the broader community. It is within this web of relationships that masculine/athletic identities began to be forged.

FAMILY INFLUENCES

Though most of the men in this study spoke of their mothers with love, respect, even reverence, their descriptions of their earliest experiences with sport are stories of an exclusively male world. When I asked them to describe their earliest athletic experiences, I was surprised to find that most of them spoke first, not of fathers, but of older brothers or uncles who served as teachers and athletic role models, as well as sources of competition for attention and status within the family. An older brother, uncle, or even close male friend of the family who was a successful athlete appears to have acted as a standard of achievement against which to measure oneself. For instance, Ray J. said, "My uncles—my Uncle Harold went to the Detroit Tigers, played pro ball—all of them, everybody played sports, so I wanted to be better than anybody else. I knew that everybody in this town knew them— their names were something. I wanted my name to be just like theirs."

Similarly, Thomas M. recalled, "I was the youngest of three brothers and everybody played sports, so consequently I was more or less forced into it. Because one brother was always better than the next brother, and then I came along and had to show them that I was just as good as they were. My oldest brother was an all-city ballplayer, then my other brother comes along and he's all-city and all-*state*, and then I have to come along . . ."

For some, the athletic accomplishments of older male family members created pressures that were difficult to deal with. Bill S. was a good athlete during boyhood, but he was always aware that his two older brothers had been better: "I had this sort of reputation that I followed from the playgrounds through grade school, and through high school. I followed these guys who were all-conference and all-state." These pressures eventually created a context in which Bill, despite his accomplishments, never felt that he was good enough. As a result, his ability to enjoy sport—and ultimately the self image he developed through sport—suffered. Most of these men, however, saw their relationships with their athletic older brothers and uncles in a positive light. Within these relationships, they gained experience and developed motivations that gave them a competitive "edge" within their peer group. As Willy S. described his earliest athletic experiences, "My brothers were role models. I wanted to prove—especially to my brothers—that I had heart, you know, that I was a man." When I asked him, "What did it mean to you to be 'a man' at that age?" he replied,

Well, it meant that I didn't want to be a so-called scaredy-cat. You want to hit a guy even though he's bigger than you to show that, you

know, you've got this macho image. I remember that at that young an age, that feeling was exciting to me. And that carried over, and as I got older, I got better and I began to look around and say, "Well hey! I'm competitive with these guys, even though I'm younger." You know? And then of course all the compliments come, and I began to notice a change, even in my parents—especially in my father—he was proud of that, and that was very important to me. He was extremely important . . . he showed me more affection, now that I think of it . . .

As Willy's words suggest, if men talk of their older brothers and uncles mostly as role models, teachers, and "names" to emulate, their talk of their relationships with their fathers is more deeply layered and emotionally complex. Athletic skills and competition for status may often be learned from older brothers, but it is in boys' relationships with fathers that we find many of the keys to the emotional salience of sport in the development of masculine identity.

Relationships with Fathers

Given the division of labor between men and women that is so common in modern, industrialized societies, boys' relationships with their fathers are often limited and problematic. In 1971, family researchers found that fathers were spending an average of thirty-seven seconds a day with infants in the first three months of life. In 1969, research indicated that fathers spent about an hour a day of direct play with their nine-month-old infants, including time spent on weekends.[4] Clearly, when the men in my study were growing up, women were performing nearly all of the work of caring for infants.

As they moved from infancy into boyhood, relationships with fathers expanded somewhat for most of these boys, but still remained limited in important ways. Six of the men I interviewed grew up in single-parent families headed by women. In the "intact" families, fathers were often absent (because of work or other public activities), and when home, they were often emotionally distant from children. As a result, according to psychologist Sam Osherson, most men "know little of their father's inner life" and tend to talk of their fathers retrospectively as "mysterious, remote figures."[5] Research performed by psychologist Zick Rubin confirms this: few fathers and sons achieve intimate connection, and many men carry a "father-hunger" with them into adulthood.[6]

The fact that boys' introduction to organized sport is often made by fathers who might otherwise be absent or emotionally distant adds a powerful charge to these early experiences. Most of the men I interviewed had startlingly clear memories of Saturday trips with Dad to a major league baseball game, or of their first games of catch with their fathers. There was often a dreamlike quality to their descriptions of these moments. Listen to the words of Jim P., who at the age of eight was gently "pushed" by his father to become involved in Little League baseball:

> *I still remember it like it was yesterday—Dad and I driving up in his truck, and I had my glove and my hat and all that—and I said, "Dad, I don't want to do it." He says, "What?" I say, "I don't want to do it." I was nervous that I might fail. And he says, "Don't be silly. Look: There's Joey and Petey and all your friends out there—You're gonna do it, come on." And in my memory he's never said that about anything else; he just knew I needed a little kick in the pants and I'd do it. And once you're out there and you see all the other kids making errors and stuff, and you know you're better than those guys, you know: Maybe I* do *belong here. As it turned out, Little League was a good experience.*

Some who were similarly "pushed" by their fathers were not as successful as Jim in Little League, and thus the experience was not altogether a joyous affair. Don W., for instance, says he "inherited" his interest in sport from his father, who started playing catch with him at the age of four. Once he got into Little League, his father, one of the coaches, expected him to be the star of the team: "I'd go o-for-four sometimes, strike out three times in a Little League game, and I'd dread the ride home. I'd come home and he'd say, 'Go in the bathroom and swing the bat in the mirror for an hour,' to get my swing level." Don laughs ironically, "It didn't help much, though. I'd go out and strike out three or four times again the next game too." Some fathers do appear to use their sons to live out their own athletic fantasies. But a more probable explanation for behavior like Don's father's is the fact that most men never learn to express love to their children directly. More often, men show their love indirectly and symbolically, through actions such as working to support the family and teaching athletic skills to sons. As a result, Sam Osherson argues, sons frequently become "trapped" into performing deeds and accomplishments as a means of demonstrating and seeking affection.[7] When I asked Don W. if he had been concerned with having his father's approval, he responded, "Failure in his eyes? Yeah. I always thought that he wanted me to get some kind of [athletic] scholarship. I guess I was afraid of him when I was a kid. He didn't hit that much, but he had a rage about him—he'd rage, and that voice would just rattle you." For boys like Don, these first athletic experiences teach them that successful performance in sport is a key to successful emotional attachment with their fathers, and that, conversely, failure to perform may destroy the tenuous bond between father and son. Neal K. describes his awe of his father's physical presence, and his sense of inadequacy in utilizing sport in an attempt to please and emulate him: "My father had a voice that sounded like rolling thunder. Whether it was intentional on his part or not, I don't know, but my father gave me a sense, an image of him being the most powerful being on earth, and that no matter what I ever did I would never come close to him. There were definite feelings of physical inadequacy that I couldn't work around." For Neal, these feelings of physical inadequacy lived on as part of his permanent self-image. He eventually became a "feared" high school football player and broke school records in weightlifting, yet he never in his own view achieved the stature of his father: "As I grew older, my mother and friends told me that I had actually grown to be a larger man than my father. Even though in time I required larger clothes than he, which should have been a very concrete indication, neither my brother nor I could ever bring ourselves to say that I was bigger. We simply couldn't conceive of it."

Using sport as a means of identifying with and "living up to" the power and status of one's father was not always such a painful and difficult task for the men I interviewed. Most of these men did not describe fathers who "pushed" them to become athletic stars. The relationship between their athletic strivings and their identification with their fathers was more subtle. For instance, Brent F. described his father as a distant "role model" whose approval mattered:

My father was more of an example. He definitely was very much in touch with and still had very fond memories of being an athlete and talked about it, bragged about it. But he really didn't do that much to teach me skills, and he didn't always go to every game I played like some parents. But he approved and that was important, you know.

That was important to get his approval. I always knew that playing sports was important to him so I knew implicitly that it was good and there was definitely a value on it.

Similarly, Eldon C. saw his boyhood athletic accomplishments as a way of receiving the approval of his father.

I wanted to play baseball because my father had been quite a good baseball player in the Negro leagues before baseball was integrated, and so he was kind of a model for me. I remember, quite young, going to a baseball game he was in—this was before the war and all—I remember being in the stands with my mother and seeing him on first base, and being aware of the crowd. I was aware of people's confidence in him as a serious baseball player. I don't think my father ever said anything to me like "play sports." [But] I knew he would like it if I did well. His admiration was important . . . he mattered.

As Eldon's words suggest, he did not hope to gain his father's admiration simply by "playing sports." He was clearly aware of the prestige his father had gained through his own athletic accomplishments. For Eldon and for many other boys, the key to gaining the approval of their fathers was not simply to play, but to play well. As a result, the process of obtaining some level of attachment with fathers became intricately intertwined with successful public achievement in competitive sport.

For the men I interviewed, while the early emotional salience of sport was related to their relationships with their fathers, the intense commitment that these young boys eventually made to the development of athletic careers is best explained as a process of developing masculine identity and status in relation to male peers.

MASCULINE IDENTITY AND EARLY
COMMITMENT TO SPORT

When many of the men in this study said that during childhood they played various sports because "it's just what everybody did," they of course meant that it was just what *boys* did. They were introduced to organized sport by older brothers and fathers and, once involved, found themselves playing within an exclusively male world. Though the separate (and unequal) worlds of boys and girls came to appear as "natural," they were in fact socially constructed. Sociologist Barrie

Thorne's observations of children's activities in schools indicates that rather than naturally constituting "separate gendered cultures," there is considerable interaction between boys and girls in classrooms and on playgrounds. When adults set up legitimate contact between boys and girls, Thorne observes, this usually results in "relaxed interactions." But when activities in the classroom or on the playground are presented to children as sex-segregated and gender is marked by teachers and other adults ("boys line up here, girls over there"), "gender boundaries are heightened, and mixed-sex interaction becomes an explicit arena of risk."[8] Sex-segregated activities such as organized sport, as structured by adults, provide a context in which gendered identities and separate "gendered cultures" develop and come to appear natural. As Thorne puts it, "Gender-marked moments seem to express core truths: that boys and girls are separate and fundamentally different as individuals and as groups. They help to sustain a sense of dualism in the face of enormous variation and complex circumstances."[9]

For the men in this study, the fact that sport was an exclusively male world made it seem natural to equate masculinity with competition, physical strength, and skills. Girls simply did not (could not, it was believed) participate in these activities. Yet it is not simply the separation, by adults, of children into separate activities that explains why many boys came to feel such a strong connection with competitive sport, while so few girls did. As I listened to men recall their earliest experiences in organized sport, I heard them talk of insecurity, loneliness, and especially a need to connect with other people as a primary motivation in their early strivings. For instance, when I asked Adam A. why he got so heavily involved in sport when he was a boy, he replied, "The most important thing was just being out there with the rest of the guys—being friends." Another athlete, Ricardo R., was born in Mexico and moved to the United States at a fairly young age. He never knew his father, and his mother died when he was only nine years old. Suddenly he felt rootless, and he threw himself into sport—but his initial motivations were not based on a need to compete and win: "Actually, what I think sports did for me is it brought me into kind of an instant family. By being on a Little League team, or even just playing with all kinds of different kids in the neighborhood, it brought what I really wanted, which was some kind of closeness. It was just being there, and being friends."

By his early teens, Ricardo started to notice, as did many other men in this study, that if he played well, was a winner, he could get attention from others:

> *It got to the point where I started realizing, noticing, that people were always there for me, backing me all the time—sports got to be really fun because I always had some people there backing me. Finally my oldest brother started going to all my games* [laughs]*—after the game, you know, we never really saw each other. But he was at all my baseball games, and it seemed like we shared a kind of closeness there, but only in those situations. Off the field, when I wasn't in uniform, he was never around.*

These boys appear to have needed and craved what was most problematic for them: connection with other people. But why do these young males find organized sport to be such an attractive context in which to establish "a kind of closeness" with others? Comparative observations of young boys' and girls' game-playing behaviors yield important insights into this question. Jean Piaget and Janet Lever both observed that girls and boys tend to play games and sports differently.[10] Girls tend to have more "pragmatic" and "flexible" orientations to the rules of games; they are more prone to make exceptions and innovations in the middle of a game in order to make the game more "fair." Boys, on the other hand, tend to have a more inflexible orientation to the rules of a game; to them, the rules ensure fairness. According to psychologist Carol Gilligan, early developmental experiences yield deep-rooted differences between males' and females' developmental tasks, needs, and moral reasoning. Girls, who tend to define themselves primarily through connection with others, experience highly competitive situations (whether in organized sport or in other hierarchical institutions) as threats to relationships, and thus to their identities.[11] For boys, the development of a masculine identity involves the construction of "positional identities," where a sense of self is solidified through separation from others.[12] Males come to fear that intimacy with others will result in loss of identity, yet they retain a human need for unity with others. This ambivalence toward intimate relationships is an important thread running through masculine development throughout the lifecourse. For the boy who both seeks and fears closeness, the rule-bound structure of organized sport promises to be a safe place in which to seek attachment with others, but it is an attachment in which clear boundaries, distance, and separation from others are maintained.[13]

Moving from what boys bring to their experiences in sport, we can now examine what they find when they get there. How does a masculine identity develop and change as it interacts with the institution of organized sport? In what ways do the structure and values of sport begin to shape the self-images and relationships of these boys?

THE STRUCTURE AND VALUES OF SPORT

Young boys may initially find that playing competitively gives them the opportunity to experience emotionally "safe" connections with others. But once enmeshed in sport as an institution, they are confronted by two interrelated realities—hierarchy and homophobia—that undermine the possibility of boys' transcending their fears of intimacy and developing truly close relationships with others.

Competitive Structures and Conditional Self-Worth

The institution of sport is extremely hierarchical, with the highest value placed on winning, on being "number one." A few years ago, I observed a boys' basketball camp organized by a professional basketball coach and his staff. The youngest boys, about eight years old (who could barely reach the basket with their shots) played a brief scrimmage. Afterward, the coaches lined them up in a row in front of the older boys who were sitting in the grandstands. One by one, the coach would stand behind each boy, put his hand on the boy's head (much in the manner of a priestly benediction), and the older boys in the stands would applaud and cheer, louder or softer, depending on how well or poorly the young player was judged to have performed. The two or three boys who were clearly the exceptional players looked confident that they would receive the praise they were due. Most of the boys, though, wore expressions ranging from puzzlement to thinly disguised terror as they awaited the judgments of the older boys.

This kind of experience teaches boys that it is not "just being out there with the guys—being friends," that ensures the kind of attention and connection they crave; it is being better than the other guys—beating them—that is the key to acceptance. Most of the men in this study did have some early successes in sport, and thus their ambivalent need for connection with others was met, at least for a time. But the institution of sport tends to encourage the development of what sociologist Walter Schafer calls "conditional self-worth" in boys.[14] As boys become aware that acceptance by others—fathers, coaches, peers—is contingent upon being a "winner," narrow definitions of success, based upon performance and winning become increasingly important to them. As Willy S. said, by the time he was in his early teens, "It was *expected* of me to do well in all my contests—I mean by my coaches, my peers, and my family. So I in turn expected to do well, and if I didn't do well, then I'd be very disappointed." This conscious striving for athletic success eventually became the primary means through which many of these young males defined themselves, as well as their relationships with others. Given the fact that one's own "success" is the flip-side of another's "failure," organized sport encourages boys to view other boys not as intimates, but as rivals. Within this competitive world, the chief question a boy may ask himself when confronted with another boy is, "Can I take him?"

Homophobia in Sport

The second element of organized sport that undermines intimate connection with other people is homophobia, the "irrational fear or intolerance of homosexuality."[15] The extent of homophobia in the sportsworld is staggering. Boys learn early that to be gay, to be suspected of being gay, or even to be unable to prove one's heterosexual status is not acceptable. Though athletes are cultural symbols of masculine heterosexual virility, however, it is not true that there are no gay men and boys in sport. There is growing evidence that many (mostly closeted) gay males are competing in organized sport at all levels. Former professional football player David Kopay wrote in his book, "Recently, I've come to the conclusion that a lot of my extra drive came from the same forces that brought black athletes out of the ghettos to the forefront of professional sports. They were out to prove that they were not inferior because of their race. I was out to prove that I was in no way less a man because I was homosexual."[16]

Indeed, gay men, having been raised *as men* in this society, tend to have most of the same ambivalence and insecurities that all men have, compounded by the knowledge that if their secret becomes known, they will be considered less than a man.[17] Furthermore, since talk of

"queer bashing" is common in male locker rooms, a closeted gay athlete knows that to reveal the truth about his sexuality can be outright
dangerous. Mike T. lived a closeted existence for years while competing
as a world-class track-and-field athlete. At a very early age, Mike discovered that athletic participation was a way to construct a public masculine identity and to hide the fact that he was gay:

> When I was a kid, I was tall for my age and I was very thin, but very
> strong. And I was usually faster than most people. But I discovered
> rather early that I liked gymnastics and dance. I was very interested
> in, and studied, ballet. And something became obvious to me right
> away—that male ballet dancers were effeminate, that they were what
> most people would describe as faggots. It suddenly occurred to me that
> this was dangerous territory for me—I'm from a small town, and I was
> totally closeted and very concerned about being male. This was the
> 1950's, a terrible time to live, and everything was stacked against me.
> I realized that I had to do something to protect my image of myself,
> that I was male—because at that time, homosexuals were thought of
> primarily as men who really preferred to be women—that was the
> stereotype. And so I threw myself into athletics. I played football, gym-
> nastics, track and field. . . . I was a jock, and that's how I was
> viewed, and I was comfortable with that.

Years later, Mike T. realized that were it not for a homophobic world,
he might have become a dancer: "I wanted to be viewed as a male,
otherwise I would be a dancer today. I wanted the male, macho image
of an athlete. So I was protected with a very hard shell. And I was
clearly aware of what I was doing. I was just as aggressive and hostile on
the football field as anyone else."

Mike's story illustrates how homophobia often leads gay males to
consciously create identities that conform to narrow definitions of masculinity. But homophobia also serves to limit the self-expression and
relationships of nongay males. Psychologist Joseph Pleck has written
that "our society uses the male heterosexual-homosexual dichotomy as
a central symbol for all the rankings of masculinity, for the division on
any grounds between males who are 'real men' and have power and
males who are not. Any kind of powerlessness or refusal to compete
becomes imbued with the imagery of homosexuality."[18]

Indeed, boys learn early that if it is difficult to define masculinity in
terms of what it *is*, it is at least clear what it is *not*. A boy is not consid-

ered masculine if he is feminine. In sport, to be told by coaches, fathers, or peers that one throws "like a girl" or plays like a "sissy" or a "woman" is among the most devastating insults a boy can receive, and such words can have a powerful impact upon his actions, relationships, and self-image. Sociologist Gary Alan Fine spent three years studying Little League baseball teams and noted clear and persistent patterns of homophobic banter and sexual talk about females among eleven- and twelve-year-old boys.[19] To give but one example, Fine described an occasion when Dan, a "high-status twelve year old," announced to his teammates that he was going to pay his girlfriend, Annie, ten cents for each sexual "base" she allowed him to reach. The boys speculated as to whether Dan would reach "third base" or "second base." In the end, a disappointed Dan reported to his peers that he had gotten only "halfway to second." But Dan added that he *would* have gone further, but for an interrupting phone call from Gordy, a "low-status" boy in the group, who was then ridiculed as "a gay one" for his transgression. As Fine concludes,

> *Dan's reputation is preserved at the expense of Gordy's. Although Dan did not meet his objectives, his reputation increased through the talk . . . whereas Gordy, a younger boy, was roundly condemned. Significantly, Annie's reputation was also affected, as players started calling her a "prostie," and Dan stopped considering her his girlfriend. Aside from Dan and Annie, no one knew the truth about what happened between the two of them; yet, it is not private actions but public talk that is ultimately significant.[20]*

Fine's observations demonstrate how homophobia and the sexual objectification of females together act as a glue that solidifies the male peer group as separate from females, while at the same time establishing and clarifying hierarchical relations within the male peer group. In short, homophobia polices the boundaries of narrow cultural definitions of masculinity and keeps boys—especially those in all-male environments such as organized sport—from getting too close. Through sport, a young boy learns that it is risky—psychologically as well as physically—to become too emotionally open with his peers: he might be labeled a "sissy," a "fag," or even be beaten up or ostracized from the group. He also finds that he had better not become too close to girls; he must, of course, establish his masculine status by making (and laughing at) heterosexist jokes, but he "must never let girls replace boys as the focus of [his] attention."[21]

For the men I interviewed, early experiences in play and sport held the promise of greater attachment with fathers, older males, and peers. For most of them, this promise was partially realized. But ultimately, the specific kinds of relationships that they developed were distorted by the hierarchical structure of sport and by the homophobic and sexist banter within the peer group.

A particular kind of masculinity was being forged among these boys and young men, a masculinity based upon status-seeking through successful athletic competition and through aggressive verbal sparring which is both homophobic and sexist. But it is important not to over-generalize the motivations and experiences of all men. As we have seen with Mike T., a young gay male might bring some very different psychological and interpersonal motivations to his athletic experiences. Furthermore, since boys from varied backgrounds are interacting with substantially different familial and educational contexts, we can expect these contexts will lead them to make choices and define situations in different ways. Boys from middle- and lower-class families and communities, for instance, relate to organized sport in quite distinct ways.

Class Differences and Early Commitments to Sport

In some ways, my interviewees' early attractions to sport were quite similar, independent of social class. Both middle-class and lower-class men spoke of the importance of fathers and older brothers in introducing them to sport. Both groups also spoke of the joys of receiving attention and acceptance within the family and among peers for early successes in sport. Note the similarities, for instance, in the following descriptions of the boyhood athletic experiences of two men. First, Jim P., born into a white, middle-class family:

I loved playing sports so much from a very early age because of early exposure. A lot of the sports came easy at an early age, and because they did, and because you were successful at something, I think that you're inclined to strive for that gratification. It's like, if you're good, you like it, because it's instant gratification. I'm doing something that I'm good at and I'm gonna keep doing it.

Second, Gene H., a black man from a poor family:

*Fortunately I had some athletic ability, and quite naturally, once you
start doing well in whatever it is—I don't care if it's jacks—if you're
doing well in it, you enjoy playing, and you try—you show off what
you do. That's your ability, that's your blessing, so you show it off as
much as you can.*

For boys from both groups, early exposure to sport, the discovery that
they had some "ability," shortly followed by family, peer, and community recognition, all led to the commitment of hundreds and thousands
of hours of playing, practicing, and dreaming of future stardom. Despite these similarities though, there are some identifiable differences
that begin to explain the higher levels of commitment to a sport career
by males from lower-class backgrounds. The most clear-cut difference
is that while men from middle-class backgrounds were likely to describe their earliest athletic experiences and motivations almost exclusively in terms of immediate family, men from lower-class backgrounds
more commonly described the importance of a broader community
context. Larry W., for instance, grew up in a poor working class black
family in a small town in Arkansas: "In that community, at the age of
third or fourth grade, if you're a male, they expect you to show some
kind of inclination, some kind of skill in football or basketball. It was
an expected thing, you know? My mom and my dad, they didn't push
at all. It was the general environment." Eldon C. describes athletic activities as a survival strategy in a poor black community: "Sports protected me from having to compete in gang stuff, or having to be good
with my fists. If you were an athlete and got into the fist world, that was
your business, and that was okay—but you didn't have to if you didn't
want to. People would generally defer to you, give you your space away
from trouble."

Nathan C. grew up in a poor black ghetto, and his words echo Eldon's: "Where I came from, you were either one of two things: you
were in sports or you were out on the streets being a drug addict, or
breaking into places. The guys who were in sports, we had it a little
easier, because we were accepted by both groups. So it worked out to
my advantage, 'cause I didn't get into a lot of trouble—some trouble,
but not a lot."

The realities faced by boys in lower-class communities gave their developing athletic identities a deeper importance than for boys from
middle-class backgrounds. Jon P., raised in a white, middle-class fam-

ily, found in sport a key means of gaining acceptance in his peer group. But he did not see his athletic role as a key to survival in a hostile environment, as Eldon C. and Nathan C. had. In addition, as Jon P. was striving for athletic success, he was simultaneously developing an image of himself as a "smart student" and becoming aware of a wide range life options outside sport: "My mother was constantly telling me how smart I was, how good I was, what a nice person I was, and giving me all sorts of positive strokes, and those positive strokes became a self-motivating kind of thing. I had this image of myself as smart, and I lived up to that image."

This is not to argue that parents in lower-class families did not also encourage their boys to work hard in school. Several men in my study reported that their parents "stressed books first, sports second." But the broader social context—education, economy, and community— was more likely to narrow lower-class boys' perceptions of real choices, while boys like Jim P. and Jon P. faced an expanding world of opportunities. For instance, with a different socioeconomic background, Thomas M. might have become a great musician instead of a great running back. When he was a child, he said, he was most interested in music: "I wanted to be a drummer. But we couldn't afford drums. My dad couldn't go out and buy me a drum set or even a guitar—it was just one of those things. He was just trying to make ends meet." But Thomas could afford, as could so many in his situation, to spend countless hours at the local park, where he was told by the park supervisor that he was a "natural": "Not only in gymnastics or baseball—whatever I did, I was a natural. He told me I shouldn't waste this talent, and so I immediately started watching the big guys then." In retrospect, Thomas knows that he had potential to be a musician or any number of things, but his environment limited his options to sport, and he made the best of it. But even within sport, he, like most boys in the ghetto, was limited: "We didn't have any tennis courts in the ghetto—we used to have a lot of tennis balls, but no racquets. I wonder today how good I might be in tennis if I had gotten a racquet in my hands at an early age."

In the summers of 1970–74, I worked as a youth sport organizer for a community recreation and park department. A major part of my job was to form boys' softball and flag football teams on each of the dozen or so parks in town, and then to organize and referee games between the various teams. It always struck me that at the parks in the parts of town populated by poor and working-class people (mostly Latino and white, with a few blacks), I had no trouble organizing teams or holding practices. There were always more than enough players on the field for games. Conversely, the parks in middle- and upper-middle class neighborhoods (mostly white, with a sprinkling of Asians) were sparsely populated. Often, I could not field a team. Or worse, I would organize a team, schedule a game for the next day, and only a few of the boys would show up. One day, at a park in an affluent part of town, I told a white boy, perhaps twelve years old, that we had a game that afternoon. He replied, "I'm bored with softball—I'm gonna go home and play with my motorbike." This sort of thing simply did not happen at the parks in lower-class neighborhoods. Lower class boys may have owned their own bikes, but never their own motorbikes, and they were far less likely than their middle-class counterparts to have a home with their own basketball hoop on the driveway.

It is within this context that many young lower-class boys found playing sport in public parks, recreation centers, and schools to be *the* place, rather than *a* place, within which to build masculine identity, status, and relationships. For instance, David P.'s father left the family when he was very young, and his mother had a very difficult time making ends meet. As David's words suggest, the more limited a boy's options appear to be, and the more insecure his family situation, the more likely he is to make an early commitment to an athletic career:

> I used to ride my bicycle to Little League practice—if I'd waited for someone to pick me up and take me to the ballpark, I'd have never played. I'd get to the ballpark and all the other kids would have their dads bring them to practice or games. But I'd park my bike to the side, and when it was over I'd get on it and go home. Sports was the way for me to move everything to the side—family problems, just all the embarrassments—and think about one thing, and that was sports.

As young boys, all of the men I interviewed appear to have brought ambivalent needs for connection with others to their first sport experiences. Those who had some early successes found that some of these needs for connection were met, albeit in ways distorted by the hierarchical structure of sport and its homophobia and sexism. Each of these men's boyhood commitment to an athletic identity amounted to what R. W. Connell has called "the moment of engagement with hegemonic masculinity—the moment at which the boy takes up the project of hegemonic masculinity as his own."[22] But despite the fact that, for all of these men, sport was the institutional context in which they experienced a boyhood "moment of engagement" with dominant conceptions of masculinity, their motivations and experiences in sport were not identical. Mike T., who knew that he was gay, made a conscious decision to pursue an athletic career as a means of constructing a masculine personality that served to hide his actual sexual orientation from public view. The men from lower-class backgrounds often saw athletic careers as a gleam of hope in an otherwise dismal future: In a choice of "fists" or football, they chose the latter. By contrast, when the heterosexual men from middle class backgrounds began to pursue athletic careers, they did so within a much broader structure of opportunity. Though all of these boys appeared to have been playing the same games, in retrospect we can see that, from a very early age, the stakes were very different.

3 : The Meaning of Success

And for the players themselves, they seem expert list-lessly, each intent on a private dream of making it, making it into the big leagues and the big money, the own-your-own-bowling-alley money; they seem specialists like any other, not men playing a game, because all men are boys [that] time is trying to outsmart.

—JOHN UPDIKE,
Rabbit, Run

When I interviewed Eldon C. in his office, he had two fortune-cookie slips taped to the wall above his desk. One read, "You can breeze through the rest of the day"; the other, "You are worried about something that will never happen." These fortunes seemed to symbolize the dual nature of his career as a world-class runner. Raised in a poor black family, Eldon found sport to be an important arena in which he and his peers competed to establish an identity in the world. But Eldon's small physical stature made it difficult to compete successfully in most sports, thus contributing to a sense of insecurity—he just never felt as though he belonged with "the big boys." Eventually, he managed to become a top middle-distance runner. But in high school, he found, it was no longer enough to do well. He felt he had to be the best: "Something began to happen there that plagued me quite a bit. I started doing very well and winning lots of races and by the time the year was over, it was no longer a question of my *placing*, but *winning*. That attitude really destroyed me ultimately. I would get into the blocks with worries that I

42

wouldn't do well—the regular stomach problems—so I'd often run much less well than my abilities, that is, I'd take second or third."

In 1956, Eldon surprised everyone by taking second place in a world-class field of quarter-milers. But the fact that he and his closest competitors broke the old world record seemed only to "up the ante," to increase the pressures:

> Up to that point I had been a nice zippy kid who did well, got into the [college newspaper] a lot, and was well-known on campus. But now an event would come up and the papers would say, "Eldon C. to face so-and-so." So rather than my being in the race, I was the race, as far as the press was concerned. And that put a lot of pressure on me that I never learned to handle. What I did was to internalize it, and then I'd sit there and fret and lose sleep, and focus more on not winning than on how I was doing. And in general, I didn't do badly—like one year in the NCAA's, I took fourth—you know, in the national finals! But I was focused on winning. You know, later on, people would say, "Oh, wow, you took fourth in the NCAA? You were that good?" Whereas I thought of these things as failures, you know?

Finally, Eldon's years of training, hopes, and fears came to a head at the 1956 Olympic trials, where he failed to qualify, finishing fifth. A rival whom he used to defeat routinely won the event in the Melbourne Olympics as Eldon watched on television.

> That killed me. Destroyed me . . . I had the experience many times after that of digging down and finding that there was infinitely more down there than I ever got—I mean, I know that more than I know anything else. Sometimes I would really feel like an eagle, running. Sometimes in practice at [college] running was just exactly like flying— and if I could have carried that attitude into events, I would have done much better. But instead, I'd worry. Yeah, I'd worry myself sick.

Why was competitive running such a struggle for Eldon? Why couldn't he carry that sense of "flying like an eagle" into his events? Many contemporary sport psychologists would treat his problem as individual pathology; modern athletes are often given complex batteries of psychological tests and then are counseled and taught to control or channel their fears into "positive thinking," all of which (it is hoped) translates into victory. I take a different approach. Eldon C.'s dilemma is best understood, not as individual pathology, but as paradigmatic among all the men I interviewed. This dilemma is not a result of individual failure; it is a sociological phenomenon, a result of the intersection of a developing masculine identity with the competitive, hierarchical world of sport.

By the time they were in high school, sport had become a central aspect (often *the* central aspect) of the developing life structures of the men I interviewed. When listening to their stories, I noticed the emergence of a fascinating duality in their descriptions of how they felt during their athletic careers. On the one hand, they spoke eloquently (as Eldon C. did) of the exhilaration, the existential high of successful athletic performance. Mike T. described competing in track and field at the world-class level as "the happiest period of my life. I loved it. I was in ecstasy." And Rick J., though never a world-class competitor, speaks similarly of a two-week period when he starred on his high school junior varsity basketball team: "I was on absolute cloud nine. It's still a thrill to look back on those times, to have the game in slow motion, not even hearing the crowd, shooting jump shots and seeing them coming down, and having the stupid things go right in [laughs]—that was an incredible thrill . . . I was really high."

Most of the men interviewed had similar stories, but there was another side to their athletic careers, a side that often dominated their memories. In addition to the "highs," they also remember (and sometimes dwell on) the pressures of competition and the painful agonies of failure, of not measuring up to their dreams and expectations.

SUCCESS, FAILURE, AND THE LOMBARDIAN ETHIC

In the 1988 Summer Olympics in Seoul, coach John Thompson and the U.S. basketball team were clothed in a shroud of failure by the media when they lost to the Soviet Union, while sprinter Carl Lewis and hurdler Edwin Moses were hounded by reporters to speak about how it felt to "lose" after they each had won silver medals in their events, instead of the gold. Celebrated diver Greg Louganis reported incredulously that after he had courageously come back to win a gold medal after hitting his head on the springboard, "A reporter told me that if I didn't win both springboard and platform, I'd be considered a failure. A failure."[1] When the San Francisco Forty-Niners completed their 1984 regular season with a record number of wins (fifteen against only one loss), coach Bill Walsh and several players stated on television that "the victories mean nothing if we don't win the Super Bowl." After winning the Super Bowl, quarterback Joe Montana stated gleefully, "Vince Lombardi supposedly said, 'Winning isn't everything; it's the only thing,' and I couldn't agree more. There's nothing like being number one."

Despite a continuing undercurrent of emphasis on fair play, doing one's best, and popular participation, the dominant message that the public gets from the spectacle of organized sport is that "winning it all" counts most. This Lombardian ethic is alive not only at the level of televised professional or Olympic-level sport—it has trickled down through the college and high school ranks, and even to Little League baseball and children's hockey.[2] Sociologist Jay Coakley quotes a high school basketball coach as saying: "Through the years, I've developed my own philosophy about high school basketball. Winning isn't all that matters. I don't care how many games you win, it's how many championships you win that counts."[3]

Dreams and Realities

The boyhood dream of one day becoming a professional athlete —a dream shared by nearly all of the men in this study—is rarely realized. In the hierarchical world of sport, the pyramid of athletic careers narrows very rapidly as one climbs from high school, to college, to professional levels of competition. For instance, only about 6 or 7 percent of high school football players ever play in college. Roughly 8 percent of all draft-eligible college football and basketball athletes are drafted by the pros, and only 2 percent ever sign a professional contract. It has been calculated that the chances of attaining professional status in sport are approximately 4 in 100,000 for a white man, 2 in 100,000 for a black man, and 3 in 1,000,000 for a U.S.-born Latino man.[4] And the average career span for professional athletes is about 7 years for a major league baseball player, 4 years for those in the National Football League, and 3.4 years in the National Basketball Association.[5]

In short, the structure of the sportsworld means that the chances of getting anywhere near "the top" are extremely small, and even if an athlete is talented and lucky enough to get there, his stay will be very brief. The stories of athletes like Joe Montana, Michael Jordan, or Greg Louganis who do come out "on top" are highly publicized and thus serve to reinforce the dominant success ethic at all levels of sport. Yet if success is defined as "winning it all," what happens to the 99 percent who fail to measure up? For many, like Eldon C., the disjuncture between the dominant ideology of success (the Lombardian ethic) and the socially structured reality that most do not "succeed" brings about feelings of failure, lowered self-images, and problems with interpersonal relationships.[6]

Some respond to the structure and values of the sportsworld by dropping out or by rejecting the Lombardian ethic and playing only "for fun." But this study concerns those who, at least for a time, were committed to athletic careers.[7] For most of these men, the structured insecurity of athletic careers led them to become consumed by their careers. As Chris H. put it, "It was totally basketball. That's all *I* was was basketball. You're talking about eighty to ninety hours a week . . ." And when one makes it to the top, it's no time to relax and celebrate, as David P. says of his arrival in major league baseball: "The pressures really come when you get to the major leagues, because you remember all those kids down in the minor leagues that are trying to get here. As Satchel Paige said, 'Never look back, because there's always someone trying to gain on you.'"

Conditional Self-Worth

It is tempting to view this system as a "structure of failure," because, given the dominant definition of success, the system is rigged to bring about the failure of the vast majority of the participants. Furthermore, given the dominant values, the participants are apt to blame themselves for their "failures." Walter Schafer argues that the result of this discontinuity in sport between ideology and experienced reality is a "widespread conditional self-worth" for young athletes.[8] In other words, the dictum "you're only as good as your last game" constantly keeps one insecure and worried about one's next performance. My interviews largely support Schafer's thesis, especially with respect to those, like Willy S., who had early successes in sport: "I expected to do well all the time, you know. I *expected* to run touchdowns. I *expected*—that was natural for me. If it didn't come, I would be really disappointed." Willy did not live up to his own expectations, and as we will see in chapter 6, this resulted in tragedy. In retrospect, he says, "Where I made my mistake is I thought you always had to be on the up side—and if you weren't on the up side, you were nothing—nobody cared—you were nothing, you had no substance to you, you were a loser. And I never wanted to be a loser." Rather than dismissing Willy's failure as a personal "mistake," we can see that the fact that his self-image hinged on always being "on the up side" was a logical result of his total commitment to an athletic career. This was a clear pattern in the lives of the men I interviewed. As one moved up the hierarchy of the sport career, one eventually had to grapple with a sense of failure. As Larry W. put it, "For me, in playing sports, early on, to be the *leader*—that was my idea of succeeding. When I got to the university, I played second team. I felt that I didn't succeed."

Despite the powerful impact of this narrow success ethic on the self-images of these men, it is important to remember that athletes are not "blank slates" onto which the sportsworld imprints its values and priorities. Some athletes do not fully accept the Lombardian ethic. Some, like Mike T., eventually rejected the "winning is everything" ethic and focused on feeling good about themselves for knowing that they worked hard and did their best: "If I've done my best, whether I've won or lost, I say fine. I walked away after finishing sixth in [my event at the] Olympics feeling like a million bucks. And people came up and said, 'How'd you do? Oh—Oh, you didn't win a medal?' I sensed this disappointment—or I projected this disappointment that *I* should feel bad because I didn't win. And I would say, '*Hell! God, sixth!*' I was so *pleased* with sixth!"

Mike's statement demonstrates that it is possible to develop one's own standards of success, yet the social context makes it difficult to do so. And it is especially difficult to do so for lower-class men who, unlike Mike, a medical doctor, have few opportunities for "making it" in public life. For most who are committed to an athletic career, winning *is* everything—or nearly so. But it is a mistake to conclude that this is simply the result of athletes being "conditioned" or "socialized" into the value-system of the sportsworld. Boys and young men bring their developing masculine identities to their experiences in athletics. It is crucial to examine how the ambivalences and insecurities of masculine identities intersect with the structure and values of the sportsworld.

MASCULINE IDENTITY AND THE CROWD

How do we account for the incredible commitment to dreams of athletic success by so many of these men—dreams that, given the struc-

ture of the sportsworld, are extremely unlikely to materialize? To begin
to answer this question, we must recall the reasons that these men, as
boys, were initially attracted to organized sport. As we saw in chapter
2, most of the men in this study were introduced to sport by immediate
family members. As they moved into adolescence and young adulthood, peers had an increasing influence, yet families continued to be of
great importance. Listen to the statements of four men discussing how
their relationships with their families had an impact on their success or
failure in sport:

- I always knew my family was behind me.
- I was lucky to have a firm foundation provided by my parents
  and my brothers at home.
- I didn't have the backing that I needed to succeed.
- My mother left me when I was five—she went off to play. I had
  weak pillars—weak foundations—I walked on a floor full of
  self-doubt holes.

Family was obviously critical to these men, but mostly as a starting
point, a basis upon which the young male builds his own life. This is
reflected in the language they used to describe family relationships—
"foundation," "backing," "pillars"—which invokes images of a hierarchical world. In this world the family is essential, not so much as a
"web of connection and caring," but rather, as the place from which the
man moves into his *real* work—competition in the world of men.[9] Thus
in the 1988 Olympics, when Greg Louganis stood atop the platform for
his final dive, a dive that would, in the eyes of many of the millions who
watched, define Louganis as a success or a failure, he reminded himself
silently, "No matter what happens, my mother still loves me." Yet it is
unlikely that he was attempting to convince himself that he could be
satisfied simply with his mother's love. Rather, he was drawing on the
emotional support of his mother as a resource—using it as an emotional
buoy—to do what he had to do to win.

Though young athletes continue to draw on family as an emotional
resource (and although those with more stable families tend to have a
"stronger foundation" to build upon), as they move into high school
and young adulthood, their athletic successes or failures increasingly
appear to them to be a result of their own personal qualities and abilities
competing in a world of male peers. As we saw in chapter 2, boys who
experience some early successes in sport receive attention from others,
which provides an emotionally distant (and thus "safe") form of con-

nection. It is through this form of connection with others that the boy begins to construct his masculine "positional identity." In childhood, the attention a successful athlete receives usually comes from immediate family members (especially fathers and brothers) and friends. As one moves into high school, college, and perhaps even into the professional ranks of sport, the attention and adulation he receives becomes more broad-based and abstract. Now it is not *simply* performing for one's friends and family that provides the raw materials for the construction of masculine identity; increasingly, "the crowd" (which includes schoolmates, anonymous "fans" in the grandstands, the public, and the media) becomes an athlete's primary relationship with the world.

Athletes may often talk of the necessity of "turning a deaf ear to the crowd" when competing, but none of the men in this study seemed fully able to do so. The attention of the crowd, for many, affirmed their existence as men, and was thus a clear motivating force. Adam A. explained that through high school, he had an "intense desire to practice and compete."

> I used to practice the high jump by myself for hours at a time—only got up to 5'3"—scissor! [Laughs]—but I think part of it was, the track itself was in view of some of the classrooms, and so as I think back now, maybe I did it for the attention. Probably, yeah. In my freshman year, I chipped my two front teeth in a football game, and after that I always had a gold tooth, and I was always self-conscious about that. Plus I had my glasses, you know. I felt a little conspicuous.

This shyness, self-consciousness, "conspicuousness," along with a strongly felt need for attention often characterizes athletes' descriptions of themselves, especially in the teen years. "The crowd," in this context, acts as a distant (and thus nonthreatening) source of attention and external validation for the insecure boy or young man. This can operate—as it appeared to do for Adam A.—on a partly imaginary level: he never really knew for sure whether anyone was watching him. It can even operate on a solely imaginary level: some adult men admit that they often engage in "childish fantasies," perhaps shooting baskets alone, while in their heads, their favorite sports announcer describes their glorious exploits as the crowd roars.[10]

For many of the men I interviewed, the roar of the crowd had been very real. Several described to me a powerful and even euphoric experience, when the crowd "gets inside you" and "lifts you." Ricardo R., in describing a heroic performance in a softball tournament, said, "It was the enthusiasm of the crowd that got me going—more than it was *me* trying, it was just that—I *had* to do well." And Willy S. described a similar feeling as a rookie playing professional football. There was, he explained, "Something about that elation—I guess, it's like dope or something—that *crowd* just turned me on, you know, just to hear them *roar*. I was young, though, definitely young . . . but that's where I thrived—just turn the crowd on. When they would introduce me, they would roar—and to me, that was my ego, that was my stimulus-response, my reinforcement. This *crowd*."

Athletes' descriptions of these kinds of moments suggest that a powerful psychological and emotional merging of self and crowd is occurring here. Yet this profound connection with others is also abstract and distant, and it thus does not push up against the young man's fears of intimacy. Feminist psychoanalytic theory would suggest that the crowd might not be as important to female athletes as it is to males. Indeed, research by sociologist Mary Duquin has confirmed this.[11] Duquin found that female college athletes, though highly dedicated to being successful athletes, tend to obtain their validation and approval primarly through their web of relationships with others. But male athletes' abstract connection with the crowd appears to be the most emotionally salient relationship through which their positional identities are constructed and affirmed. The problem, of course, is that there is a flip side to the lift that the crowd can give an athlete. Ultimately, whether the crowd roars or boos, whether one gets headlines or is criticized in the press, whether one is adored by one's schoolmates or has to deal with embarrassed silences or even taunts, is determined largely by the success or failure of one's most recent performances. The roar of the crowd lifted Willy S., but this created expectations in his mind that he always had to win: "In the newspaper, I remember one time they said, 'This person here is the greatest running back in the history of the league,' and, you know, I ate that up. I believed my own clippings, and I had a big head: That's me, I'm *that good*. [So] I always thought I was supposed to win—*every game, I was supposed to win!* [Chuckling ironically]—You're not supposed to *lose*, you know?"

That Willy credits the media ("I believed my own clippings") with the development of his "always a winner" identity is not unusual. Sociologists Patricia and Peter Adler concluded from their five-year participant observation study of a nationally prominent college basketball team that star athletes who are in the public limelight often develop identities that are both aggrandizing and constricting.[12] What the Adlers call "the gloried self" becomes the athlete's dominant self-image. But as Willy S. eventually discovered, the press clippings and the roar of the crowd, which served as the major basis of his self-image, were contingent on his continuing to win: "Every game, I was supposed to win!"

The contingent nature of the self, as developed through athletics, was also evident among men who never became "big time" athletes. As we have seen, Ricardo R. discovered at an early age that sport gave him a "kind of closeness" with an otherwise distant brother and with male peers: "It got to the point where I started realizing that people were always there for me, backing me all the time." This kind of attention motivated him to commit himself to athletic excellence, and by the time he got into high school, it was clear that he was a very good athlete. In retrospect, he can see how the resulting performance pressures contributed to his conditional self-worth: "I'd say I really started getting down on myself when I was as young as fifteen. I already had a good reputation as a good baseball player and a strong hitter in football—and already, that was what I was *supposed* to do—already in my freshman year. So right off the bat I was against the wall." However, Ricardo never felt as though his accomplishments were delivering what he craved most. Perhaps, he surmised, he just wasn't trying hard enough. Perhaps if he hit just one more home run, made one more all-star team, won one more championship for his school, everything would be all right: "I could hit three home runs in a game, and I wouldn't be satisfied. Maybe on the fourth time up, I'd ground out, so I wouldn't be satisfied. I've always got to find another plateau to reach. The things that I do well, I just tend to kind of leave behind in the back of my head, because that's just what I do."

"Never be satisfied with your performance" is, of course, a common dictum in the sportsworld, lauded by coaches and by the media as part of the formula of success. Yet what is evident from my interviews is that it is not simply the "socialization" of boys and men into the world of organized sport that accounts for the development of conditional self-worth. Rather, it is the dovetailing of the competitive structure and values of the sportsworld with the tendency of boys and young men to define themselves positionally that explains the intensity of men's commitments to athletic careers. In other words, there tends to be a neat fit—an affinity—between the structure of sport and developing masculine identities.

SCHOOLS, PEERS, AND CLASS DIFFERENCES

As we have seen, even in childhood, middle-class boys were aware of an expanding range of life options, while lower-class boys had fewer choices. This made it more likely that boys from lower-class backgrounds would see athletics as *the* career option rather than *a* career option. The stories of these men suggest that relationships with teachers, coaches, and peers in junior high school, high school, and college more often than not reinforced these class differences.

"Respect" for Lower-Class Men

For the lower-class young men in this study, success in sport wasn't an added proof of masculinity; it was often their only socially legitimate means of achieving public masculine status.[13] Larry W. and Calvin H., two black men from lower-class backgrounds, were able to utilize athletics as a vehicle to get college educations and become, respectively, a high school teacher and a college professor. As Calvin H. said, "The opportunities that were presented to me to develop came from athletics. I took that, and I've since been able to generalize and expand upon it."

More common, though, were the words of Ray J., who, in describing the options available to him, concludes that his youthful focus on sport stardom and his concomitant lack of effort in academics made sense:

> You can go anywhere with athletics—you don't have to have brains. I mean, I didn't feel like I was gonna go out there and be a computer expert, or something that was gonna make a lot of money. The only thing I could do to live comfortably would be to play sports—just to get a contract—doesn't matter if you play second or third team in the pros, you're gonna make big bucks. That's all I wanted, a confirmed livelihood at the end of my ventures, and the only way I could do it would be through sports. So I tried. It failed, but that's what I tried.

Why would a young male restrict himself so completely to sport? The answer lies in how the social structure of opportunity for young lower-class males interacts with the perceptions that a given individual has of his opportunities (which are affected by role models, familial values, peer group relations, schools, teachers, and coaches). For young men from lower-class backgrounds—especially blacks—the road to upward mobility through education is a psychological, cultural, and structural minefield.

Schools and teachers in poor black communities tend to be of lower quality.[14] If an athlete from a poor background manages to get a college scholarship, he is often at an academic disadvantage to his peers. This was documented by a 1984 sociological study of 10,000 U.S. athletes that revealed that athletes in general are less well prepared for college than are nonathletes; this is especially true of scholarship holders, black athletes, and participants in football and basketball.[15] Lower-class athletes' poor academic preparation is often grounded in the tendency of teachers, coaches, and counselors to stereotype young black males, from a very early age, as "dumb jocks" and to channel them into easy (not college prep) classes to keep them eligible for athletic participation. The gifted young athlete receives a dual message: First he learns that if he simply continues to work hard in practice and star in athletic competitions, he will be taken care of in school. As Willy S. said of his high school years, "I'd hardly ever go to classes and they'd give me C's. My coaches taught some of the classes. And I felt, 'So what? They *owe* me that! I'm an *athlete!*' I thought that was what I was born to do—to play sports—and everybody understood that."

This sort of treatment is experienced by the young male as privilege: "They *owe* me that!" But second, he is also receiving—and too often internalizing—the message that others believe he is incapable of intellectual growth and achievement. Ricardo R., from a poor Mexican immigrant family, said of his high school years:

> I wasn't a student, and never professed to be one. If I went through my [high school] grades now, I'd probably crack up! I had a bad attitude, you know? And [the coaches and teachers] knew I didn't really give an effort other than in athletics—so they treated me that way too. My whole junior year was a farce, because I really didn't try and I got C's all the way through . . . the coaches were finding ways to keep me eligible all the time, and I just laughed at it, you know, just went along with it [laughs].

We can see from Ricardo's statement how others' definition of one's lack of intellectual ability can become a self-fulfilling prophecy, resulting in a low self-image: even in his mid-thirties, he still concludes that he "had a bad attitude." Similarly, Thomas M. says that in high school, "I was the good dumb athlete . . . I just got by." But, as sociologist

Harry Edwards has argued, "The 'dumb jock' is not born; he is systematically being created."[16] In addition to lowering the athlete's self-image, this social context further reinforces his perception that sport is his only chance to excel. As Ricardo R. said,

In high school, that was my self-identity, being a good ballplayer. At that time, I was realizing that whatever you excel in, you put out in front of you. In other words, it's almost like a product—if you're a good baseball player, bring it out. Show it. Be the jock. If you're a good athlete, or student, or something like that, stick out like a sore thumb. And that's what I did. That was my protection. That was my saying, "Hey, I'm better than you." It was rotten in high school, really. Sports got to be a product at that time—before, it was just fun, and having acceptance, you know. Yet I had to work for my acceptance in high school that way, just by being a jock. So it wasn't fun anymore. Not that much. I put a lot of pressure on myself, and I tried really hard to work myself into the ground just to show that I excelled in something. Athletics was the one thing that I excelled in, and that was the one thing I had to use. That was my tools. That was my attention-getter.

Once a person is committed to a sport career, it takes a huge amount of time, energy, and concentration to succeed. At each level, the competition becomes more fierce for fewer positions. The "raised stakes" at these higher levels call for more commitment and directed focus on athletic accomplishment. By the time one gets into college athletics, according to Calvin H., "It becomes a full-time job." According to Harry Edwards, the modern university scholarship athlete is required to carry a full load of classes while putting between forty-five and sixty hours a week into practice, preparation, and travel for athletic contests.[17] If he is poorly prepared to start with, the scholarship athlete has little chance to take advantage of the opportunity to become college-educated. Indeed, in their study, Patricia and Peter Adler observed that freshmen athletes began with high expectations of playing ball and getting a college degree. But over the next four years, the amount of time that their athletic roles demanded, the amount of reinforcement they received from peers, fans, and the media for their athletic accomplishments and their relative isolation from academic life undermined their commitment to academic goals. Gradually, the Adlers observed, these college athletes became "pragmatically detached" from academic life.[18]

Peer group values interact with this limited structure of opportunity to shape further the goals and perceptions of these young males. The interviews suggest that these lower-class boys and young men were not simply duped or "channeled" into putting all their eggs into one basket by an all-powerful system. The development of masculine status within male peer groups played a key role in their active participation in making themselves into "athletes." By the high school years, class and ethnic inequalities had become glaringly obvious, especially for those who attended school with students from wealthier backgrounds. Cars, nice clothes, and other signs of status were often unavailable to these young men, and this contributed to a situation in which sport took on an expanded importance for them. Ricardo R. describes what it was like to be "one of the very few Mexicans" in his high school:

> *Off the field, I was low-key. I always kind of put myself down because I didn't have a block sweater or a school ring—I didn't have any of those things. A lot of times, I would even walk [several miles] home— I'd even jog all the way home, just because I was too embarrassed to be asking for rides, you know? I was really never accepted by the students—to them I was just some dumb jock who was supposed to be a terror on the football field. The only time I got any attention was when I was out on the field playing.*

David P., who grew up in a poor white, single-parent family, was also acutely aware of his lower-class status in his high school:

> *I had one pair of jeans, and I wore them every day. I was always afraid of what people thought of me—that this guy doesn't have anything, that he's wearing the same Levis all the time, he's having to work in the cafeteria for his lunch. What's going on? I think that's what made me so shy . . . But boy, when I got into sports, I let it all hang out [laughs]—and maybe that's why I became so good, because I was frustrated, and when I got into that element, they gave me my uniform in football, basketball, and baseball, and I didn't have to worry about how I looked, because then it was me who was coming out, and not my clothes or whatever. And I think that was the drive.*

Similarly, Thomas M. described his insecurities as one of the few poor blacks in a mostly white, middle-class school and his belief that sport was the one arena in which he could be judged solely on his merit:

> *I came from a very poor family, and I was very sensitive about that in those days. When people would say things like "Look at him—he has dirty pants on," I'd think about it for a week. [But] I'd put my pants on and I'd go out on the football field with the intention that I'm gonna*

*do a job. And if that calls on me to hurt you, I'm gonna do it. It's as
simple as that. I demand respect just like everybody else.*

"Respect" was what I heard over and over when talking with the men
from lower-class backgrounds, especially black men. I interpret this
type of "respect" as a crystallization of the masculine quest for recognition through public achievement, unfolding within a system of structured class and race inequities and constraints. The institutional context of education (sometimes with the collusion of teachers and
coaches) and the limited economic opportunities made the pursuit of
athletic careers appear to be the most rational means of achieving respect. As Gene H. put it, "I like people to respect me more than anything. If that respect has to be with football, well, I'll accept that. Athletics has been my attention-getter throughout my life."

The same is rarely true of young lower-status women. Writer Margaret Dunkle points out that from junior high school through adulthood, young black men are far more likely to place high value on sport
than are young black women, who are more likely to value academic
achievement.[19] Sociologist Clyde Franklin has argued that many of the
normative values of young lower-class black males (little respect for
nonaggressive solutions to disputes, contempt for nonmaterial culture)
contribute to the constriction of their views of desirable social positions, especially of education.[20] Calvin H., who did succeed in beating
the odds by using his athletic scholarship to get a college degree and
eventually become a successful professional, says that his boyhood peer
group rejected the "feminized" world of books, teachers and schools in
favor of physical expressions of status: "By junior high, you either got
identified as an athlete, a thug, or a bookworm. It's very important to
be seen as somebody who's capable in some area. And you *don't* want to
be identified as a bookworm. I was very good with books, but I was
kind of covert about it. I was a closet bookworm. But with sports, I was
somebody, so I worked very hard at it."

For most young men from lower-class backgrounds, the poor quality
of their schools, the attitudes of teachers and coaches, as well as the
anti-education environment within their own peer groups, made it extremely unlikely that they would be able to succeed as students. Sport
therefore became the arena in which they attempted to "show their
stuff." For these lower-class men, as sociologists Maxine Baca Zinn and
Richard Majors argued in studies of chicano and black men, when in-

stitutional resources that signify masculine status and control are absent, physical presence, personal style, and expressiveness take on increased importance. What Majors calls "cool pose" is black men's expressive, often verbally and physically aggressive, assertion of masculinity.[21] This self-assertion often takes place within a social context in which the young man is quite aware of inequities. As Ray J. said of his high school years:

> See, the rich people use their money to do what they want to do. I use my ability. If you wanted to be around me, if you wanted to learn something about sports, I'd teach you. But you're gonna take me to lunch. You're gonna let me use your car. See what I'm saying? In high school I'd go where I wanted to go. I didn't have to be educated. I was well respected. I'd go somewhere, and they'd say, "Hey, that's Ray J., yeah, that's a bad son of a bitch!"

Majors argues that although "cool pose" represents a creative survival technique within an environment that is hostile to black males, in the long term, this masculine posturing is likely to result only in educational and occupational dead ends. Lower-class men's responses to a constricted structure of opportunity—responses rooted, in part, in the developmental insecurities and ambivalences of masculinity—serve to lock many of them into limiting activities, such as sport careers.

"Small Potatoes" for Middle Class Men

Sport was very important to the boys from middle-class backgrounds as well. But in contrast to lower-class male peer groups, athletic accomplishment, though highly respected, was not as singularly valued in the middle-class male peer group. Larry W., now a junior-high school coach, described differences in the ways that lower-class boys from "the flatlands" and middle-class boys from "the hills" relate to sport and intermale competition:

> For kids in the flatlands, the poorer kids, [sports] is their major measuring-stick. You'll hear a verbal callout or putdown, like, "Hey, man, I took you to the hoop! In your face!" It's an extremely verbal putdown. They constantly remind each other what they can't do in the sports arena. It's definitely peer-acceptable if they are very good at sports—although they maybe can't read, you know—if they're good at sports, they're one of the boys. Now I know the middle- and upper-class boys,

*they do sports and they do their books . . . and the rich kids, I'll see
them doing a different kind of argument, on vocabulary and stuff. They
never call each other out—sports callouts, that is—they might on records or something, like "who hit the most home runs in 1912?" or
something—historian-type of stuff. Knowledge, not performance.
They get away from performance, because quite a few of them are very
weak in athletic performance. But as a whole, the kid from the hill,
he's putting less effort into it—he reads more, you know, and he emphasizes different things. As you slide down the hill, the kids become better
in sports.*

There are similar, yet class-specific, forms of masculinity being expressed here. In each case, boys are using sport to compete for status
and recognition within the male peer group. But in the case of the boys
from "the flatlands," the competition is physical; for the boys from "the
hill," the competition is intellectual. As we shall see, this differential
appropriation of sport as a "measuring stick" eventually contributes to
the reconstruction of class differences among men.

What was the process through which these differences emerged?
Boys from middle-class backgrounds developed their identities within
a context that afforded them a wide range of options, and their family,
educational, and peer-group experiences tended to expand their awareness of these options. Clarence T. describes a relationship to school and
to teachers that stands in stark contrast to those of most lower-class
men: "There was a whole lot of pressure from my father and mother to
succeed and accomplish stuff. The game was to get into the most pres-
tigious college possible. I studied a lot. I was home every night studying. I was a model student if there ever was one. Teachers loved me."

Sport was an important part of his life, but education was at least as
highly valued within his family and schools. Jon P., born into a white,
middle-class family, loved sport, and hoped that being an athlete would
give him the sort of camaraderie and respect from peers that he did not
feel he received from getting straight A's or from working on the school
yearbook. Being on the basketball team was important to him, but not
the "most" important thing:

*It was one of the really important things . . . I was really shy, I had
terrible acne that really stifled my being confident. I was the premier
student at that school. There was nobody else at that school that even
compared in terms of what I was getting with grades and testing and*

all that. But I didn't think anybody in the world gave a damn about that, and probably nobody did—and I wanted so badly for that to mean something. So basketball, somehow I wanted that to be it—it was a conscious thing on my part.

Here we can see that for Jon, sport played a similar role in constructing a public image as it did for lower-class men like Ricardo R. Yet for Jon, sport was used to bolster his public image, not as the basis of identity. It is very significant that he already had other options in life—high grades, a nice car, knowledge that he was college-bound—even though they may not have seemed to deliver what he wanted and needed most at the time. On some level, he knew even then that his future was not dependent on his being good in sport, and this was probably reinforced by the fact that he was a second-string player. As he said, "Most of the time, I just enjoyed being on the team. I loved practice and I worked my butt off in practice, somehow thinking it would get me a chance to play [in games]. [Laughs]—it never really did."

Many other middle-class men I interviewed had dreams of becoming professional stars—but most of them say (at least in retrospect) that these were more pipe dreams than realistic hopes. As a boy, Clarence T. says he idolized Mickey Mantle and Roger Maris, wore their jersey numbers, and fantasized of one day playing for the Yankees: "I'd have to say it was more of a fantasy. I don't think I ever grew up thinking I was going to be a professional player. No, I never really had that dream. Yet I still love to fantasize about it—it's great fun." By junior high school, some of these boys consciously began to shift their attentions away from sport and directed energies elsewhere. Brent F. suggests that as early as junior high school, he was becoming aware that the world of sport was a "structure of failure": "By junior high, I started to realize that I was a good player—maybe even one of the best in my community—but I realized that there were all these people all over the country and how few would get to play sports. By high school, I still dreamed of being a pro—I was a serious athlete, I played hard—but I knew I wasn't heading anywhere. I wasn't going to play pro ball."

These kinds of realizations are, of course, most common among athletes of marginal talent. But one of the striking findings of my research is that lower-class males rarely came to this conclusion early on, while several middle-class males, even some who were excellent athletes, did. For instance, Steve L. had been a successful college baseball player.

Despite considerable attention from professional scouts, he decided to forego a shot at a baseball career and entered graduate school to pursue a teaching degree. He explained this decision: "At the time I think I saw baseball as pissing in the wind, really. I was married, I was twenty-two years old with a kid. I didn't want to spend four or five years in the minors with a family. And I could see that I wasn't a superstar, so it wasn't really worth it. So I went to grad school. I thought that would be better for me." Perhaps most striking is the story of Jim P.—high school student body president, top-notch student, and "Mr. Everything" in sport. This young white man from a middle-class family received attention from the press and praise from his community and peers for his athletic accomplishments, as well as considerable interest from college athletic departments, and even some professional baseball scouts. But by the time he completed high school, he had already decided to quit playing organized sport. As he said, "I think in my own mind I kind of downgraded the stardom thing. I thought that was small potatoes. And sure, that's nice in high school and all that, but on a broad scale, I didn't think it amounted to all that much. So I decided that my goal is to be a dentist, as soon as I can."

How and why do many—even highly successful—male athletes from middle-class backgrounds come to view a sport career as "small potatoes," as "pissing in the wind"? How and why do they make an early assessment to shift away from sport and toward educational and professional goals? The white middle-class context, with its emphasis on education and income, makes it clear to them that choices exist and that the pursuit of an athletic career is not a particularly good choice to make. Where the middle-class boy once found sport to be a convenient institution in which to construct masculine identity and status, the young adult simply transfers these same strivings to other institutional contexts: education and careers. As a result, as we examine the higher levels of the sport career hierarchy, we find that an increasingly disproportionate number of the athletes come from lower-class and minority families.

4 : The Embodiment of Masculinity

Your spine is very important. You get it knocked out of alignment every game. You have to treat your body like a car. You get your tuneups and wheel alignments.

—Running back ROGER CRAIG before the 1989 Super Bowl

The pain principle is crudely evident in the "no pain, no gain" philosophy of so many coaches and athletes. . . . It stifles men's awareness of their bodies and limits our emotional expression. We learn to ignore personal hurts and injuries because they interfere with "efficiency" and "goals" of the "team." . . . We become adept at taking the feelings that boil up inside us . . . and channeling them in a bundle of rage which is directed at opponents and enemies.

—DONALD F. SABO, 1986
"Pigskin, Patriarchy, and Pain"

Barry B. had, by nearly any standards, a very successful college and professional football career. He played in the Pro Bowl twice, and when he retired in the early 1980s, he held the single-season rushing records for two professional football teams. But while he was "at the top," he, like most other professional athletes, had to deal with constant pressures:

When you get to that level, you think that you are the epitome of what a man's supposed to be. But in essence, you are still a kid. Mentally, you have not reached the level of maturity to handle the pressures that

61

are gonna come upon you . . . and all those things that you don't know how to handle have the effect of causing you to question your manhood, your role as a man. So your realm is the football field: That's *where I'm a real man—where it comes to being* physical. *That's where you feel most comfortable, on the football field—it's something that you know you can do well.*

In effect, Barry said, he became a "one dimensional person," his insecure masculine identity shored up through "being physical" on the playing field. Similarly, R. W. Connell, in his analysis of the life of an Australian "Iron Man," concludes that the Iron Man's "whole person has become caught up in practices that centre on his body and its performances. . . . In effect, the body becomes the focus of the self in a quite radical way."[1]

Indeed, my research suggests that a young man's imperative to prove himself, to perform, achieve, and win, dovetails with the hierarchic world of athletic careers in such a way that he tends to develop a certain kind of relationship to his own body. It's not simply that an athlete's body becomes "the focus of the self," but that the athlete is often encouraged to see his body as an instrument. An "instrumental male" is an alienated creature: he is usually very goal-oriented (in his work and in his personal relations), and he frequently views other people as objects to be manipulated and defeated in his quest to achieve his goals.[2] The ultimate extension of instrumental rationality is the alienation from one's own body—the tendency to treat one's body as a tool, a machine to be utilized (and "used up") in the pursuit of particular ends. Tender feelings (toward oneself and toward others) come to be seen as an impediment, something that needs to be repressed or "worked on."[3] Physical or emotional pain are experienced as a nuisance to be ignored or done away with (often through the use of alcohol or other drugs). A common result of this focus on the body as an instrument is violence expressed toward others, and ultimately toward oneself.

"PSYCHING UP": BODY AND MIND

Ultimately, success in athletic careers is predicated on training the body to perform certain tasks on command. Yet training is not enough. Any armchair fan can tell you that there are some athletes who seem to have all the "tools," yet never "come through in the clutch." There are others who always seem to "rise to the occasion." Clearly, successful athletic performance is only partly the "training" of the body—it is also "a head game." As we have already seen, Eldon C. had trouble dealing with the pressures of world-class competition as a middle-distance runner. His descriptions of his races sound as though he was a spectator within his own body. Not until he was part-way into a race would he "discover" whether he was running well or not, as this description of one of his best races illustrates:

> *The impetus of being at that level of competition completely changed the way I used my body—I felt completely out of control in some respects. It's like my whole lower body became unhinged, and I was reaching and doing things that I'd never done before. I'd never used my body that way before. I was keeping up with this very fast field, and I* clipped *as I came off the final turn. I realized I was in the race, and there was some feeling of excitement there, and then I went deeper down and got more stuff that I didn't know I had, and not only did I stay in the race, but I began to gain on the big guys, and then* passed *the big guys, and almost caught [the first place finisher] at the tape . . . We ran the fastest times in the world in the quarter mile at that time, and it was a two-second drop for me in my time! [laughs incredulously]*

In this race, his body's "autonomous" action had pleasantly surprised him. Yet in later races, his body would seem to betray him: "My head was full of these thoughts, and it would just basically freeze up my body. I would say it was just fear—and anxieties that interfered with the freedom of my body." Looking back, Eldon can see that the basis of his anxieties was the fear of not winning. He was so intent on beating other people to the finish line, he lost touch with his body's capabilities. He was, he can now see, a "racer," instead of a "runner":

> *A runner is much more aware of autonomously where their body is, and maybe works relatively independent of the pack. They know what speed their body's going at, they know how they are feeling, they have some sense of how much distance is left and what they can do, and very often will run against the clock, no matter what is going on in front of them; so they are not thrown off by people who are running foolishly fast or foolishly slow. [But] I was always locked into the competition and racing against people, rather than autonomous running.*

It is commonly a goal of coaches and sport psychologists to encourage athletes (especially those in individual performance sports like running or swimming) to focus on this autonomous performance ("running"), but given the Lombardian ethic of the sportsworld and the imperative to develop a positional identity for young males, it is far more likely that young athletes will become "racers," focusing on competing against people, rather than on doing one's best. Under these conditions, the natural unity of body and mind is split: Athletes attempt to "use" their minds in order to "get the most out of their bodies." Having the "right attitude" and "psyching up" come to be seen as keys to achieving the kinds of peak performances that translate into winning. As Thomas M. put it, "In order to have control, you've got to control yourself." Rather than being a surprised spectator of one's own body, the successful athlete must learn to block or ignore fears, anxieties, or any other inconvenient emotions, while mentally controlling his body to perform its prescribed tasks. As Connell concludes, in his study of the Australian Iron Man, "the decisive triumph is over oneself, *and specifically over one's body.* The magnificent machine of [the athlete's] physique has meaning only when subordinated to the will to win."[4] To mentally and emotionally subordinate one's body toward the goal of winning is to make of the body a tool, separate from the mind. As we shall see, that tool is to be used against other people.

THE BODY AS WEAPON: SPORTS VIOLENCE

With the possible exception of boxing, perhaps the position in modern sport that requires the most constant levels of aggressive body contact between opponents is that of the lineman in U.S. football. Though television cameras focus primarily on those who carry, throw, catch, and kick the ball, the majority of the players on the field are lining up a few inches apart from each other, and on each play, snarling, grunting, cursing, and slamming their large, powerful, and heavily armored bodies into each other. Blood, bruises, broken bones, and concussions are commonplace. Gene H. was a lineman in professional football for nine years, following successful high school and college careers. Obviously an intelligent and sensitive man, he seemed stung when I asked how he was able to submit himself to such punishment for so many years.

You know, a lot of people look at a lineman and they say, "Oh, man, you gotta be some kind of animal to get down there and beat on each other like that." But it's just like a woman giving birth. A woman giving birth. Everybody says, you know, "That's a great accomplishment: she must be really beautiful." And I do too—I think it's something that's an act of God, that's unreal. But, she hasn't done anything that she wasn't built *for. See what I'm saying? Now here I am, 260, 270 pounds—and* that's my position. *My physical self helped me. I can* do that. *I can* do that. *I couldn't run out for a pass— I'd have looked like a* fool *runnin' out for a pass, see what I mean? But due to my good speed and my strength and my physical physique, that's what I'm built for. Just like a truck carrying a big caterpillar: you see the strain, but that's what it's built for, so as far as that being a real big accomplishment, it is, but it's not. That's all you were built for.*

Gene's comparison of the aggressive uses of his body in football with a woman's giving birth and with a truck is telling: it suggests one of the major paradoxes of men's construction of meaning surrounding the uses of their bodies. On the one hand, many of the men I interviewed felt a strong need to naturalize their capacities for aggression and violence: men wearing helmets and pads repeatedly engaging in bone-crushing collisions with each other is simply "an act of God," "like a woman giving birth." Yet on the other hand, there is the clear knowledge that the bodies of successful linemen are, like trucks, "built" by human beings to do a specific job. Time after time, I heard former athletes, almost in the same breath, talk of their "natural" and "God-given" talent, and of the long hours, days, and years of training, work, and sacrifice that went into the development of their bodies and their skills.

For instance, Nathan C., who in his years as a professional football player was known as "The Destroyer" for his fierce and violent "hits" on opposing receivers, described himself as a "natural hitter." But his descriptions of his earliest experiences in high school football tell a different story. Though he soon began to develop a reputation as a fierce defensive back, hitting people bothered him at first:

When I first started playing, if I would hit a guy hard and he wouldn't get up, it would bother me. [But] when I was a sophomore in high school, first game, I knocked out two quarterbacks, and people loved it. The coach loved it. Everybody loved it. You never stop feeling sorry for [your injured opponent]. If somebody doesn't get up, you want him

to get up. You hope the wind's just knocked out of him or something.
The more you play, though, the more you realize that it is just a part of
the game—somebody's gonna get hurt. It could be you, it could be
him—most of the time it's better if it's him. So, you know, you just go
out and play your game.

Nathan's story suggests that the tendency to utilize violence against
others to achieve a goal is learned behavior in sport. Social scientific
studies of young ice hockey and U.S. football players corroborate this:
violent adult athletic role models as well as rewards from coaches,
peers, and the community for the willingness to utilize violence successfully create a context in which violence becomes normative behavior.[5] Sociologist Edmund Vaz, for instance, found that violence is virtually nonexistent among young boys just starting to play hockey. But
as they are influenced by older players and professionals, and by the
reward structure of youth hockey leagues, rough play is encouraged
and "under certain conditions, failure to fight is variously sanctioned
by coaches and players."[6] Athletes who earn reputations as aggressive
"hitters" are afforded high status in the community and among peers.
Anthropologist Douglas Foley observed that among high school football players, conversations often center on the enthusiastic recounting
of the most impressive moments of "hitting," "sticking," or "popping"
an opposing player. Indeed, those individuals who deliver the most
"bone-crushing hits" are afforded a sort of "folkloric immortality" in
the male peer group.[7] The praise, respect, and status that "hitters" receive from those around them can anchor (at least temporarily) an otherwise insecure masculine identity. As former professional football
player David Meggyesy wrote in his book, "I developed a style the
coaches loved. We moved in Oedipal lockstep: the more approval they
gave me, the more fanatically I played. From an early age, I had learned
to endure violence and brutality as simply a part of my life. But in
football, the brutality became legitimate, a way of being accepted on
the football field and off."[8]

Despite the socialization and the pressures to participate in violence,
many young boys have a problem with it. Neal K., for instance, said
that everyone was always reminding him that he didn't have the same
"killer instinct" on the high school football field that his father had
displayed years earlier. So he "faked it": "When people told me that I
wasn't an animal and didn't have the killer instinct, it really hurt. So I

faked it as best I could and it usually worked. I growled and swore and did all those manly things, but my heart wasn't there, because I kept thinking, *knowing*, that I was *acting!* But when my father played football, I knew *he* wasn't acting—he was a killer, an animal, a man. And I wasn't."

As this story suggests, it is not enough to explain away the use of physical violence in sport as simply the result of rewards and punishments handed out by coaches, peers, and the community. Despite the intentions of some coaches and sport psychologists, athletes are not "made" through a Pavlovian system of reward and punishment. They are human beings, often incapable of doing the kind of "emotion management" that is necessary to participate in competitive athletics.[9] They are, however, capable of critical reflection, moral deliberation, and change. David Meggyesy, for instance, reacted against the fanatical "violence and brutality" of professional football by quitting while his career was in full swing. Their decision to participate—or not participate—in violent sport takes place within a complex social/psychological context. And, as we shall see, such decisions—and the meanings that the athlete attributes to them—depend in complex ways upon the athlete's gender.

Masculinity, the Rules, and Violence

Young males come to sport with identities that lead them to define their athletic experiences differently than female athletes do. Despite the fact that few males truly enjoy hitting and being hit, and that one has to be socialized into participating in much of the violence commonplace in sport, males often view aggression, within the rule-bound structure of sport, as legitimate and "natural."[10] Moreover, highly aggressive sports often feel psychologically "safe" to young males because they provide clear-cut boundaries around boys' and men's affiliations with each other. As Carol Gilligan has argued, because men fear intimacy, they tend to perceive vulnerability, danger, and thus the possibility of violence, not within situations of competitive achievement, but rather, in situations of close affiliation.[11] As Gilligan has written,

> *If aggression is tied, as women perceive, to the fracture of human connection, then the activities of care, as their fantasies suggest, are the activities that make the social life safe, by avoiding isolation and preventing aggression rather than by seeking rules to limit its extent. . . .*

Rule-bound competitive achievement situations, which for women threaten the web of connection, for men provide a mode of connection that establishes clear boundaries and limits aggression, and thus appears comparatively safe.[12]

Mary Duquin and Brenda Bredemeier, in two separate studies aimed at testing Gilligan's theory of gender difference, found that male and female athletes indeed engaged in different kinds of moral reasoning around issues such as rule-breaking and aggression.[13] Female athletes tended to fear that aggression—even "within the rules"—threatened their connection with others, and thus the basis of their identities. By contrast, male athletes tended to feel affirmed by, and comfortable with rule-bound athletic aggression.

These social-psychological analyses of athletic aggression reveal the affinity between developing masculine identities and the structure and values of the institution of sport. Within the athletic context, young males can develop a certain kind of closeness with each other while not having to deal with the kinds of (intimate) attachments that they tend to fear. Here individuals' roles and separate positions within hierarchies are determined by competition within a clearly defined system of rules that governs the interactions of participants. Although many athletes will "stretch" the rules as much as they can to gain an advantage over their opponents, most have a respect, even a reverence, for the importance of rules as a code of conduct that places safe boundaries around their aggression and their relationships with others. Without the rules, there would be chaos—both physical and psychological; there would be a frightening need to negotiate and renegotiate relationships constantly. This is what feels truly dangerous to men. So to Gene H., the constant physical aggression that is part of being a lineman in football felt more than "natural"—it also provided a comfortable context within which he developed a certain kind of relationship with other men.[14]

This guy we played against in Denver by the name of Walt B. . . . we battled. He enjoyed it, and I enjoyed it. But never was it a cheap shot, never did he have me down and just drive my head into the ground, you know, unnecessary stuff. We played a good, clean game of football, because we respected each other. Now, if he could knock me on my butt, he'd do it. And I'd do it to him and help him up. Talk to him after the game. Sit and talk with him like I'm sitting here talking to you. But while we're out there, now, we go at it. And I loved it. Yeah, I loved it.

For most of the men whom I interviewed, this sort of aggression "within the rules" was considered legitimate—even desirable. In fact, sociologist Peter Lyman has observed that aggression is usually not defined by men as "violent" so long as it is rule-governed, rather than anger-induced.[15] But what happens when legitimate aggression results in serious injury, as it so often does in sport? Two of the men I interviewed, football player Nathan C. and former professional baseball player David P., were involved in frighteningly violent collisions, each of which resulted in serious injury. In each incident, the play was "legal"—there was no penalty issued by officials. But in the aftermath of each case, there was a lively public controversy concerning "violence in sport." Nathan's and David's retrospective definitions of these situations are instructive in drawing a link between, on the one hand, the athlete's experience and understanding of his participation in violence, and on the other hand, the larger social meanings surrounding such public incidents.

By the time Nathan C.—"The Destroyer"—got to the pros, he had become the kind of fearsome hitter that coaches dream of. Though he took pride in the fact that he was not a "dirty" player (his hits were within the rules), his problem was that he was perhaps too good at his craft. "Intimidation" was the name of the game, but there was a growing concern within football and in the sport media that Nathan C.'s "knockouts" were too brutal. Eventually, the inevitable happened: Nathan delivered one of his patented hits, breaking his opponent's neck and paralyzing him for life. All of a sudden, Nathan was labeled as part of a "criminal element" in the NFL. He was confused, arguing that this had been a "terrible accident," but nevertheless a "routine play" and "within the rules."

> *I guess the thing that mystified me was that I could play for [several] years, and one guy gets hurt and then everybody comes down on me, you know. It's just like for all this time I've been playing the game the wrong way: but I've made All-Pro, I've got all the honors playing exactly the same way. So, you know, it just kind of mystified me as to why there was just all of a sudden this stuff because a guy got hurt. It*

wasn't the first time a guy got paralyzed in football, so it really wasn't that unusual.

David P. was the recipient of a violent hit in a major league baseball game. The situation was simple: It was the final inning, and an opposing player, steaming around third base, needed only to touch home plate in order to score the winning run. David's job as the catcher was to block the plate with his body and hope that the ball arrived in time for him to catch it and tag the runner out. The runner arrived a split second before the ball did and, looking a lot like a football player delivering a "hit," drove his body through David, and touched the plate safely. David's shoulder was separated, and despite his youth, he never fully regained the powerful home run swing that he had demonstrated earlier that summer. Again a serious injury had resulted from a technically legal play. The player who scored the winning run was seen by some as a hero, but others criticized him, asking if it was right for him to hurt someone else simply to score a run. He seemed as mystified by these questions as Nathan C. had been. "I play to win," he responded, "I just did what I had to do."

When I interviewed David P. years later, well into his retirement as a player, he lamented the effect of the injury, but he saw it not as the result of a decision on the part of his opponent, but rather as "a part of the game." It was fate, an impersonal force, that had broken his body—not an individual person. In fact, he felt nothing but respect for the man who had so severely injured him:

> *I've seen that play a million times since [in the] replays they keep show-ing and showing, but I never once believed that he hit me intentionally. He's just a competitor, and I only wish that every other major league ball player played as hard as he did, 'cause then you wouldn't have fans upset because players [are] making so much money and they're not performing. But he's a competitor—But I would say that that was the beginning of a lot of pain and problems for me.*

Nathan's and David's cases offer examples of what Brenda Bredemeier and David Shields call "contextual morality": the reification of the rules of the game free the participants from the responsibility for moral choices.[16] As long as the participants "play by the rules," they feel not only that they should be free from moral criticism but, perhaps subcon-sciously, that they are entitled to "respect," that emotionally distant connection with others so important to masculine identity. Flagrant rule-violators, it is believed, are "violent" and must be sanctioned; others like Nathan C. and the man who injured David P.'s shoulder are "aggressive competitors," deserving of respect. But this distinction is shaken when serious injury results from legal actions and public scrutiny raises questions about the individual morality of the athletes themselves. Both Nathan and David were nonplussed by the framing of the issue in terms of individual choice or morality: they just play by the rules.[17]

THE COSTS OF VIOLENCE: INJURIES AND HEALTH

I interviewed former pro football star Thomas M. in the upstairs office of the health spa that he owns and manages. Retired now for several years, he appears to be in excellent physical condition, and he makes his living helping others achieve strong, healthier bodies. He was relaxed, sitting in a chair and resting his feet on a table, talking about basketball. When I asked him how tall he was, I received a startling reply: "Oh, I used to be about 6'2"—I'm about 6 even right now. All the vertebras in my neck, probably from all the pounding and stuff, the vertebras used to be farther apart—just the constant pounding and jarring. It hurts all the time. I hurt all the time. Right now, that's why I put my legs up here on the table, to take the pressure off my lower back." Here is one of the ultimate paradoxes of organized combat sport: top athletes—especially boxers and those who play in the more aggressive and violent team sports—are often portrayed as the epitome of good physical conditioning and health, but they suffer a very high incidence of permanent injuries, disabilities, alcoholism, drug abuse, obesity, and heart problems. The instrumental rationality that teaches athletes to view their own bodies as machines or weapons with which to annihilate an objectified opponent comes back upon the athlete. The body-as-weapon ultimately results in violence against one's own body. In fact, a former professional football player in the United States has an average life-expectancy of about fifty-six years (roughly fifteen years shorter than the overall average life-expectancy of U.S. males). Football, of course, is especially brutal: Barry B. told me that in his pro career "six of eight off-seasons I had surgery, twice a two-for-one—they cut me twice." In a recent survey of retired professional football players, 78 percent reported that they suffer physical disabilities related directly to football, and 66 percent believe that having played football will negatively affect their life spans.[18]

Playing Hurt

It is not difficult to understand how athletes often get injured.[19] What is sometimes perplexing, though, is why so many athletes continue to "give up their bodies" by playing while injured, knowing that it may cause them permanent damage. The reasons are twofold: First, there are external pressures to play hurt. The values of the sportsworld are such that if one refuses to play hurt, he will be judged negatively by coaches, teammates, fans, and the media. Second, the internal structure of masculine identity results in men's becoming alienated from their feelings, thus making them more prone to view their bodies instrumentally. Though I discuss these "external" and "internal" factors separately, it should be kept in mind that they are mutually reinforcing and connecting factors.

EXTERNAL FACTORS. In a situation where "you are only as good as your last game," the respect one receives from being a winner is precarious. Bill S., for instance, was respected as an aggressive intimidator on the high school football field. But Bill discovered, as have many athletes, that the use of his body as a weapon—and the support of the community—can cut both ways. His athletic career, and his sense of identity that came with it, unraveled quickly when he injured his knee just before the state championship game:

> I was hurt. I couldn't play, and I got a lot of flack from everybody. The coach [said], "Are you faking it?" And I was in the whirlpool and [a teammate] came in and said "You fucking pussy!" I still remember that to this day. That hurt more than the injury. Later, people told me it was my fault because we lost, and I just couldn't handle that—not just coaches and other players, but people in the whole town. It hurt; it just really hurt.

Bill's "sin" was refusing to conform to "the pain principle," so important a part of the values of the sportsworld. Don Sabo writes that largely because of these sorts of external pressures, most male athletes tend to "adopt the visions and values that coaches are offering: to take orders, to take pain, to 'take out' opponents, to take the game seriously, to take women, and to take their place on the team. And if they can't take it, then the rewards of athletic camaraderie, prestige, scholarships, pro contracts, and community recognition are not forthcoming."[20] Bill S. couldn't (or wouldn't) "take it." As a result, he lost not only his status in the community, but also that fragile masculine identity he had built up through his sport successes. Just as he had previously found himself rewarded for using his own body to punish other people, he now found himself ostracized, his masculinity called into question, when he refused to "give up his body for the good of the team." It is significant that an objectified, sexualized female body part is the point of reference for the ultimate insult ("You fucking pussy!") to Bill's manhood.[21] In this athletic context, misogyny is a key mechanism through which the male peer group enforces its alienated, violent embodiment of masculinity.[22]

Given the system of rewards and punishment attached to the pain principle, many athletes do continue to "take it." The precarious nature of the athletic career makes it difficult for an injured player to stay out of competition until his injury is fully healed. As Barry B. said, "You play hurt. You play under a lot of pressure because you know somebody's behind you. Now, more than ever, when you turn pro, you have to be aware [that] you can't relax now. Moreso than ever, you pay a price, because now you've reached the last level—and it could end any day. It could end any minute." A number of men I interviewed said they had "paid the price" by coming back from injuries too soon, only to reinjure themselves almost immediately. This often led them to be labeled "injury-prone," which is similar to being called "lazy" or a "faker." An injured player—especially an often-injured player—is commonly treated as a pariah, a nonperson. As Willy S. lay in his hospital bed with a serious knee injury in his rookie year as a pro football player, the roar of the crowd seemed distant indeed:

I was thinking, "Everybody should feel sorry for me," you know? I'm hurt, you know? [Laughs]—and everybody, they just kept playing football! And I kept saying, "Well, man, they don't even need me." And here I had been getting all this attention, and now, I realize that, well, that's how you run your business—the show must go on, regardless. But then, I was thinking, "Boy, you guys shouldn't be playing! I'm hurt! Don't you see, I'm the star of the show!" That went on for a

month or so. Then I made my mind up to come back. I began my
workouts. I accelerated my program.

These kinds of pressures are not limited to professional athletes. When
Brent F. injured his ankle in high school basketball, he lost his position
to another player: "The coach found someone to replace me. After that,
I found it impossible to redeem myself. . . . I should have quit playing,
but I'd always start playing again before I should have—I'd never let it
heal all the way."

It is telling that Brent used the phrase "impossible to redeem myself" to describe the way he felt about having been injured. It was
as though he had done something shameful by getting hurt. Indeed,
David Meggyesy writes that "an atmosphere of suspicion" often sur-
rounds an injured player: "Coaches constantly question the validity of
a player's complaints, and give him the silent treatment when he has a
'suspicious' injury. After a few days of this treatment, many players
become frantic. They will plead with the team physician to shoot them
up so they can play. The player will totally disregard the risk of permanent injury."[23]

David P.'s interview was an almost endless chronicle of injuries, surgeries, rehabilitations, and rapid comebacks. When someone got hurt,
he explained, "We had a saying: 'Throw dirt on it, spit on it, go play.'"
And David always did "go play," despite his myriad aches, pains, and
injuries. The season that his shoulder was separated, he said he continued to play, often with "a lot of cortisone and just anything to kill the
pain, just to go out and play. I don't know how many shots I had—I
know I had a lot, because it was killing me. And now, as I rotate my left
arm, I can hear bone to bone, you know [laughs ironically]—because it
healed back wrong."

INTERNAL FACTORS. Nearly every former athlete I interviewed had at
least one story of an injury that disabled him, at least for a time. Many,
like David P. and Thomas M., had incurred serious injuries that had a
permanent impact on their health. Yet the tendency of athletes to "play
hurt" and endanger themselves cannot be attributed simply to the
greed of owners, the manipulation of coaches, or the cutthroat competition for positions on teams. There is a powerful motivating force
working in conjunction with external factors, that makes it likely that
the athlete will "choose" to play hurt: the internal structure of masculinity.

On the average, men die at a younger age than women do. Men are usually less emotionally expressive and engage in more dangerous and unhealthy behaviors (such as driving cars recklessly, smoking, and consuming alcohol), and men do not take adequate physical care of themselves (and are less likely to ask for medical help) than women.[24] These factors, along with the tendency for men to view their bodies instrumentally, are amplified in the competitive and insecure world of sport careers. It starts very early. Even in Little League baseball, according to sociologist Jay Coakley, "many participants do not report small injuries for fear that they will be taken out of the game or be accused of being babies. Those injuries may then become more serious or lead to other injuries."[25] By the time one gets to the professional level, according to Barry B., one "must know the difference between being hurt and being injured." But there is a fine line between being "hurt" and being "injured," and to recognize the difference one has to have a clear understanding of one's own body. David Meggyesy wrote that near the end of his professional football career it was hard to come to terms with his body: "I realized, paradoxically, how cut off and removed I was from my body. I knew my body more thoroughly than most men are ever able to, but I had used it and thought of it as a machine, a thing that had to be well-oiled, well-fed, and well-taken care of, to do a specific job."[26]

Given this "paradoxical" (I would say "alienated") relationship that many athletes have with their bodies, it is not surprising that many injuries are simply ignored until they cannot be ignored any longer. As David P. explained about one of his final seasons in major league baseball, "I actually played the second half of the season with a torn cartilage in my left knee, not knowing. I wore a brace at times, and it locked two more times on me. I should have known something was wrong, but I didn't." At the beginning of the next season, David had surgery on his knee, and he wore a cumbersome leg brace for eight long weeks that summer. His body had, for thirteen professional seasons, served as an effective means toward success, status, and fame. In fact, his athletic body had served as the center of his masculine identity, an identity constructed largely to counter the low self-esteem he had experienced as a child from a lower-class, insecure family. As his body began to break and disintegrate, so did his self-esteem. The indignity of the injury, the inactivity, and the brace on his leg brought his childhood and adolescent fears back to the surface. He was "just totally miserable": "I felt

kind of embarrassed—I went back to my feeling of my high school days
of what people thought about me with this brace on. We would go to
Tahoe, and I would not take my jeans off and show this brace . . . I just
felt very self-conscious."

This deep-rooted insecurity and self-consciousness are behind the
seemingly limitless determination David P. showed, year after year, in
coming back from serious injuries to play baseball. When asked what
his motivation was to do this, his answer seemed to sum up all of the
"external" and "internal" factors I have discussed:

> *I think coming up in professional baseball at a time when if you got
> hurt, you got no sympathy, and obviously I didn't get any—especially
> the shoulder injury. You know, "Throw dirt on it, spit on it, go play."
> So without somebody telling me to go play, you know, I was just too
> stupid to say I couldn't play. So I played. And I just felt that, you
> know, I've had the drive in me from a very young child, that drive to
> succeed in sports because that was the way out—and I wasn't going to
> let an injury get me down to the point that I wasn't going to play any
> more. And I saw it happen a lot of times with players. I guess it was a
> gift that God gave me to rehabilitate myself, to keep pushing, to keep
> going.*

Despite the fact that most of the athletes, like David, wore their scars
and permanent injuries with pride, as badges of masculine status, there
was also a grudging acknowledgement that one's healthy body was a
heavy price to pay for glory. But to question their decisions to "give up"
their bodies would be to question the entire system of rules through
which they had successfully established relationships and a sense of
identity. Since this is usually too threatening, former athletes instead
are more likely to rationalize their own injuries as "part of the game"
and to claim that the pain contributed to the development of "character," gaining them the respect of others. To continue to be somebody—
indeed, to be a man—one must "keep pushing, keep going." But sometimes one's will is not enough.

Drug Use among Athletes

In recent years, the "drugs in sport" issue has been defined as a major
social problem.[27] Largely because of the extreme visibility of athletes
and their traditional position as paragons of virtue, conservatism, and
role models for "America's Youth," the drug suspensions of stars such

as pro football player Lawrence Taylor have created a great deal of furor and media attention. Discussion of the "drugs in sport" issue has been framed largely in terms of individual choice and morality: Canadians reportedly responded with shame and a sense of disgrace when they learned that sprinter Ben Johnson had been stripped of his Olympic gold medal for taking steroids. How could he have *done* this?[28] Instead of simply assuming that Johnson and other athletes should "just say no," it is important to analyze the social context of drug use among athletes. It is therefore important to differentiate between different kinds of drugs. I will discuss three: painkillers, performance-enhancing drugs, and recreational drugs.

PAINKILLERS. What many of the critics and those ready to impose controls over individual athletes usually do not recognize is that drug use in the sportsworld (and not just in professional sport) has been accepted behavior for many years. Especially, but not exclusively, in sports where athletes must constantly play in pain, the use of painkillers, often administered by team doctors, is widespread. David P. played out an entire season with an injured shoulder, with "a lot of cortisone and just anything to kill the pain." Athletes are rarely "forced" to play hurt or to take painkillers. Yet we have seen how external and internal factors lead many athletes to "choose" to play hurt, and once the choice is made, many team doctors willingly supply painkillers to facilitate this decision. The man who chooses to take a shot in the knee and play hurt may be elevated to the status of hero for the moment, but he is the one who may have to live out the rest of his life in pain, or even crippled.

PERFORMANCE-ENHANCING DRUGS. We have seen how, in the world of the sport career, the body becomes an instrument that is consciously shaped and conditioned to do a job. As an athlete moves higher in the sportsworld, his personal commitment becomes greater, the stakes get higher, and the competition becomes more intense. Where, for instance, an athlete might have been able to dominate opponents in high school simply with his size and "natural ability," he finds when he gets to college that everybody is big, and everybody has ability. He then might start to look for something to give him an "edge." In the 1960s and 1970s, there were reports of widespread use of amphetamines in certain sports. One study, in 1972, concluded that 67 percent of NFL players used amphetamines, and in many cases, the drugs were supplied by team trainers or doctors.[29] Despite the fact that these drugs were addictive and dangerous, many players took them while coaches looked the other way. Eldon C. told me that in the world-class level of competition that he was in as a middle-distance runner, any slight advantage can make a difference between winning and second, or third, place. "I've discovered that there was more drug usage than I knew. Speed, stuff like that. Basically, it makes a slight difference, depending on who you are. I tried it a couple of times, not in events, but just in workouts. It was kind of shocking, you know, the difference. But I was real puritanical about that stuff. Now, if I had it to do over again, I'd do it. Definitely." Many players, apparently, do not have Eldon's "puritanical" attitude. Many, because of the "win at all costs" values of the sportsworld and the instrumental relationships they have with their own bodies, tend to feel that the short-term efficiency or confidence that is gained through drug use will outweigh any possible problems that might ensue from the drug. This appears to be true of the recent upsurge of steroid use among athletes.

In terms of the dangers to health, steroids make amphetamines seem tame. Yet large proportions of weight-lifters, football players, even track-and-field athletes, are estimated to take steroids because they clearly increase body mass, power, and strength. Tommy Chaikin revealed in a 1988 article in *Sports Illustrated* that when he began his career as a college football player, he opposed drug use. But he found that he was too small and was "getting the crap knocked out of [him]" by larger, stronger, more aggressive players—many of whom were taking steroids. He "took it as a challenge to [his] manhood," and he eventually joined the culture of steroid users, as coaches and trainers turned a blind eye. The results were immediate: in eight weeks, he'd gained size, strength, and aggressiveness. The troubling physical and psychological "side effects" of steroids were largely ignored—Chaiken did not want to give up the edge the drug gave him. Eventually, though, he nearly committed suicide, and he ended up in the hospital, severely depressed and physically damaged by the steroids.[30]

What is most striking about reading stories like Chaikin's is that despite the obvious dangers of steroids, given the structure of high-level competitive sport and the values of the sport culture, the question is not "how could he take this dangerous drug?" Instead, one wonders, how could he *not* have taken it? After all, steroid use does improve certain kinds of athletic performance. Evidence suggests that steroid use has become commonplace, perhaps even widespread, among body-builders and among athletes in sports that require muscular bulk and explosive power.[31] Though only 6 percent of players in the NFL tested positive for steroids in league-sponsored drug tests in 1988, this may be a reflection of inadequate testing procedures. NFL players who testi-fied in a 1989 session of Congress estimated that steroid use among pro football players is "epidemic," perhaps reaching as high as 75 percent.[32] There is growing evidence that steroid use has filtered down to high school sport. A 1989 study of 3,403 high school seniors in forty-six schools in the Southern California area indicated that 6.6 percent of them had used steroids.[33] Ben Johnson may be merely the visible tip of the iceberg.

In addition to the motivation to take steroids in order to improve one's athletic performance, there is growing evidence that steroid use has become a way to achieve instant respect within some athletic male peer groups. For instance, sociologists John Fuller and Marc La-Fountain conducted interviews with fifty steroid-using weight lifters and found that despite the fact that "medical evidence is overwhelming as to the deleterious effects these drugs have on the human body and the psyche," within the athletes' subculture, the medical evidence was discounted as exaggerated and alarmist.[34] In fact, Fuller and La-Fountain report, within the gym, "a certain amount of importance is attached to steroid use as signifying athletic commitment. Some of the subjects presented drug use as the only indicator of a serious attitude, almost as if steroid use meant instant authenticity, not to mention ath-letic competence."[35]

Here, in the athletic male peer group, we can see a collective con-struction of the athletic male body as machine. As sport scholar John Hoberman has pointed out, contemporary sport has grown directly out of "the fundamental law of this civilization . . . the performance prin-ciple."[36] To illustrate how this principle is embedded in the culture of American sport, Hoberman quotes Frederick C. Hatfield, the scientific editor of *Muscle and Fitness* magazine, who wrote in 1983: "Drugs are not inherently evil. . . . I believe that drugs have been, and will con-tinue to be an important source of man's salvation. I also believe that there can be no nobler use for drugs than improving man's performance capabilities. Society demands bigger, faster, and stronger athletes. The sacrosanctity of the sports arena, however, has been a hindrance to meeting this demand."[37] Athletes' use of performance-enhancing drugs meshes with the contemporary emergence of what Hoberman calls "the technological image of man." Surely, if the body is viewed as a machine whose raison d'etre is "maximum performance," then the addition of a bit of "high performance fuel" is all to the better. Don Atyeo quotes a professional football player: "If they say, 'It's not whether you win or lose but how you play the game,' then fine, a lot less guys will use drugs. But they've never said that. And as long as winning is the name of the game, you have to take what you can."[38]

RECREATIONAL DRUGS. Athletes' use of "recreational" drugs (alcohol, marijuana, cocaine, etc.), which are not intended as performance-enhancers, is best explained as a reflection of the larger society's use of these drugs. In fact, the social scientific research is unclear on the question of whether or not athletes do more or fewer recreational drugs than those in the general population. There is some evidence that recreational drug use among athletes is widespread. For instance, sociologist Charles Gallmeier, in his study of a professional hockey team, found that nearly every player on the team participated in some form of "juicing, burning, and tooting" (alcohol, marijuana, and cocaine use).[39] But there is also some evidence that the public perception of widespread drug use and abuse by athletes is overblown, resulting largely from the high-profile of athletes who are arrested or suspended for drug use.[40]

That drug use in sport is a reflection of drug use in society can be illustrated by looking at possibly the most abused drug in society and in sport: alcohol. Alcohol, especially beer, is closely associated with the sportsworld. Beer manufacturers and distributors are among the largest sponsors of sporting events, and from city-league to professional sport, the most common thing to do after a sporting event is to go out and have a few beers "with the boys." For the top-level athlete, alcohol, as a depressant, can be used to relax from the extreme pressure of the game.

Alcohol also tends to play a very important role within male peer groups. Young men often compete to "drink each other under the table." Sometimes this excessive alcohol use within male peer groups can contribute toward group sexual violence against women.[41] But in addition to sometimes triggering (and serving as an ex post facto justification for) aggression and violence, alcohol use in male peer groups can also be seen, sociologist Lillian Rubin points out, as "an inchoate wish to relax some of the constraints that bind [men] in their human relationships."[42] In short, the particular form of masculinity that is constructed within the athletic male peer group requires the suppression of feelings, especially "softer" feelings such as sorrow and hurt. It also enforces severe limits on direct (verbal and physical) displays of tenderness, empathy, and nurturance. Alcohol, as a depressant, can help a man suppress or deaden these feelings, but it also can give men permission to "open up," to be more expressive ("I'm really drunk, so I'll tell you this")—even to be physically supportive and affectionate with each other. I have observed young male athletes, after several hours of drinking, pouring their hearts out to each other, even crying and hugging. But the next day, not a word is spoken of this shared intimacy. The fact that alcohol can lubricate the male peer group in ways that makes expression of intimacy more acceptable might explain much of the appeal of many of the televised beer commercials that show men drinking together and being close.

Thus, whether we are looking at painkillers, performance-enhancing drugs, or recreational drugs, our analysis of them as "problems" should not be couched in a rhetoric of individual morality. Better we should examine these issues in the broader context of the sportsworld (and indeed, of the larger society) and the alienated relationships that men are encouraged to develop with their bodies and with each other.

SOCIAL CLASS, RACE, AND ATHLETIC EMBODIMENTS

Despite the external and internal pressures to use one's body as a weapon against others and to "play hurt," there are moments of resistance to—even rejection of—the pain principle, even among top-notch athletes. For instance, San Francisco Forty-Niners twenty-seven-year old tight end John Frank retired before the 1989–90 season while still very early in his career. He cited the "brutality" of football as his major reason for quitting and giving up his $357,500 salary. In his final season, Frank had several bones in his left hand crushed in a game. He described the incident to a *Sports Illustrated* reporter: "It sounded like I cracked all my knuckles at once. . . . The hand went numb. I wanted to cry. Lindsey McLean [the Forty-Niner trainer] said, 'We'll cast it, John, and you can block in the second half.' At that moment I realized how barbaric football is. I thought, you've got to be kidding. I only get one left hand. I told Lindsey no."[43]

Soon Frank made the decision to quit the game altogether. "I just couldn't [mentally] block out the injuries any more."[44] In refusing to play injured, and by leaving the game for good, Frank had rejected the dictates of the pain principle and delivered a searing critique of the sport of football. But despite his rejection of football, hundreds of thousands of boys and young men, from pee wees to professionals, continue to line up each autumn to play the game. A key to understanding the uniqueness of Frank's rejection of the world of football is the fact that he was in medical school, and he saw possible football injuries as real threats to his career as a surgeon. But in quitting football, he was most assuredly not rejecting masculine status and power. He was making a rational decision that was likely to yield him a secure (and less physically dangerous) economic future. As boxing promoter Chris Dundee once said, "Any man with a good trade isn't about to get himself knocked on his butt to make a dollar."[45]

Most athletes, especially by the time they reach the professional ranks, do not have the range of career options that John Frank had. Among the men I interviewed, young athletes from lower-class backgrounds, especially poor black males, were far more likely than their middle-class counterparts to become committed to careers in violent sports. There are a number of reasons for this. First, middle-class males are more likely to leave a sport career earlier, owing to a wider range of educational and career options. Second, middle-class males who do choose to pursue athletic careers have greater access to sports such as tennis, golf, and swimming, and they are thus likely to opt out of dangerously violent sports at a fairly early age. Lower-class males are more likely to be channeled into sports such as boxing, football, basketball, and baseball, where aggressive, even violent body contact or collisions are "a part of the game."[46] Once involved in these sports, there is considerable evidence that they are likely to be "stacked" in lower-prestige, higher-risk positions.[47]

In addition to these structural reasons, lower-class males are more likely to value physicality as a means of gaining status among other males. Nathan C. and Ricardo R. both stated that they received "respect" from their peers for being tough, aggressive "hitters" and "intimidators" on the football field. And Thomas M., when asked whether he liked the contact in football, stated, "Yeah—the *respect* that I got from it." The use of aggression, intimidation, and violence as a means of gaining respect was sometimes taken to extremes, beyond the rules.

For instance, before being injured himself, Bill S. had developed a reputation as a very successful high school athlete, largely because of his ruthless aggressiveness. By his own admission, he would often "do mean things, like beat people up. On the football field, I'd be dirty, like I'd kick guys in the groin . . . or in basketball, I'd undercut people. And I think it was mainly to earn their respect. It was like I had to let them know that, hey, I'm superstud and you, you're second class—you're not as good."

Sometimes this kind of aggressive intimidation would take on racial undertones. Ray J., for instance tells a story of a basketball game in high school where he was the only black on his team, playing against a team which also had one black player:

> We play against each other and he's supposed to be the best around. Well, hey, fuck you, buddy! Let's see who is the best. I can dominate you, buddy! You know, I'm gonna slap you upside the head if the referee turns his head—I might do a lot of things just to show you who's boss out here. I slapped him upside the head once, and they got a little riot out there. They hated me, you know, everybody hated me because I was good. [Laughs]—I'd intimidate people.

When I asked Ray whether he liked being "hated," he replied, "Well, you got respect. They didn't really hate me, they respected me. I was the villain that was gonna win. We won that game, and it was just the idea that I had to show that I was the best black around. I had fun. I was recognized, you know."

This sort of "black villain" role is sometimes appropriated by an athlete in order to play on white fears and "get the edge." Gerald M., who at the age of thirty still plays a lot of basketball, on mostly white playgrounds, told me that he has consciously constructed a "fearful" persona in order to intimidate "white boys": "I'm tall, I'm thin, I'm a black person with a shaved head, and I'm fearful. You have to intimidate mentally, because that's the advantage you have. But you're not really out to hurt that individual—it's competitiveness—the whole realization is that you've gotta talk shit in this game, you *have to* say, you know, 'If you come close to me, I'm gonna *hurt you!*' "

As Richard Majors has argued, young black males often find sport to be a context in which they can actively embody "cool pose," an aggressive, expressive style that sends the message, "See me, touch me, hear me, but, white man, you can't copy me!"[48] But though cool pose is an embodied masculine style that is, in some ways, resistant to the class constraints and racial oppression these young men face, essentially this form of resistance is mostly symbolic, and probably self-defeating. Though it may benefit a few black men by giving them specific tools with which to successfully compete within masculine hierarchies such as sport, it ultimately does not challenge—indeed, it may actually support—the logic of racial domination. It is ironic that large numbers of poor black men such as Ray J. and Nathan C. are channeled into sport, where to be successful, they must become intimidating, aggressive, and even violent to survive. Then, commentators turn around and use these "data" to "prove" that black men are indeed naturally violent and aggressive.[49] Placing irony on top of irony, some black men, like Gerald M., will theatrically appropriate this socially constructed stereotype, using it to play on white fears, to seize an advantage in a world that has offered them so few alternatives.

5 : Friendship, Intimacy, and Sexuality

The locker room had become a kind of home to me. . . . I often enter tense and uneasy, disturbed by some event of the day. Slowly my worries fade as I see their unimportance to my male peers. I relax, my concerns lost among relationships that are warm and real, but never intimate, lost among the constants of an athlete's life. Athletes may be crude and immature, but they are genuine when it comes to loyalty. The lines of communication are clear and simple. . . . We are at ease in the setting of satin uniforms and shower nozzles.

—BILL BRADLEY, 1977
Life on the Run

On 17 September 1990, *Boston Herald* reporter Lisa Olson routinely entered the New England Patriots locker room to get her postgame interviews. Several players responded to her presence by harassing her with lewd comments and sexually aggressive gestures. The following week, Cincinnati Bengals coach Sam Wyche barred a woman sportswriter from the team's locker room, in violation of the National Football League's long-standing equal access rules. In the days and weeks following these incidents, the NFL levied fines against the New England players and Wyche, and reporters and athletes debated the issue in public forums. On the one side it was argued that in order to get her story and meet her deadline, a woman reporter's "right to access" to the postgame locker room must be respected. On the other side, it was asserted that athletes should have a "right to privacy" in the locker

85

room. According to a *Sports Illustrated* survey of 143 NFL players, only 38.5 percent were in favor of women reporters entering the locker room, while 47.6 percent were opposed, and 13.9 percent were undecided. Among those who were opposed to the presence of women in the locker room, the common factor appeared to be their view that the locker room is a male preserve, separate from women. Atlanta Falcon quarterback Scott Campbell said, "When women start playing in the NFL, then they should be allowed in the locker room." Phoenix Cardinals running back Ron Wolfley put it this way: "The locker room is a sweaty place. You want to belch. Maybe you want to scratch. It doesn't seem like a good place for women to be." On the other hand, the statement by Dallas Cowboy defensive tackle Danny Noonan seemed to sum up the feelings of the sizable minority of players who favor women reporters in the locker room: "I don't know why all of a sudden now it's coming out. I thought that this stuff was resolved in the '70's." [1] Indeed, in an informal survey I conducted among acquaintances and my students, the dominant reaction appeared to be a yawn and slightly irritated sense of déjà vu: Hadn't the "women reporters in the locker room issue" been dealt with over a decade ago?

Why does this issue continue to surface every few years, often in the form of ugly confrontation between male players and women reporters? Is it simply a clash of "rights"—the women reporters' right to pursue their profession, the players' right to privacy in the locker room? I think the issue runs much deeper than this. In order to understand its persistence—and especially the depth of anger it periodically brings out in male athletes—it is necessary to examine the specific kinds of relationships that male athletes develop. How do male athletes define their friendships with each other? What do men talk about in locker rooms? What is the role of sexuality in male athletes' relationships with each other? Finally, how are men's relationships with each other shaped by—and in turn, how do they shape—their attitudes about and relationships with women?

"LIKE FAMILY": FRIENDSHIP ON THE TEAM

Years after the end of an athletic career, it is not uncommon to hear men talk almost reverently of their relationships with teammates. Gene H., for instance, said,

The guys I played with, I had the utmost respect for. Because once you've been through training camp together, and those hard times together, you learn to know and feel things about them that no one else can ever feel if they haven't been in those situations with them. The most important persons are your teammates, and to be loved and respected by them means more than anything—more than the money aspect, if a guy would tell the truth about it.

These kinds of statements are not reserved for former professional athletes. Jim P., who only played organized sport through high school, spoke of his relationships with teammates with similar reverence:

I'd say that most of my meaningful relationships have started through sports and have been maintained through sports. There's nothing so strong, to form that bond, as sports. Just like in war too—there are no closer friends than guys who are in the same foxhole together trying to stay alive. You know, hardship breeds friendship, breeds intense familiarity. . . . You have to endure something together—sweat together, bleed together, cry together. Sports provide that.

This (often highly romanticized) sense that close friendships between men are forged in "adversity," through "enduring hardship" together, was a common theme in former athletes' discussions of their relationships with teammates. But despite almost universal agreement that sport provided a context in which this kind of mutual respect, closeness, even love, among men developed, there was usually a downside to men's descriptions of their relationships with teammates. Brent F., for instance, said that in his early teens, his relationship with his best friend was a "sports rivalry." He described this friendship as "a sort of love-hate relationship. There were times when we—I remember fighting him. I remember getting into fights, but at the same time I remember going to his house and having good times. It was never a real deep relationship." It is this sort of ambiguity that was most characteristic of men's descriptions of their relationships with teammates. "Forged in battle," these are often the closest relationships that these men ever have; yet the battles as often take place between teammates as they do with other teams. This paradox can be examined as a manifestation of the development of masculine identities within the competitive, hierarchical world of athletic careers.

The Team Structure: Antagonistic Cooperation

The public face that a team attempts to present to the rest of the world
is that of a "family" whose shared goal of winning games and championships bonds its individual members together. But the structure of
athletic careers is such that individuals on teams are constantly competing against each other—first for a place on the team, then for playing
time, recognition, and "star" status, and eventually, just to stay on the
team. Rather than being a purely cooperative enterprise, then, athletic
teams are characterized by what sociologist David Riesman called "antagonistic cooperation."[2] In sport, as Christopher Lasch has pointed
out, just as in the modern bureaucratic corporation, "a cult of teamwork conceals the struggle for survival."[3]

Coaches attempt to mitigate the potentially negative consequences of
this individual struggle for survival by emphasizing the importance of
"team play."[4] In fact, several men said that having learned to "play a
role" on a team, rather than needing to be the star, was a valuable lesson
they learned through sport. For them, teamwork was an exciting and
satisfying experience. As Jon P. put it, "I like the feeling of getting on a
team where you might not have the best individuals, but with teamwork and somehow a sense of togetherness, you can knock somebody
off that's better than you." This sort of satisfaction, though, was probably easier to experience and appreciate for young players like Jon, who
knew that they were not "stars," who knew that their futures did not lie
in athletic careers. As he put it, "I would never have gotten my name in
the paper—maybe if I had been a better scorer, but I never was. The
way I would make my niche in basketball was obviously by being a
good passer—I always got a thrill out of it."

For those who did see themselves as stars (or as potential stars), for
those who were committed to an athletic career, the competition with
teammates was very real, and often very intense. Athletes have developed their own ways of dealing with the hard reality that one teammate's success might mean one's own demotion. For instance, the fact
that new players on a team often pose a threat to the veterans is dealt
with through ritualized testing and hazing of rookies. Willy S. said that
as a rookie on his college football team, he had to "earn the respect" of
the older players before being accepted as a teammate. He did this, he
said, by "getting knocked on my butt by them," and then in turn,
"knocking them on their butts. After that, they respected me." Nathan

C. agreed that "you get your respect, but you have to earn it. . . . They won't just give it to you right off." Part of the ritual involves showing the proper deference to the veteran players, not appearing too "cocky." One year, Nathan said,

> *A rookie came in, and the veterans hadn't even come to camp yet, and this guy was talking about what he was going to do to [the team's defensive stars], how he was gonna be the leading pass receiver. He lasted about two days. They hurt him, and I think he stayed in the training room about two weeks. Came out, lasted another day, and they sent him back. Finally he had to be cut from the team. People were popping him, right, just because he had a loud mouth.*

Once a team is formed, a coach does his best to channel these internal antagonisms toward an external "enemy." As Gene H. explains, "No matter what you hear about teams—they don't get along, they fight each other—you just try to let some outsider come in and come up fighting one of them. It'd be like two brothers who fight like cats and dogs, but you let *somebody else* mess with one of them and he's got to be ready to deal with both of them at one time. Same thing: a team *is* a family. It *has* to be." Lurking just below the surface of this "family" rhetoric, though, lies intense, often cutthroat competition. A number of men told me of difficult, even destructive relationships that developed between themselves and teammates as a result of competition for individual rewards and recognition. This was especially true in cases where two players were vying to be seen as the star of the team. Jim P. told of a high school basketball game in which his teammate/rival was "basket-hanging" and had gotten twenty-six easy points by half-time, which put him within five points of the school record.

> *I must have fed Tim [the ball] eight times in the first half. At halftime, our center says to me, "Hey, this is bullshit. I'm getting all the rebounds, and I haven't gotten a shot. Why can't Tim get a few rebounds instead of all the [easy ones] at the other end?" So I said, "Oh, I'll take care of that," because I was the one throwing him the ball all the time. So I'd get the outlet pass and I'd just bring it up. Tim ended up with twenty-eight points. I'm sure he still begrudges that—I mean, he could have broken every record in the book, but anybody who could make a layup could have done that.*

The intensity of competitive antagonism between teammates often increases as one moves up the ladder of athletic careers, where the stakes are higher. Chris H. said that through college, relationships with teammates were important and meaningful to him, but when he got to the professional ranks, he found it was "all business," with little room for the development of close friendships:

> [*When you get*] *to pro ball, all of a sudden you got assholes out there. It's the money. The competition is greater. You're dealing with politics. I was drafted second round. They had a lot of draft picks and it was real cutthroat. So you see a lot of good players come and go. It was tight. You're dealing with money. You're dealing with jobs. It's a business, and that really turned me off. I had dreamed it would be* everything, *and I got there and it was a job. You know, a fucking job where a man screams at your ass.*

At times, the antagonisms are racial. Thomas M., for instance, described his shock in his first year of pro football in finding that black players were second-class citizens on his team:

> *There was no togetherness on that team. Race had a lot to do with it. And money. They didn't want a brother making any money. You know, a white player would walk into the damn locker room and tell one of the brothers, "Turn off that damn nigger music! I don't want to hear that shit!" And the brother would go over and turn the music off! Boy, oh boy, when the guy turned off the music, that just about blew my mind! I said to myself, this cat's got no heart. And then they went after me, because I'm the rookie, the number one draft choice. They wanted me to sing.* I ain't singing: Fuck 'em. I'm a grown man. I ain't gonna sing. *Then they tried to get me on the football field and I ended up fucking around and hurting a couple of people 'cause I knew what they were gonna do. It didn't take me very long to get 'em quiet.*

Few men described such overt racial conflicts, yet most did say that informal friendship networks on teams tended to be organized along racial lines. Nevertheless, several white and black men told me that through sport they had their first real contact with people from different racial groups, and for a few of them, good friendships began. Unfortunately, most of these friendships were not strong enough to persist outside the context of the team, where social, cultural, peer, and familial pressures made it difficult to nurture and maintain cross-racial friendships.[5]

MASCULINE IDENTITIES AND MEN'S FRIENDSHIPS

An interesting consensus has emerged among those who have studied gender and friendship in the United States: Women have deep, intimate, meaningful, and lasting friendships, while men have a number of shallow, superficial, and unsatisfying "acquaintances." Several commentators have concluded that men's relationships are shallow because men have been taught to be highly homophobic, emotionally inexpressive, and competitive "success objects."[6] Lillian Rubin, employing a psychoanalytic perspective, has argued that men tend to place a high value on "spending time" with other men, but their early developmental experiences have left them with a deep fear of intimacy (which she defines as the ability and willingness to share one's inner life with another person). As a result, Rubin says, men tend to distance themselves from each other by organizing their time together around an activity that is "external" to themselves. As Jim P. stated above, "Sports provide that": Here men can enjoy the company of other men—even become "close"—without having to become intimate in ways that may threaten their "firm ego boundaries," and thus their fragile masculine identities. As a result, men's friendships with each other are, according to Rubin, "emotionally impoverished."[7]

Within this theoretical framework, we can begin to make sense of former professional basketball player Bill Bradley's seemingly paradoxical description of his relationships with his teammates as "warm and real, but never intimate."[8] Bradley seems comfortable with the simultaneous existence of a certain kind of closeness and a clear sense of boundaries and distance. This is understandable when considered in light of the affinity between masculine gender identity and the gendered structure of sport as a social institution: The hierarchical and rule-bound pattern of athletic careers, and especially of "antagonistic cooperation" on the team, dovetails with men's ambivalent need to develop "closeness without intimacy" with other men. In short, competitive activities such as sport mediate men's relationships with each other in ways that allow them to develop a powerful bond while at the same time preventing the development of intimacy.

But to simply leave it that men's friendships constitute "bonding without intimacy" belies the depth of affection that so many of these men expressed for each other. Sociologist Scott Swain has suggested that negative views of "male bonding" are distorted and unfair. Drawing on Francesca Cancian's observation that since the industrial revolution, social conceptions of love and intimacy have become "feminized," Swain argues that Lillian Rubin and others have been guilty of judging men's friendships against the standard of the type of intimate relationships that women tend to develop.[9] Women tend to place a very high value on talk—and indeed, for a relationship between women to be "intimate," there must be a willingness and ability to mutually share their inner lives. In this light, since men friends tend to "do things" with each other, rather than spending their time talking about their inner lives, they are judged to be engaged in "bonding without intimacy." Swain asserts that if we instead examine men's friendships from the point of view of men, rather than through a "feminine model," we see that men's friendships are in fact characterized by a "covert style of intimacy." Men, Swain asserts, already have an "active style of intimacy" and should not be forced to learn "feminine-typed skills to foster intimacy in their relationships."[10] In short, women and men experience and define intimate friendship in different ways, and neither should be judged by the standard of the other.

When I asked Gene H. whether or not he and his closest teammate/ friend shared their thoughts and feelings, he replied, "We didn't *have* to talk about everything; We just *knew* we were on the same page." These kinds of statements are consistent with Swain's contention that men share a covert intimacy, and that "men and women have different styles of intimacy that reflect the often-separate realms in which they express it."[11] But there is a danger in viewing men's and women's friendships as "separate but equal." For example, Swain discusses a man who told him that "a couple of girls picked [him and his friend] up and we got laid and everything. . . . After, [he and his friend] went out and had a few beers and compared notes." Swain concludes that "though this sort of quote might imply sexual exploitation, . . . the commonality gained from a shared life experience did provide meaningful interaction among the men."[12] Clearly, this talk among men is "meaningful interaction" when viewed from the point of view of the men. But whatever this implies about the operation of male friendships, it is also crucial to examine the ways that sexual talk among men about women might contribute to certain kinds of attitudes toward and relationships with women. In other words, I am suggesting that we move away from examining men's friendships with each other from a "feminine" standpoint (Rubin) or from a "masculine" standpoint (Swain), and instead ask feminist questions: How are male athletes' friendships with each other affected by—and in turn how do they affect—their attitudes toward and relationships with women?

SEXUALITY AND SEXUAL IDENTITY

"Big Man on Campus." "Sexual Athlete." For many, these terms conjure up the dominant cultural image of the athlete on campus: He is extremely popular, self-assured, and (hetero)sexually active. Other boys and young men are envious of the ease with which he can "get women." My interviews at times revealed a grain of truth to this popular stereotype of the athlete. Chris H. said that even as a second-string professional basketball player, it was "just the good life." He laughed, "I mean, you could wave at one way up in the fifteenth row, and after the game, she's standing right there by the locker room . . . that's what makes it fun, you know." Similarly, when asked how he related to others when in school, Thomas M. said, "I liked to be the big man on campus, and sports was a highlight because it gave me that opportunity. *Everybody* knew who I was. Big Tom. *Everybody* knew who I was."

On the surface, these two statements affirm the stereotype of the athlete as a confident young man at ease with himself and with his sexuality among his peers. Interestingly though, when asked about their specific relationships with girls and women, a very different picture emerged. "Big Tom," for instance, stated that "girls, in high school, were really not prime in [his] life." He laughingly continued, "When I was in high school, I thought I was an ugly guy. You know, being under a lot of pressure, and being so much bigger than everybody, and everybody's always looking at you. In high school, you don't know what looks *mean*—it could be good, it could be bad. At one time I felt I was a freak, so I was more or less into myself. I don't think I had one girl-friend." This youthful awkwardness and insecurity with respect to girls seemed almost universal among the men I interviewed. David P.'s shyness was compounded by his family's difficult economic situation, so for him, sport became an escape from dealing with girls: "No doubt I was shy, and I think it had to do with the fact that if I did make a date with a girl, how was I going to go? What was I going to spend? Because I had none of it. So I just used sports as an escape." Clarence T., who had no trouble paying for dates, nevertheless had similar problems with girls:

> *In my senior year [of high school], I remember dating all these girls. It was real bizarre: I had this list I kept of all the girls I wanted to go out with, and it was like twenty-five people, and I went out with twenty of them. I was just going out with people. I wasn't sexually active—I hadn't had intercourse—I might have done a little petting, but never any genital stuff. I think I was popular, and was seen as an attractive boy, but I didn't have a sense of it. I just thought I was absolutely ugly as hell.*

Several of the men I interviewed recalled hoping that being an athlete would give them the confidence to overcome their "lameness" with girls. Jon P. said that he had hoped that being on the basketball team would help him overcome his shyness "and make it easier to talk with girls. It didn't." But several of these men reported that they did eventually develop ways to talk to girls, despite their shyness. Eldon C., for instance:

> *[In high school], I was lame, as they called it. So I didn't know how to do women so well. My stepmother threw a sixteenth birthday party for me and invited a lot of friends, and I remember that day, trying on a lot of the roles that I saw guys playing, and it kind of shocked me because the women took it seriously, you know. That was a big turning point for me. I didn't particularly like—some of the black modes of relating to women, I thought were* stupid. *Like: "you know, sugar, you know"—just* nonsense—*sweet nothings seemed silly to me. [But] anyway, I tried it, my version of it, and to my surprise some woman took it seriously. That meant it was possible [laughs].*

Calvin H. describes a similar transformation from tortured shyness with girls in high school to a smooth "rap" with women in college:

> *I was just scared, and bashful and shy. I did not know what to say or what to do. It was very uncomfortable. One of the things that were the rewards of being a good athlete, and you didn't really want it—I mean, you wanted it, but you didn't want it—you know, like, a girl likes you, but then, clamming up and not being able to communicate very effectively. This was a very bad time, because you're always*

around a lot of girls at parties. [I was] very uncomfortable in groups and with individuals. Finally [I went] off to college and went to the extreme of trying to attract a lot of girls, [and was] semisuccessful. You knew you had to have a date on Fridays, and knew you had to have one on Saturdays, and so you just walked through the student union, and you'd just have this rap you'd thought of, and you'd just put it on. It was peer pressure. I'm naturally a shy person. But somehow in college I was able to somehow fall into the right kinds of things to do and say.

We can see from these stories that developing a "rap" with women becomes an almost ritualized way that a young man helps himself overcome an otherwise paralyzing shyness, a sense of "lameness" when trying to relate to young women. This sort of verbal game involves a certain dramaturgy, a conscious self-manipulation ("you'd just put it on"), and one result is that girls and women become the objects of men's verbal manipulation. This kind of manipulation of women does not spring naturally or magically from men's shyness. Rather, it is socially learned through the male peer group. Notice that Eldon C. learned to "do women" by watching his friends. Calvin H., though somewhat mystified as to how he was able to overcome his shyness and "fall into the right things to say," also cites "peer pressure" as a motivating force. Clearly, an analysis of the development of men's sexual relationships with women must take into account the ways that male peer groups influence attitudes and feelings about sexuality and emotional commitment to women.

Peter Lyman, in his study of college fraternities, argues that there is an erotic basis to the fraternal bond in male groups.[13] In the past, the key to maintaining the male bond was the denial of the erotic. Organized sport, as it arose in the late nineteenth and early twentieth centuries, was based in part on a Victorian antisexual ethic. First, it was believed that homosocial institutions such as sport would masculinize young males in an otherwise feminized culture, thus preventing homosexuality.[14] Second, the popular (and "scientific") belief in the "spermatic economy" held that "the human male possessed a limited quantity of sperm, which could be invested in various enterprises, ranging from business through sport to copulation and procreation. In this context, the careful regulation of the body was the only path to the conservation of energy."[15] As sociologist Todd Crosset has pointed out, in a society in which it was held that young men's precious energies would be drained off should they expend too much sperm, sport was elevated as the key "to regenerate the male body and thus make efficient use of male energy." [16]

Some of the older men in this study went through adolescence and early adulthood when remnants of the ideology of the "spermatic economy" were still alive. Eldon C. reports that as a young runner, from the late 1940s through the mid-1950s, he had been "a bit cautious about sex, because [he] still had some old-fashioned notions about sexual energy [being] competitive with athletic stuff." Most of these men, though, came of age during the sexual revolution of the 1960s and early 1970s, when the dominant credo became, "if it feels good, do it." [17] As a result, the male peer group, within the athletic context, became a place where sexual activity and talk of sexual activity (real or imagined) was a key component of the status system.

But if the bond among men is erotic, and the culture is increasingly telling them, "if it feels good, do it," what is to prevent the development of sexual relations among young men who are playing, showering, dressing, and living in such close quarters? The answer is that the erotic bond between men is neutralized through overt homophobia and through the displacement of the erotic toward women as objects of sexual talk and practice. In boyhood, adolescent, and young adult male peer groups, "fag," "girl," and "woman" are insults that are used almost interchangeably. In this way, heterosexual masculinity is collectively constructed through the denigration of homosexuality and femininity as "not-male." Bill S. described nicely how his high school peer group helped to build his own public presentation of his sexuality: "I was shy [with girls]—I hung out more with guys. I never dated. I never was real intimate with anyone. It was just kind of scary because I thought I'd get teased by my peers." When I asked him whether he'd be teased for not being involved with women, he replied,

For being *involved! But* you've got to *be involved to the point where you get 'em into bed, you know, you* fuck *'em, or something like that, yeah, that's real important* [laughs]—*but as far as being intimate, or close, I wasn't. And that wasn't real important. Just so I could prove my heterosexuality it was real important. But I always wanted to look good to females—because I didn't have the personality* [laughs]—*to* get 'em into bed! *So I wanted to be able to have the* body, *and the sort of friends around who admired me in some sort of way, to have that pull.*

This sort of use of women as objects of sexual conquest is important for gaining status in the male peer group, but it also impoverishes young males' relationships with females. As Bob G. put it, in high school, he and his friends would "tell a lot of stories about girls. I guess it was a way to show our masculinity. [But] I never got emotionally involved with any of the girls I went out with. I never got close to any of them." The link between young males' tendency to "tell [sexual] stories about girls" and their lack of intimacy with girls is an important one. As Peter Lyman points out, young males commonly use sexually aggressive stories and jokes as a means of "negotiating" the "latent tension and aggression they feel toward each other." They also are using this joking relationship to "negotiate the tension they [feel] between sexual interest in the girls and fear of commitment to them. [They use] hostile joking to negotiate their fear of the 'loss of control' implied by intimacy."[18] While talk of sex with females, then, bonds the males together, the specific forms of sexual talk (sexual objectification and conquest of women) helps them deal with their terror of intimacy with women (described, by many, as "shyness" or "lameness" etc.). Again, in the words of Lyman, "In dealing with women, the group separate[s] intimacy from sex, defining the male bond as intimate but not sexual (homosocial), and relationships with women as sexual but not intimate (heterosexual)."[19] In a very real sense, these young males' relationships with females—whether sexual or not—were constructed through (indeed, were often distorted by and subordinated to) their relationships with their male teammates. One logical result is the kind of attitude toward women that former pro football star Jim Brown describes in his book, *Out of Bounds*. When he played football for the Cleveland Browns, he explains, his male "partners started calling [him] the Hawk" because he was so successful in "chasing women." Now at age fifty-three, Brown continues to view women primarily as young, sexual bodies and as objects of consumption: "My lady right now is nineteen. . . . When I eat a peach, I don't want it overripe. I want that peach when it's peaking."[20] Clearly, this attitude tends to preclude Brown's developing a long-term intimate relationship with one woman.

After all, every woman eventually ages, her body changes, and she can be discarded and replaced by what Brown sees as an endless supply of younger, firmer bodies.

Unlike Brown, many male athletes do yearn for, and manage to develop, more or less exclusive relationships with one woman. But this happens despite the fact that the male peer group tends to police its own members in terms of intimacy with females. Male peers might taunt boys and young men who start to spend too much time with a girlfriend, who are becoming too attached, telling them that they are "pussywhipped." Don Sabo, in writing about his own football career told this tale: "Once when I was a high school junior, the gang in the weight room accused me of being wrapped around my girlfriend's finger. Nothing could be further from the truth, I assured them, and in order to prove it, I broke up with her. I felt miserable about this at the time and I still feel bad about it."[21] Sociologist Timothy Curry found in his participant-observation study of two college male locker rooms that sexually aggressive talk about women usually takes the form of a loud public performance.[22] Curry also observed that any serious discussions between two men about actual relationships with girlfriends usually takes place in hushed tones, often at the edges of the locker room. If this sort of talk is discovered by the group, the speakers are often ridiculed and taunted to reveal details about the woman's body and whether or not the she is sexually "putting out." The result of this locker room culture, according to Sabo, is that many men end up suffering a kind of "'sexual schizophrenia.' Their minds lead them toward eroticism while their hearts pull them toward emotional intimacy."[23] Some young men deal with this split by keeping their emotional attachments with women a secret, while continuing to participate in locker room discussions about sexuality with their male peers. Bob G. had one such relationship in high school: "We started sneaking around and going out late at night and no one else knew. I didn't tell any of my friends. We got along great, sexually and emotionally, though she said I didn't express my feelings enough."

At times, the male peer group's policing of its members' relationships with females took on a racial angle. Larry W., for instance, said that when he was in college "the biggest conflict we had was black males dating white girls. The white males would call up the white females and call them whores, bitches, and prostitutes—you know, insulting language, like 'If you ball him, you'll ball anybody, so come over here and ball me too.'" In this case, the peer group was not only policing intimacy with women, but also imposing controls on interracial sexuality.

The need to prove one's manhood through sexual conquests of women was experienced as a burden by many young heterosexual males, and was sometimes complicated by racial tensions, but it was especially oppressive for gay men. As we saw in chapter 2, Mike T. threw himself into sport, rather than into dancing, largely because he was terrified that people might find out that he was gay. Sport allowed him to project a masculine public image. But this meant that he also had to project a heterosexual image:

> I hated high school. I mean, I just didn't know who I was. I think I had quite a bit of negative self-esteem at that time, because I really felt different. I mean, I didn't drink, I didn't like to screw around, and this was what all my friends did, so I felt compelled to go along with this stuff, and all the time hating it. I dated some women, some that I loved because they were just really fine people—[but] physically, there was not a great deal of passion. For males, there was a passion. [But] homophobia was rampant, especially in athletics. You see, I think a lot of athletes go into athletics for the same reason I did. They need to prove their maleness. And I did, I readily admit it. I felt I've got to hide this thing—because I know what they were thinking: If I were gay, they would see me as less than a man, or not a man. So I'm going to be a man, because that's what I am.

Though his secret knowledge of his own homosexuality made this process a much more conscious one for Mike, ("I was *clearly* aware of what I was doing"), his public construction of manhood-as-heterosexual was not all that different from what his nongay teammates were doing. Whether gay or heterosexual, the denial and denigration of gayness and femininity (in oneself and in others) were important to these young men's construction of masculine identities and status in their male peer group.[24] As Mike T. said,

> Go into any locker room and watch and listen, and you'll hear the same kind of garbage—I call it garbage now, and I thought it was garbage then, but I felt compelled to go along with it, because I wanted that image. And I know others who did, too. I know a lot of athletes are gay. And I think a lot of athletes are attracted to athletics because they're fighting feelings of tenderness—not necessarily gay—but they're fighting feminine qualities. I know a lot of football players who

very quietly and very secretly like to paint, or play piano, and they do
it quietly because this to them is threatening if it's known by others.

The pressure to be seen by one's peers as "a man"—indeed, the pressure to see oneself as "a man"—kept most young males in conformity (at least on the surface) with this homophobic and sexist locker room "garbage." Conformity with locker room culture was a way for both gay and heterosexual men to construct their public masculinity. But gay men were far more likely to see this process as a strategy than were heterosexual men. As Arthur Brittan explains, "Gender identity . . . is a set of reflexive strategies which are brought into play whenever gender is put on the line. In everyday life most heterosexuals do not have to do too much identity work because they tend to function in contexts in which heterosexuality is taken for granted."[25] In the locker room, gay athletes must constantly engage in "identity work." Nearly every gay athlete that social scientist Brian Pronger interviewed agreed that being around all of those naked male bodies in the locker room "feed[s] the homoerotic imagination and provide[s] homoerotic contact." One gay athlete told Pronger, "[There is] a surprising amount of sexual cruising and activity in the university locker rooms and shower. I've certainly had sex there."[26] But since homosexual behavior—or even more subtle expressions of desire—violate the kind of masculinity that is common in the locker room, most gay men develop a strategy of identity construction that is "ironic": On the surface, they conform to the heterosexist masculine culture, while underneath, they view the locker room through their hidden knowledge of its highly charged eroticism.

Even for a few heterosexual men, the "garbage" of the locker room led them to question—even reject—the jock culture and the specific form of masculinity and sexuality that predominated there. Brent F., for instance, says that toward the end of high school, he "really got turned off to the way the guys were relating to the girls":

It was really ugly in certain ways, like just treating them like objects,
totally judging them by their surface appearances, talking amongst
themselves in really abusive language about girls, how they're going to
do this or that to them. I thought it was wrong. I thought that people
shouldn't be treated that way. I started to realize that the way I related
to women was not the way these guys were relating to them, and there-
fore I didn't want to relate with them on that level. So I started to

distance myself from the same activities, and started to feel really alienated from my buddies.

This rejection of the sexist treatment of women was a rare exception to the rule. It is significant that this realization was made by a young athlete who several years earlier had decided that he was not a "career athlete." That he had already begun to disengage from his athletic career meant that he had less invested in the athletic male peer group. For young men who were fully committed to athletic careers, this sort of rejection of one of the key bonds of the group might have amounted to career suicide. So whether they liked it or not, most went along with it. Furthermore, when the "garbage" went beyond verbal sparring and to sexual behavior, peer group values encouraged these young men to treat females as objects of conquest. Eric M. described a night on the town with his male peers. He was in high school, a virgin, and terrified at his own lack of sexual experience. But when they hit the town, he said, "We were like wolves hunting down prey. Dave told me, 'If a girl doesn't give it up in sixty seconds, drop her!'"

It is this dynamic that is at the heart of what feminists have called "the rape culture."[27] One study of date rape revealed that college men who have experienced pressure from their current male friends to engage in sexual activity are more likely to commit acquaintance rape.[28] Similarly, a 1988 national study found that "involvement in peer groups that reinforce highly sexualized views of women" is an important predictor of "sexually aggressive behavior" by college males.[29] Robin Warshaw concluded from her research on date and acquaintance rape that "athletic teams are breeding grounds for rape [because they] are often populated by men who are steeped in sexist, rape-supportive beliefs."[30] Indeed, sportswriter Rich Hoffman reported in a story in the *Philadelphia Daily News* that between 1983 and 1986, a U. S. college athlete was reported for sexual assault an average of once every eighteen days.[31]

The sexual objectification of women among male athletes is probably, in most cases, a "rhetorical performance" that rarely translates into actual aggression against women.[32] But there is considerable evidence that men pay a price for these performances. As sociologist Miriam Johnson has argued,

That the peer group's pressure to be heterosexual occurs in a context in which women are sex-objectified may well have the consequence of making it difficult for males to become sexually aroused in a relation-

ship in which they do not feel dominant over the female. If one learns
about sexuality in the context of being rewarded by other males for
"scoring," for "getting pussy" or just "getting it," then this does not
augur well for egalitarian sex.[33]

Though this socially structured denigration of women truly does
hurt young males, in terms of making the development of true intimacy
with women more difficult to develop, ultimately, it is women—the
"prey"—who pay the price for young men's fear of intimacy with each
other.

Young men don't totally "go it alone" in constructing masculine
identities and relationships. Athletic teams and organizations, after all,
are organized and run by adult men. It is to young men's relationships
with their coaches that we turn next.

RELATIONSHIPS WITH COACHES

There are two common cultural stereotypes of "the coach."[34] First, the
coach is traditionally seen as a father figure: a strong, solid, and secure
man who acts as a role model to boys and young men, teaching them
the skills and values necessary to become responsible and successful
citizens. On the other hand, coaches are also commonly viewed as path-
ological or authoritarian types who, while working out their own insecurities, drive young athletes into destructive and self-destructive values and practices. How do athletes experience coaches? My interviews
indicate that these two stereotypes of coaches—the responsible
"builder of men" and the authoritarian "slave driver"—live side-by-
side, each reflecting a different aspect of the same social reality.

At least through the mid–1960s, the view of coaches as responsible
adult role models was probably most common. This is largely because,
as Sabo and Panepinto point out in their study of former football players, coaches were acting as the "social-psychological managers of boys'
gender identity development." Drawing on anthropological literature,
Sabo and Panepinto argue that young male athletes' relationship with
their adult male coaches is akin to traditional patriarchal rites of passage into adult manhood in preindustrial societies. Here, the initiates
to manhood are isolated from women, subjected to adult male authority
and control, and taught (largely through the use of pain) deference to
male authority. Sabo and Panepinto quote a man saying of his former
coach, "We all worshipped the ground he walked on but he was also a

huge prick. He beat the shit out of us and we loved him for it. It sounds weird now, but that's the way it was."[35] Many of the men I interviewed expressed, in retrospect, this puzzlement about their own compliance with the authority of, and their own need to be affirmed by, their former coaches. Clarence T., for instance, said:

> The coaches would push us in ways that didn't seem fair, and I would do it! But I have this memory of looking at them and thinking, what the fuck is all this stuff about? [But] it wasn't that I got angry back at them. I think I was perceived as real coachable because I wouldn't talk back to them. And winning their respect was real important. I remember one time the head football coach was walking around the gym in P.E. class and he walked by me and said, "Hey, Clarence, you've got to quit that smoking!" And I wasn't smoking. And I wanted to say, "But Mr. Smith, I don't smoke!' I was really concerned and scared that he thought I smoked. I just wanted to get on my hands and knees and say "I don't smoke. I don't smoke."

For Jim P., the respect he automatically gave his coaches was connected to their position, but there were certain coaches for whom he felt he would do anything:

> Even if a guy wasn't a good coach, I still respected him, just [for] the fact that he was a coach. You were supposed to respect him. But there were particular coaches I didn't want to let down, [because of] the fact that they were so involved with our teams and with me as an individual. I think they cared, and the fact that they cared, just as you wouldn't want to fail your parents, you wouldn't want to fail these guys. So if they ask you to run through a brick wall, you know, I probably would have done it.

Such descriptions of coaches as being "like gods" or "like fathers"— and of athletes' willingness to "run through a brick wall" for them— can be seen largely as a function of the coach's social role in the development of masculinity. Here, young males are learning to identify with adult male power and authority, and in the process, a powerful emotional bond often develops between them and their coach.

Since the late sixties, though, the role of the coach as a builder of men has been eroded by two changing social realities (and the athletic careers of many of the men in my study spanned this era of change): First, the steady commercialization of sport and the concomitant rise of the Lombardian ethic. As top-level sport increasingly became a business, the "winning is everything" ethic began to eclipse the more traditional emphasis on the importance of character, on how you play the game. As was discussed in earlier chapters, the Lombardian ethic has now permeated college, high school, and even youth sports. With this shift, the idea that the coach is primarily a "builder of character," a man who "shapes boys into men," has been largely supplanted by the reality that coaches are increasingly judged by their employers and by the community in terms of their wins and losses. This sort of system tends to weed out or discourage many of the coaches who are less concerned with winning and more concerned with the lives of their players. It tends to reward coaches who are motivated by narrow goals of public status and success to be gained by winning games and championships. The pressure to win—and to keep winning—encourages coaches to view their players, not as young, developing human beings, but as instruments of their own public success. As Thomas M. put it, "Coaches encouraged me to get better in sports because that mean[t] they [would] be successful. I don't think that coaches were that concerned with the athlete's education, they were just concerned about the athlete. I think they cared about what you could do for them—at least this was true of some of them."

Just as coaches were increasingly treating athletes as the means to a successful career, a second social transformation was taking place that further undermined the coach's traditional role as a builder of men: the "youth rebellion" of the late 1960s and early 1970s. Coaches came to be viewed as paradigmatic examples of destructive adult authoritarianism and regimentation.[36] In particular, as the black power movement increasingly defined liberation in terms of "black manhood," black athletes began to rebel against the absolute authority of their (nearly always white) coaches.[37] Thomas M., for instance, described an intolerable situation that led him to ask to be traded from a professional football team:

They brought in a new coach and he thought he was a drill sergeant. You couldn't have sideburns, you couldn't have a mustache below your lip, all this kind of shit, and I just thought, "fuck, the war is over! I can't live under these situations where I can't go out of my room unless I've got my tie on." It was just regimented and I couldn't handle it. So I told them, "I'm a grown man and I am not going to be treated like a damned dog or a military person where I've gotta be here or there at some time. I can't have sideburns, I can't have a mustache." I said, "No. I have to go."

Unlike Thomas, a star, most athletes could not afford to rebel against coaches so openly, lest they be "tossed out of the barrel before they spoil all the other apples." Those who were not so secure in their positions described more subtle or passive froms of resistance against authoritarian coaches. One man said that his college coach "was like a drill sergeant, and everything had to be done exactly his way—no ifs, ands, or buts about it. But me, I had my own ways of doing stuff. But I had to *act* as if I'd do it his way. So if he said, 'Shit,' I'd shit—but I'd shit where and when *I* wanted to." Revolts against coaches have never been total, have not completely undermined coaches' authority over players. Nor have the criticisms eliminated the emotional bond that connects young men to their coaches, even years after their athletic careers end. This is because, despite many negative or ambivalent feelings about coaches, most men still have memories of at least one coach who did care about them, who did seem to make a difference in their lives. It is also because, though it has been undermined by social changes, the coach's role as an adult male "officient" in a cultural masculinity rite has remained extremely salient. The athlete's relationship with his coach takes place during boyhood and young adulthood, when the young male's masculine identity is being formed, when he is most insecure about his public status, about his relationships, his sexuality, his manhood. Coaches can and do sometimes help young males negotiate their way through the minefield of adolescence and early adulthood. Unfortunately, though, many coaches see these masculine insecurities as convenient psychological levers to be manipulated to "get the most" out of their players. As David Meggyesy wrote, coaches often "develop a talent for emasculating a player over and over again without quite killing him." Once, he recalled, a coach told him at halftime of a game that he looked "almost feminine" in making a tackle. As Meggyesy put it, "This sort of attack on a player's manhood is a coach's doomsday weapon. And it almost always works, for the players have wrapped up their identity in their masculinity, which is externally precarious for it not only depends on not exhibiting fear of any kind on the playing field, but is also something that can be given and withdrawn by a coach at his pleasure."[38]

LIKE FAMILY

I began this chapter with the question of why many male athletes today still (often virulently) oppose the presence of women reporters in the locker room. My research suggests that the answer to this question lies in understanding the kinds of relationships that male athletes develop with each other. Moreover, it is crucial to understand the specific roles that women (and talk of women) play in constructing these male relationships. The existence of living, breathing women (as opposed to abstract, sexualized female objects) in this masculine environment threatens to undermine a major basis of men's relationships with each other.

When I asked former athletes to talk about the kinds of friendships that they had with teammates, most of them immediately dropped into the language of "family." This was not too surprising. Like family relations, friendships with teammates are often among the closest that young men ever develop. But underneath the talk of respect, love, and closeness among teammates lies another reality: Athletic teams, like families, are are also characterized by internal antagonisms rooted in hierarchy. These socially structured competitive antagonisms among teammates are exacerbated by boys' and young men's tendency to fear certain kinds of closeness with others.

This is not to say that men do not develop "intimate friendships" among athletic teammates. The men I interviewed developed a kind of "covert intimacy," an intimacy characterized by "doing" together, rather than by mutual talk about their inner lives. That the men I interviewed valued these friendships is beyond question. But I have suggested in this chapter that in evaluating men's friendships, it is desirable to move beyond either judging them (negatively) from a "feminine standpoint" or observing that from a "masculine standpoint," men value the particular kinds of intimacy that they have with male friends. That is, we must look at men's friendships in the larger context of structured power relations between men and women, and between men and other men. When examined in this way, we can see that though men often "feel good" about their athletic friendships, the fact that these friendships are often cemented by sexist and homophobic talk (and at times, actions) suggests that men's relationships within sport play a part in the construction of a larger gender order in which men's power over women is reasserted, often sexually. Moreover, through these kinds of athletic friendships and peer-group dynamics, heterosexual men marginalize gay men, while policing and limiting any "feminine" tendencies in themselves. Homophobia discounts the possible existence of erotic desire between men, while aggressive sexuality expressed toward women displaces the erotic bond between men toward a devalued female object. As a result, the male bond is cemented, while the ability to develop egalitarian relationships with either males or females is impoverished.

6 : Out of the Limelight: Disengagement from the Athletic Career

> [*The high school coach*] *knew these kids had no soft cushion. The second the season was over they became vague, fuzzy shapes, as indistinguishable as the thick clouds that skimmed across the sky into the horizon. They might come back to the locker room after a big game. Their favorite coach might give them a big, sincere hello and then quickly drift off because of more pressing needs, and they would paw around the edges of the joyous pandemonium and it would become clear that it wasn't theirs anymore—it belonged to others who had exactly the same swagger of invincibility that once upon a time had been their exclusive right.*
>
> —H. G. BISSINGER,
> *Friday Night Lights*

Willy S. was born to win, born to be rich and famous. Or so it seemed for the first twenty years of his life. You'll recall that Willy grew up in a poor black community, and that he found early on that he could successfully compete with the "big boys" in sport. Soon he came to think of himself as "a natural," and that was confirmed for him in high school, when the local newspaper called him "the greatest running back in the history of the league." He came to believe that he was destined for greatness: "I thought I was supposed to win—*every game, I was supposed to win!*" And win he did. But his high school coaches and teachers were also giving him another message: As long as you run the football so well, you don't have to be responsible for anything else. Minor infractions of team rules and of community laws were covered up. Lack of effort and attendance in classes was smoothed over by coaches who would see that he would pass each year. He felt it was only his due: "They *owe* me that! I'm an *athlete!* I thought that was what I was born to do—to play sports—and everybody understood that."

Willy's mother felt that he "needed discipline," so she sent him to a highly structured military-oriented junior college, where he made the Junior College All America football team. He was actively recruited by major universities but soon found himself in jail after a spree of writing bad checks. He was unexpectedly bailed out of jail by a coach who had drafted him onto a professional football team outside the United States. He was told that if he agreed to sign a contract that started him off at a paltry $15,000 a year, he could go free in the custody of the coach. Seemingly magically, his legal problems were cleared up. He was nineteen years old, and he was off to training camp.

In his first pro exhibition game, he "ran all over the defense" for about two hundred yards and two touchdowns, and everything seemed to be coming together for him. The local media touted him as a rising star, and the crowd loved him. But it all ended quickly: in his second regular-season game, he received a serious knee injury:

I was nineteen years old. I was starting. I had made first string already. First string! Bang! Knocked out that quick. . . . I had had all that high expectation—I was on my way, you know? I thought, well, this is where I've got to get, and then—there's nothing. I was hurt, and I felt like everybody should feel sorry for me. I had been getting all this attention, and now, you know, "We've got more important things to do." Now I realize that, well, that's how you run your business, the show must go on, regardless. [Laughs]—But then, I was thinking, "Boy, you guys shouldn't be playing! I'm hurt! Don't you see that I'm the star of the show?" [Laughs]—So I fell into that syndrome for maybe a month or so. Then I made my mind up to come back. I began my workouts. I accelerated my program.

Only twenty-eight days after making the decision to "come back," he was on the playing field again, this time playing cornerback. In his first game back, he was hurt badly:

I got clipped again. Same leg! [Laughs ironically]—Same leg! So, operation again, right? But this time, they had a different doctor, and I find out that my leg wasn't operated on right the first time. And he told

me, "Don't even think about playing football." Well this really de-
pressed me. So I went out and tried to work my leg back and it never
bent more than 90 degrees, and I had to have maybe 110 or 120 to
run—I mean to run the speed I had been running and make the cuts. I
couldn't stand it any more. If I tried to [make a sharp move] off this
leg—oh, tremendous pain. . . .

[I was feeling] bad. Real bad. I was on my way to being rich and
famous, you know—this was going on in my mind—and now I'm
hurt. I left. I just quit and left. I had gotten big. I was up to around
260 then. Eating a lot. No working out. That was probably how I
dealt with it, eating. I felt a tremendous sense of failure. Tremendous
sense of failure. I thought my whole life was over. That was it! I would
never be able to get to be where I had to go, you know. I was nineteen,
twenty years old. I went back to different places. I wanted that recog-
nition, but I couldn't get it. And then my girlfriend came out to [stay]
with me—I called her and she came out. Then she went back.

[Did your relationship with her change?]

Well, yeah, I can see a change in some aspects—because if you don't
feel good about yourself, then you can maybe lash out at a person—
your hostility is transferred.

His life was shattered. His future seemed wiped out. But he still had a
powerful desire to "be somebody." He had a gun. He passed by a bank.
He put two and two together: "I said, 'Shit, I can *still* be rich and famous! I've just gotta get that money,' you know? [Laughs ironically]—
I said, 'Well, shit, I'm gonna rob this bank!' " During the course of the
robbery, shots were fired, and a guard was killed. This time, though,
no football coaches were there to cover up Willy's mistakes. He was
arrested, tried, and convicted. At the age of twenty-one, he found himself facing a life term in prison. Now, at age thirty-three, and still in
prison, he remembers: "I'm glad it's over. I feel relief. Relief that all
this pressure's over, you know? I don't have any pressure on me. I'm in
prison. I'm here for the rest of my life, and that's it. All the pressure's
gone. So now I'll just play basketball."

The tragedy of Willy S.'s athletic career was not typical of the men I
interviewed. Yet the various problems and crises he faced as his career
fell apart—loss of identity, separation from teammates and from "the
crowd," problems in relationships with women, injuries, obesity, and
other health problems, aborted attempts to recapture lost status in non-

athletic contexts—are common themes, experienced in varying degrees by most retiring athletes.

THE END OF THE ATHLETIC CAREER

For some, the end of the athletic career approaches gradually, like an unwanted but not unexpected houseguest. One can thus at least plan for the inevitable. For others, like Willy S., the athletic career ends with the shocking suddenness of a violent thunderclap that rudely awakens one from a pleasant dream. But whether it approaches gradually or emerges suddenly, the end of the playing career represents the termination of what has been central in the man's life, and the change signals a crisis in the lifecourse. As sociologist Daniel Levinson has pointed out, a "marker event," such as the end of the athletic career, can disrupt and drastically alter a man's relationships with the world, with other people and with himself. During such a marker event, according to Levinson, "One is suspended between past and future, and struggling to overcome the gap that separates them. Much from the past must be given up—separated from, cut out of one's life, rejected in anger, renounced in sadness or grief. And there is much that can be used as a basis for the future. Changes must be attempted in both self and world.[1]

Nearly all of the research on the retirement (or "disengagement") of athletes has focused on the lives of professional athletes. This makes some sense, given the fact that sport, for the professional athlete, is a living in a way that it is not for high school or (most) college athletes. Sport is his livelihood as well as his life. Furthermore, the structure of the profession suggests that "the higher one goes, the farther one falls" when he finally steps off, falls off, or is pushed off the competitive pyramid of athletic careers. My research generally confirms this, but even high school and college athletes often must deal with some difficult, even traumatic problems upon disengagement from sport.

Retiring athletes often face problems similar to those faced by men retiring from other jobs and professions. But there is one factor that sets the experiences of athletes apart from those of the more general male population: athletes retire at a comparatively young age. As one researcher put it, the trauma of retirement for an athlete is "more critical" than for the nonathlete, because "retirement at age twenty-five or thirty-five is not as socially-sanctioned as it is at age sixty-five."[2] In fact, athletics is one of the few professions where a twenty-seven-year-old man can be referred to as a "veteran," a thirty-five-year-old as an "old man."[3] As former pro basketball player Chris H. told me, "I've seen guys come out [as] hardship [cases] and then be on out of the league at twenty-four! Shit, where do you go then? Your career is over and you never really did get off into it! You played, you know, you did your thing—and you're out of the league at twenty-five, twenty-six. *Out* of it! And you've been a *veteran!* A *star* in that league! It's a little bit too soon, a little too soon."

Athletes who retire "voluntarily," researchers have suggested, face an easier transition than those who try to "hang on" and are finally forced out. Unfortunately, as sociologist Barry McPherson points out, "most athletes do not, or are unwilling to recognize that their skills are declining," therefore, most athletes face a retirement imposed by coaches and management.[4] The short career of the athlete, along with the fact that one of the key personality traits of a "successful" athlete is refusing to be a "quitter," makes for a situation where very few athletes ever quit or retire voluntarily.[5] In fact, an analysis of the retirement of athletes suggests that the dichotomy of voluntary versus involuntary retirement is a false one that ignores the interaction between external determinants and internal motivations. A seemingly voluntary decision to quit may be a grudging and face-saving recognition of the hard truth. For instance, Don W. told me, "I thought I could have played baseball in college too, but I had had such a bad experience in high school that I didn't want to see it happen again. I was afraid to go out—afraid of getting cut again. Or of being on the bench."

The increasingly competitive and cutthroat nature of sport as one moves up the career ladder often leads people to make the decision to retire. Yet as Eitzen and Harris point out, this decision is often facilitated by coaches, who commonly "cool out" and "degrade" an unwanted player, leaving the responsibility for the decision to quit on the shoulders of the player. This process, they point out, often leaves the athlete open to "self-criticism and self-denigration." In his final attempt to make it in college football, for instance, Ricardo R. said that he knew that coaches were unfairly "blackballing" him, not giving him the chance to prove himself in a game situation. But notice how he ultimately puts blame on himself for his failure to make it:

I really thought that I still had it enough to go out the next year. [The coaches] decided that I just wasn't in their future, in their plans, but I just stayed out there and practiced, went through the motions. I really never got a shot. I finally realized that there was just no chance, that they didn't even want me out there, you know? And that's where I hung it up. Heck, I figured I was gonna try out, but they didn't need me. In my mind, I thought I did okay. I felt like I, you know, I tried. I put a little blame on myself, though, because I really did enjoy football, but at that time I really wasn't mentally ready. I had lost my aggression, and you need serious aggression to be a good football player. You've gotta have that mental strength, you know.

Chris H. said that during his athletic career, he always tried to protect himself emotionally by "expecting the worst." Yet his explanation of his attempt to "hang on" a bit longer as a marginal professional basketball player reveals the pain involved in coming to the realization that his career was over. It also demonstrates his need to save face by demonstrating to his wife that *he* is in control, despite the fact that his fate is clearly in the hands of others:

One year, I was supposed to go to the Lakers' camp. The camp opens that morning at 10:00 and I get a call at 5:30: "Hey, Chris, look, we're not gonna be able to bring you." What are you supposed to do? Tear the phone out of the wall? Go kick the windows out? Go whip your wife's ass? You know, I just [went] and lay back in bed, and she didn't even know about it for a week. [Finally,] she said, "Hey, I thought you were supposed to go to camp." I said, "Ah, I decided not to go."

Eventually, at the age of twenty-six, a veteran of the NBA and of professional basketball in Europe, Chris H. decided to hang it up for good:

It was tough. I more or less made that decision. I would rather have it sooner than later. A lot of people say, "Well, you should have done it later." It was a hell of a decision. My mother says, "you sure you want to quit?" [But] I know what I've gotta do. I've got about all I can get out of it. This is about it. I've been playing since I was eight. And of course, I had lost interest. If you no longer have the desire to really be competitive, and to play ball all the time, then you might as well forget it.

In effect, what happened with Ricardo R. and with Chris H. is that the "cooling out" by coaches and management forced them to begin to disengage psychologically from their athletic careers at the very time they were still desperately trying to hang on. When it was finally all over, they saved face with others by claiming that it was, in fact, their choice. Truth be told, though, both Richard and Chris would have continued to play if they thought it was possible. Despite their face-saving decision, inside they felt a certain sense of failure and self-blame, which was fully consistent with the individualistic ethic of sport: If success in sport is defined as a combination of "natural talent" and "hard work and determination," then failure in sport can only be interpreted as a clear indication that the individual lacks these characteristics. As Chris H. put it, "You can't expect anyone to give you anything out there. It's on *you*." Though Chris and Ricardo had clearly responded in a rational way to the social dynamic of "cooling out," they interpreted their emotional/psychological distancing from their athletic careers in individualistic terms. Though they had worked hard, they had ultimately failed on some level. They had "lost aggression," "mental strength," "desire."

As these examples demonstrate, with the exception of sudden career-ending injuries, the decision to retire from sport is a complex social-psychological process. Rather than categorizing them as either voluntary or involuntary, we can see that most retirement decisions fall on a continuum between these two polarities. Whether a given individual leans more toward the voluntary or involuntary end of the continuum is largely determined by how much emotional and psychological investment he had in his athletic career. As we have seen in previous chapters, this factor is often connected to the man's range of nonsport options, and thus to his socioeconomic status.

Class Differences in Retirement and Disengagement

From early boyhood, the choices and options of youngsters from lower-class (especially black) families and communities were far more constricted than those of boys from middle-class (predominantly white) families. This different structure of opportunity led athletic boys from lower-class backgrounds to see sport careers as *the* means of constructing masculine status and identity in the family, the male peer group, and the community. On the other hand, athletic boys from middle-class backgrounds were facing a much wider range of options—recreational, educational, and ultimately, occupational. As a result, despite the importance of sport to these boys and young men, they were much less likely to become highly committed to athletic careers. These class differences emerge clearly in the the stories of Ray J. and Jim P., who in the late 1960s attended the same high school and were teammates in baseball, basketball, and football. Ray and Jim were both stars in all three sports, but most of the similarities ended there.

Ray J., born into a working-class, black family, recalls realizing very early on that "the only thing that [he] could do [to] live comfortably was to play sports." He threw himself into athletic competition whole-heartedly, but his efforts in sport were not accompanied by much effort in the classroom. Like Willy S.'s, Ray's social environment—peers, teachers, coaches—told him that if he was good on the athletic field, he was not expected to take responsibility for his studies, or for other aspects of his life. By the time his senior year in high school rolled around, he was a great athlete, but his life was "a mess." He was married and was having "family problems." He had very poor grades and couldn't realistically think of going to a university, at least right away. So he escaped. The U.S. Marine Corps invited him to be a member of their baseball team; he enlisted in 1969. Over a decade later, he says:

It was a stupid decision—impulsive, man. I wanted to be one of the best, you know, and that was the worst place you could go, but you had to be a domineering person to make it through it—your mind had to be strong. I felt that I could manipulate in there well enough to get over pretty good, you know. And I would have, except they wanted me to do a lot of extra shit, and I said, "To hell with it," you know, "I play baseball!" That's what I was supposed to do there. [My high school coach] talked to them, other people talked to them: that's what I was supposed to do. But I got into a bunch of little problems with them, and they just sent me to 'Nam.

[Did you ever play any baseball?]

In the service? I played catch a lot. But I never played anything. They told me, "Take your fucking glove to 'Nam with you!" And I did [laughs ironically]—I took my glove when I packed everything else. I wasn't gonna send it home, you know, I was supposed to play baseball! I took my glove to 'Nam with me, and they said, "Catch a goddamned grenade with the sonofabitch!" Well, the only way I screwed up was I ended up catching a mortar instead of a grenade. You know, they told me my future. . . .

His description of how he was wounded in Vietnam suggests that he was attempting to recapture the experience of athletic heroism in this new context, warfare:

I was only there six or eight weeks—they had stuck us out in a zone where people were always getting fucked up and shit, and we used to get constantly mortared and shit from the time I got there. We were being hit one night, and we were running to positions and there were a few of us all together and then in comes a round and landed on the ground—and instead of using my head and running away like every- body else did, I tried to get rid of it, throw it away, which was stupid. There was really nowhere to throw it away—it was just a stupid reac- tion on my part. You know, I used to watch G.I. Joe shit on television when I was a kid—you know, jump on a grenade—I just reacted in my mind and I did it—stupid. It blew up in my hands. . . . . It's a part of life, man, just a part of life. It happened, man.

When he returned home from Vietnam, Ray was told by a doctor that he would never pitch again. Indeed, on his right (pitching) hand, only the thumb and forefinger remained, and the tips of three fingers on his left hand were missing. When I asked what he was feeling at the time, he replied: "That I had to play sports, to show I was still good. They told me that I couldn't ever do anything else again with my hands. I played basketball that same day, you know, with *pins* sticking out of my finger about an inch and a half. I played ball, you know, with three fingers here and one here: *I played ball—I came back!*" He played one year of basketball on a community college team, but mostly sat the bench: "It was the first time I had to learn to be not a first stringer— that was *a lot* to accept, man, *a lot* to accept." Then, he went into a tailspin. Divorced, having trouble getting a job and feeling unappre- ciated and unwanted as a partially disabled veteran, his future appeared to him to be "nothing."

I didn't know where I was going, what I was gonna do. You know, I was just left with a big space, man. I just played a lot of pool, man, played pool for money and constantly ran the streets. Got high a lot. And that's about it, man, you know, there was nothing else to do. Hey, I was, you know, nothing. I was a Vietnam veteran and I couldn't get a job. I couldn't go nowhere, man. I had gone and got a license to drive big trucks, came back and put in applications all over the state, man. You know, I never even got a call about a job, man, so I kind of gave up, man, because I didn't have nowhere to go.

Like Ray J., Jim P. always viewed himself as a sort of athletic under- dog, who achieved success by being hungrier, by "working harder than the next guy." Like Ray, Jim constructed his identity and received high status among his peers and in the community largely through his athletic accomplishments. Yet important differences in Jim's relationship with sport emerged early on, and as we have seen, these differences were rooted in the white, middle-class world in which he grew up. By the time he was a high school junior, he had realized that athletic stardom was "small potatoes," that he needed to "get serious" and focus on building a future, and that meant leaving athletics behind and focusing on academics. He went off to college with the goal of getting into dental school in three years. Throughout college, his desire to play ball was stimulated by the basketball coach, who told him that someday he would wonder if he "could have done it":

> And I thought about that. But I thought, so what if I can spend two years playing basketball? I'm not gonna be a basketball player forever, and I might jeopardize my chances of getting into dental school, you know. I've always been one that if I'm gonna do something, I'm gonna sink everything into it, I'm not gonna do it half-assed or half-heartedly. And if I was gonna be a college basketball player, I was gonna do it. And the studies, I'm sure, would have suffered.

So he fended off the coach's pleas and his own inner yearnings to play ball and transferred his energies, competitiveness, and even his internal "fears of failure" into his academic work:

> The biggest scare I ever had was the first test I took in college—the general chemistry test. I really studied for that sucker, and I just choked. It ended up that I aced the rest of the class, ended up second in the class or something. That's the worst grade I ever got. When I think back on it, I was so afraid of failing—I went through some real mental gymnastics over that: Boy, how am I ever going to become a dentist? We had a hundred guys who wanted to be dentists in my freshman class, and as it turned out I was the first guy to get into dental school after three years instead of four. Yeah, it worked out good.

Both Ray and Jim worked very hard to "make themselves" through successful competition within hierarchies of intermale dominance. In their youth, each had experienced success doing so through organized sport. But Jim, like many males from middle-class backgrounds, began to disengage from his athletic career while he was still playing, whereas Ray, like many males from lower-class backgrounds, invested everything in his athletic career. Jim P. enjoyed a wide range of educational and career options, and he could see that shifting his efforts toward education was the rational choice in terms of continuing to construct a successful masculine identity as he moved into adulthood. Though in retrospect he sees some of his choices as "stupid," Ray J.'s decisions too can be seen as "rational," given the options available to him. These two men's "career decisions"—to quit sport and go to college, to join the Marines in order to keep playing sport—demonstrate how the social structure of race and class inequality contextualizes young men's choices (and their perceptions of their choices). As a result of what on the surface appears to be individual choices, Jim ended up in dental school, where "it worked out good." But, the path that Ray took left him partially disabled, unemployed, and feeling that he was "nothing," with "nowhere to go."

DISENGAGEMENT AS A CRISIS OF MASCULINE IDENTITY

Most of the men I interviewed had already traversed the three-to-five-year period of disengagement from athletic careers. I did interview one man, twenty-six-year-old Rick J., who was still in the middle of disengagement from a high school and college basketball career. He discussed his ambivalence about playground and recreational basketball, as well as his confusion about the directions his life was now taking:

That saying "you're only as good as your last game" is painful for me to hear, and I know why. It's because it still feels that way to me. So I feel a bit tenuous about [playing basketball] right now. This summer, I haven't played at all. I felt I needed a break from it. It takes a lot of hard work to play at the level I was playing at, and maybe it's just not worth it.

[What are the costs of all that hard work?]

[Sighs]—*A real intense dedication. And then after it's over, after the playing is over, I'm expecting a whole lot more strokes and support for it than I'm gonna get now.*

[Are there things in life that you get strokes for now?]

[Sighs]—*Yeah, there are. These past few months I've been trying a lot of different things, thinking about different careers, things to do. So there's been quite a bit of stumbling—and I think that part of my ten-*

*uousness about committing myself to any one thing is I'm not sure I'm
gonna get strokes if I go that way*—[nervous laugh]. *It's scary for me.
I feel a little bit shaky, a little insecure. Yeah, a lot sometimes. I guess
a lot of fits and starts over the last year, and I wish one of the starts
would take hold, you know? I guess you could say I'm stumbling in
my relationships, too—stumbling in all parts of my life*—[laughs]. *I
feel like I'm doing a lot, but not knowing what I want.*

Surely there is nothing unusual about a man in his mid-twenties "stumbling" around a bit as he seeks direction in his work and in his relationships. But for the former athlete, this stumbling is often more confusing and acute precisely because he has lost the major focus of his life
and identity. As Carol Gilligan has written of the personality under crisis, "Freud, in tracing development through the exposure of crisis,
compares the psyche under stress to a crystal that is thrown to the floor
and breaks not into haphazard pieces, but comes apart along its lines of
cleavage into fragments whose boundaries, though they were invisible,
were pre-determined by the crystal's structure."[6] Though I prefer to
view the construction of the personality as a tapestry that is woven and
changes as a person interacts with the social world, Gilligan's analogy is
useful in viewing disengagement as a crisis of masculine identity. I have
argued that young males have an internalized ambivalence toward intimacy—both a need for and a fear of closeness with others. Organized
sport offers them a context in which they can develop nonintimate connection with other males, with women, and, more abstractly, with "the
crowd." But the competitive, hierarchical structure and values of athletic careers (as well as the homophobic and misogynist culture of athletic teams) tend to create an insecure and conditional sense of worth,
as well as exacerbating men's difficulties developing truly intimate relationships. Thus, though a successful athlete may appear to be a confident young man, these insecurities and fears of intimacy are "invisible
cleavages" running through his developing identity. As long as he en-
joys continued success in his athletic career, these insecurities and fears
rarely surface as "problems." The public status gained through his role
as successful athlete is usually enough to lay a neat veneer over these
weaknesses. But when the athletic career ends, they too often crack the
surface.

The development of the athlete's identity is an interactional process.
At first, it is primarily interaction with family and peers, but as one

moves up the ladder of an athletic career, increasingly it becomes one's relationship with that more abstract entity "the crowd" that forms the basis of one's identity. This interaction between self and other is what sociologist Charles Horton Cooley called "the looking glass self."[7] If we view the athletic activity and the crowd as a sort of mirror into which the athlete gazes, we can begin to understand how devastating it can be when that looking glass is suddenly and permanently shattered, leaving the man alone, isolated, and disconnected. As retired baseball player Steve Hamilton told Studs Terkel, it's easy during their careers for athletes to get a "false sense of importance": "People are always saying good things about you and treating you like you're something special. You start believing you're something special. Now they're out of baseball. They feel: 'I was great.' But nobody remembers them. It doesn't make any difference what your name is. You find people no longer want to be associated with you when you're out of the limelight."[8] The shock of being "out of the limelight," of having one's precarious connection with the crowd severed, was a common theme when I asked men about their disengagement from their careers as athletes. Gene H., for instance, spoke eloquently about how, as a professional football player, he had "strong foundations" and developed a sense of "personal priorities" that served him well later in life. But when I asked him to describe his retirement after a nine-year career in the NFL, he paused and sighed deeply:

Now that's a completely different story. I sat here and talked to you about being satisfied with myself inwardly. I sat here and talked to you about my foundations, and I talked to you about respect. I talked to you about all those different things. But when that skeleton comes out of the closet—and that's retirement—it's a completely different thing. I mean you find yourself just scrambled. You don't know which way to go. Your light, as far as you're concerned, has been turned out. My retirement initially was very hard. Of course you miss the financial deal, but you miss the camaraderie of the other ballplayers. You miss that—to be an elite, to be one of a kind —that's a hell of a feeling, you know? It's just that—whew!—It's a feeling that's unreal! But most athletes at retirement, the game itself you don't miss. I'm talking about the beating and all that. You don't really miss that. You miss the camaraderie of the fellas. You miss too the roar of the crowd. And you'll notice that with most ballplayers, especially those who have been in spectator sports, most of them hang around bars, wherever there's a lot of people—it's the roar of the crowd. Once you've heard it, you can't get away from it. And the ones who try to hide themselves inside get into a lot of trouble, become super depressed, and get really lost, no direction. It's like if you lose someone that you love—doesn't matter if you knew they'd been sick for thirty or forty years—if you lose them, it's a shock. There's an empty feeling—you feel like everything you wanted is gone. The same way when all of a sudden you wake up and find yourself twenty-nine, thirty-five years old, you know, and the one thing that has been the major part of your life is gone. It's gone. And you can't just walk away [into] retirement all of a sudden, because you don't know how people are going to react to you—you don't know— you wonder and question.

Gene's words capture several facets of disengagement trauma that were common among the men I interviewed. In terms of identity, you feel "scrambled." You miss "the fellas" and the "roar of the crowd." Since the major basis of your identity is now gone, "you wonder and you question" how others will react to you. In what follows, I will look at two aspects of this crisis of identity. First, what happens to athletes' self-images and to their health once their bodies are no longer the in-struments of their public success? Second, what changes in relation-ships with other men and with women are precipitated by retirement?

The Body and Identity

As we saw in chapters 3 and 4, the athlete's identity hinges largely on successful athletic competition. This public success entails the devel-opment of an instrumental relationship toward one's body as a "tool" or even a "weapon" to be developed and utilized in athletic competi-tion. The ironic result is that athletes often become alienated from their bodies. Pain and injuries are seen as nuisances and brushed aside or covered up with pain-killing drugs. But these injuries take their toll. For many athletes like Willy S., a single debilitating injury brings their career to an abrupt end. Mike T., like Willy, had a serious injury at the end of his career as a world-class decathlete:

In 1972 when I was competing for the last time, my kneecap came off and I ruptured a hamstring before the Olympic trials. So I sat—and I was lying in bed with my knee in a cast during the trials. But I never felt that I achieved my potential, and that sort of saddens me. The injuries prevented me from going back to it on that level again. My knee never healed properly. My kneecap came right off. I've never run the same, and I could never run properly again.

Most of the men I interviewed did not experience a single, career-ending injury. More common were tales of a gradual accumulation of smaller, "nagging" injuries that gradually wore their bodies down and led to retirement. As we have seen, David P.'s pro baseball career was constantly interrupted and hampered by injuries, surgeries, and painful rehabilitation periods. He often played when he was nowhere near "100 percent." In his last two pro seasons, he rarely played, yet he remained determined to come back. He worked out hard, and was "in the best condition of [his] life." But on the first day of the exhibition season, David awoke with a "crick" in his neck. His neck did not respond to therapy, and the doctor told him that he needed to have another disk in his neck fused, a dangerous operation he had been through once before:

> [*My team manager*] *told me, "Okay, you're gonna have to make a decision whether you can play." So I said, "All right, I'll play." And I got to the point where I couldn't hold my head up to give a sign—I had to kind of peek at the pitcher and I just prayed to God that nobody would hit a pop fly. I caught two innings and then two more innings in a game in spring training. [Then I was told:] "The manager wants to see you." He said, "David, we're gonna put you on waivers—tried to trade you and couldn't trade you, so we're gonna put you on waivers for your release if nobody claims you." And twenty-five years of playing baseball from age eight to that point—fifteen years of a dream come true was ended, in a clubhouse by a manager telling me that it's all over.*

[What was your immediate reaction?]

Shock. I mean it was just—you talk about the world coming to an end—and then I had to go back and tell my wife. And for her, ten years of being in that life—it was just very sad and heartbreaking to have it happen. I decided not to have the surgery. I just made an instant decision right there. I said, "Hey, that's it." I think it just hit me: Hey, face it, you know? I knew it was gonna come one day or another. I knew that. But I wanted to hang on. I wasn't ready to face the outside world. It was kind of scary more than anything. I had felt that the way I had conditioned myself and taken care of myself that I would play until I was thirty-seven, thirty-eight.

This last statement is especially telling: David seemed somehow betrayed by his body. He assumed he could play another five years or so, given the way he had "conditioned and taken care" of himself. Yet when one recalls the incredible chronicle of pain and playing hurt that had been an integral part of his life for many years, it is not at all surprising that his body finally began to say "enough" at the age of thirty-three. That he was shocked is only further indication of the extreme alienation that top-level athletes develop with the body-as-machine.

Since the conditioned body is so integral to the athlete's success, and is thus a major basis of his public identity, the termination of the athletic career entails the transformation of his experience of—and the meanings surrounding—his body. Since the conditioning of an athlete's body was always oriented toward a particular goal, rather than the achievement of "health," when the goal is removed, the conditioning may cease. Indeed, some men reported to me that when their careers ended, they quit sport altogether, sometimes for several years.[9] When this happened, the true irony of athletes' relationships to their bodies emerged. Once public paragons of athleticism, they were now likely to "let themselves go": inactivity, obesity, overeating, alcohol and drug abuse are common problems for recently retired athletes. As we saw with Willy S., eating was one way to deal with the sudden end of a football career. After his knee injury, his graceful and powerful body had lost its raison d'etre. So he quit working out and got fat.

For others, inactivity and overeating were a means rather than a result of disengagement. Clarence T., for instance, had been in "great shape" in high school. Despite his prominence as a high school athlete and as a student, he was very unhappy, and he can see in retrospect that his unhappiness had a lot to do with the incredible pressures to succeed that he had internalized from his family and his peer group. When he got to college, he began to disengage from these pressures, but not in a fully conscious manner: "What's puzzling is as soon as I got to college, I stopped playing sports, basically for three years. I put on probably twenty-five or thirty pounds. I might have entered college around 160, but then I got up close to 190. I just stopped doing stuff. I think at the time there was just stuff piling up about how unhappy I was. Basically, I didn't do anything—I didn't run, I didn't do shit. And I got really heavy."

Another common pitfall for recently retired athletes is substance abuse. As we have seen, many athletes begin a relationship with drugs and alcohol during their playing careers, often with covert support, tolerance, or approval of team management, coaches, and peers. But for most athletes, the need to stay in shape in order to perform their craft successfully makes them moderate their use of "recreational" drugs and alcohol during their playing careers. After the career is over, however, there is no such check on their behavior. Furthermore, feelings of loss, isolation, and uncertainty about the future may create anxiety that leads to increased use of alcohol or other depressants as coping mechanisms. Professional baseball player Ron Bryant already had a drinking problem during his playing career, but when it all ended, alcohol really became his refuge:

> Bumming around was the only thing I could do. I had to forget; I could only think of how close I got to really being a superstar. What a down it was to think of what I had lost. And for what? When I realized that I didn't have enough velocity on my fastball to break a pane of glass, that my baseball dream was over, I just scrounged up money for more drinking. Nothing mattered. I didn't care if I was a bum. I only thought booze. Eventually I had to ask myself: "What's Ron Bryant going to do now? Was it worth it to keep living?"[10]

This sort of extreme abuse of alcohol or other drugs appears to be more common among athletes who were forced to retire suddenly as a result of being cut by a team or suffering a severe injury. One man I interviewed had been an all-conference community college athlete. Though he had dreamed of becoming a pro, he "realistically" knew that his best hope was to transfer to a state college and play two more years. But at the end of his sophomore year, a freak accident led to a serious injury that spelled the end of his athletic career. He did return to college, but feeling directionless in life, he never completed his degree:

> I missed the competition, you know. After being in it like I was, there's really nothing that can take that place. You know, you just have that void.

[Did you do anything to try to fill that void?]

[Pause, then a nervous laugh]—*Probably got more into drugs and drinking, I think. It just seemed a lot easier to drink and forget about it basically. It's disappointing, but rather than dwell on it, you just drink on it. When I was playing, I really didn't do any drugs at all.*

Barry B., who after his own retirement from pro football formed a nonprofit organization aimed at educating and counseling athletes about drug use, pointed out to me that former athletes' drug abuse can be linked to their disengagement from the crowd. Brown explained that an exhilarating high comes from performing in front of the crowd, but this high is temporary—it just doesn't last. But the need for that high, that exhilaration, goes on after the game is over, after the career ends:

One of the things that we don't often realize is that athletes seek— have, do, and always will—seek immediate gratification because they do get that on the field. And then in life, the feelings are the same.

[When you lose that immediate gratification on the field, does it amplify the need to get it somewhere else?]

Somewhere else—that being through drugs or alcohol or the physical- ness of bikes and things. Because you're immediately accepted when you run the touchdown, catch the big pass. Millions of people, thou- sands of people and your teammates are accepting you, and you know if you do this, you'll get that. And the same thing with drugs. You know that if you do drugs, you'll get a good feeling; you try to duplicate the highs you get on the field off the field. Because after you get off the field, you go back to normality and become normal again. And after you've just left being on one of the most extreme highs that you'll ever get in life—then you have to come back to life.

Interpersonal Relationships

We have seen how the athletic environment provides a context in which men commonly develop a sort of intimacy with each other. Despite the limitations of these friendships, powerful bonds often develop between men who are sharing the adversity of athletic competition. On a very basic level, the team often comes to be experienced as a family. When a man's relationship with the team is severed, he often feels disconnected, cut off from his friends and "family." For professional athletes, this break is often extremely abrupt. When a pro athlete retires or is cut from a team, it is common for him to be treated as a nonperson by former teammates. Former baseball player Jim Bouton pointed out in his book that the day-to-day language used by athletes in the clubhouse lays bare this grim reality: "When a guy got cut we'd say he died. . . . A player who wasn't going well was said to be sick, very sick, in a coma or on his deathbed, depending on how bad he was going." When someone on the team was greeted by the "grim reaper," according to Bouton, "You walk into the clubhouse and you see a guy packing his bag and you both try not to look at each other. Most guys won't pack until they know everybody is busy on the field, but sometimes you surprise somebody in there and it's always awkward. . . . It's funny what happens to a guy when he's released. As soon as he gets it he's a different person, not a part of the team any more. Not even a person. He almost ceases to exist." [11]

This seemingly cold-hearted treatment of a person who yesterday was your teammate is less a reflection of the superficiality of friendships on the team than it is a manifestation of the career insecurities that each player must constantly deal with. In order to play well, one must have confidence. But how can an athlete play with confidence when he knows that all athletic careers are short, that his can end any day? The answer is that a culture of denial has been built into the structure of the team. The loss of yesterday's teammate, roommate, card-playing buddy can't be mourned; to do so would be to remind oneself of one's own "mortality," and that might lead to worry and ultimately to poor performance on the field. [12] When David P.'s time finally came, he asked to be kept on in some capacity. He was a bit puzzled and hurt when the team said no:

> *I appreciate their feelings of not wanting me around because of what I might do to bring down the morale of the club. So it was best that I leave the organization. I guess they felt that by having me around I might start doing something like badmouthing the organization or something. But you know, that's how much they knew about me, because I would never do that anyway. I was willing to earn my money, that's what I was saying: "Let me do something and stay in the game."*

So he was abruptly cut off from his team and from baseball:

> *Sometimes you just have to think, "Did I actually play this game?" [Laughs]—You know, Bob Euker tells this story about when he was*

released by the Milwaukee Braves: He went to the clubhouse in spring training and his bag was sitting outside the door and the equipment manager said, "Sorry, no visitors allowed." [Laughs]—*You know, he said it as a comedian, but in essence, that's what it means: "Don't come in here, man, you're not part of us anymore. Just take your stuff and take a hike. We don't want to see you anymore." You know, you're a piece of—you're cattle. It's time to butcher you. It's a hard feeling for a lot of players.*

It certainly was hard for Barry B. He had been released by one pro football team and was immediately picked up by another, but before he could begin practicing with his new team, his mother died. A week after the funeral, his new team released him, and it was all over. He was feeling as low as he had ever felt:

When you put so many years of your life into something—and I put sixteen years of my life into sports—you eat, you sleep, you fight, you cry, and you live together, and they become a part of your family. These guys become like family. So when you're released or cut from there, it's like you're a bastard child, you know. They cut you straight off and so that takes some real adjustment. Even if you are prepared, it's still gonna take some adjustment. I saw a psychologist—not for the drugs, but to find out, you know, was I a bad person? I was having problems: self-image, self-esteem, self-motivation . . . As you go higher up the ladder, what you end up being is a highly skilled, highly trained individual, only to have it end at an early age with nowhere to transfer your skills. We're in one of the most highly stressed jobs in this country, sports, and there's no assistance, so it's gonna continue to turn out guys who are mentally unstable, bankrupt, divorced, alcohol and substance abusers. Athletes are set up to be very high-risk people in terms of being abusers of things—money, substances, everything. These problems have to be dealt with by attacking the problem, and not the symptom. And the problem is being ill-prepared for life.

For Barry, as with many other retiring athletes, it was not just relationships with teammates that were strained or terminated during disengagement, but relationships with other friends as well: "It was starting to become really clear as to the kind of life that it was going to be after football, because friends had stopped calling, and people had stopped coming by. I didn't get many calls to say, 'Hey, man, I'm sorry about your mother, and I'm sorry about you being out of the game,' and so forth. So that was reality."

Men's relationships with women—especially wives and lovers—are commonly strained during disengagement as well. Willy S. said, "if you don't feel good about yourself," you may "lash out" at the woman you are close to. In addition to displaced anger, men's relationships with women are often strained because their own identities are strained. More than one man told me that during the disengagement period, "I don't know how she put up with me." Like Chris H., they were often brooding and noncommunicative with their spouses and lovers. Barry B. told me, "a lot of guys lose their wives" because they "can't open up to [them]." Many of these men report having relied heavily on their wives for emotional support during disengagement. In retrospect, David P. credits his wife with being his "emotional anchor" during this difficult time. It is of course not unusual for women to perform the family "emotion work" for inexpressive men.[13] However, in the case of retiring athletes, this can be a nearly impossible task, as the man is likely to be both extremely emotionally needy and extremely incommunicative (except, perhaps, for anger). Women's usual burden of family emotion work, then, is often much greater during disengagement.

7 : Life after Sport

> *Every man in the Mid-life Transition starts to see that*
> *the hero of the fairy tale does not enter a life of eternal,*
> *simple happiness. He sees, indeed, that the hero is a*
> *youth who must die or be transformed as early adulthood*
> *comes to an end. A man must begin to grieve and accept*
> *the symbolic death of the youthful hero within himself.*
> *He will gradually discover which of the heroic qualities*
> *he can keep, which new qualities he can discover and de-*
> *velop in himself, and how he might be a hero of a differ-*
> *ent kind in the context of middle adulthood. Humanity*
> *has as yet little wisdom for constructing the "portrait of*
> *the hero as a middle-aged man."*
>
> —DANIEL LEVINSON,
> *The Seasons of a Man's Life*

At age thirty-five, Chris H. had been retired from professional basketball for nine years, and he seemed painfully aware that his public
status was now in the past: "I *was* somebody!" When I interviewed
him, he was working "sixteen-hour days" as a social worker and in his
new job as an assistant college basketball coach, which edged him back
toward the public limelight. Once again, he said, there was a chance to
be a success, to "be somebody":

> *When I say "successful," that means somebody that the public looks*
> *up to just like a basketball player. Yet you don't have to be playing*
> *basketball. You can be anybody: you can be a senator or a mayor, or*
> *any number of things. That's what I call successful. Success is recog-*
> *nition. Sure, I'm always proud of myself. But there's that little goal*

there that until people *respect you, then* [*snaps fingers*] *anybody can say, "Oh, I know I'm the greatest thing in the world," but* people *run the world, and when* they *say you're successful, then you* know *you're successful.*

His social work job is satisfying on some level, but the coaching job is clearly more salient in terms of his identity. He clearly feels better about himself when he's in the public eye. But the two jobs have their costs: He spends a lot of time away from his family. When I asked him whether he spent enough time with his children, aged ten, six, and three, he replied,

No. No, you never do. I plan to someday. Very seldom do you have enough time to spend with your kids, especially nowadays, so I don't get hung up on that. The wife does sometimes, but as long as I keep a roof over their heads and let them know who's who, well, one day they'll respect me. But I can't just get bogged down and take any old job, you know, a filling station job or something. Ah, hell, they'll get more respect, my kids for me, right now, than they would if I was somewhere just a regular worker. You know, my daughters, they never saw me play, but as far as they're concerned, I was great. They can look at the papers and see Daddy, and shit, "He must have been some-body!" [Laughs]—"Daddy must have been pretty damned good." And that's where I get most of my satisfaction, from that.

Chris obviously cares deeply about his family, but the *way* that he ex-presses his care—working, providing, establishing himself as "some-body" in the world—has the effect of removing him from day-to-day contact with his family. He hopes to "someday" spend more time with his children, but for now, he is a man with goals to achieve in the world of men:

There's some things that I still want to do. I'm still half-way young. I've still got some time. You've got to pay your dues. Now in my early thirties, I'm a lot more serious because that's a point where it's, you know, do or die—just like in basketball. Can't be any bullshit now. Whereas when you're twenty-seven, twenty-eight, you've got all these things on your mind. Age—I don't feel old. At thirty-five, you've got a chance to really do something, if you're in a position to. And right now, I'm trying my best.

Chris was experiencing what Daniel Levinson calls a "surge of mascu-line strivings" common to men in their early adulthood.[1] His struggles suggest several themes descriptive of the lives of retired male athletes. First, retired athletes feel compelled to pick up the pieces of their shattered identities, to reconstruct them in terms of work and success in the public world. This usually means both redefining success and coming to some resolution about one's severed relationship to sport. Second, since these young men have largely developed relationships with other people through their public status as athletes, in their postathletic career years, they must find or forge some new way to relate to others, especially loved ones.

WORK, SUCCESS, AND IDENTITY IN EARLY ADULTHOOD

Like Chris H., many retired athletes seek to reconstruct their relationships with the crowd that earlier served as the primary foundation of their identities. For David P., being out of baseball brought up his old insecurities about what other people thought of him and led to a confusing scramble to recapture his lost public status. He dabbled in real estate, worked with a sporting goods manufacturer, got involved in producing sport videos, but couldn't really settle into one thing: "So I'm wearing all these different hats, and my wife is going totally berserk, because she never knows from day to day when I'm gonna come in with another great deal that I'm involved in. She wanted me to get into something that I knew about and just *do it*. So I would do all these things and say, 'Hey, got a great idea, gonna do this,' then a week later, 'gonna do that.' And it just became very frustrating."

David's confidence did not return until he, like Chris H., found a way "back into the game." His former professional baseball team offered him a job with their speakers' bureau. In the past year, he estimated, he had delivered 150 public talks for the team. At times, he said, his old insecurities about his lower-class status (and now, his lack of a college education) surfaced as he spoke to groups of successful businessmen and community leaders. When this happened, he drew on his past athletic accomplishments to buoy his confidence: "Hell! *They* never hit a curveball from Nolan Ryan! To *hell* with them! What if they don't like what I'm saying? The hell with them! Because I've done a lot more than a guy who's a multimillionaire, you know, and that's a good feeling to be able to think in those terms and not really care. I wish I had known that many years ago [*laughs*]—I would have been a lot better off."

David P. and Chris H., unlike most former athletes, were able to get back into sport occupations. The joy they displayed when discussing what it meant to them to be back in sport suggests that there was an almost womblike comfort to be found for them there. Most former athletes, however, move (by choice or not) into nonsport occupations. Though there is usually a certain amount of trauma attached to the move away from sport careers, for some it can be a very liberating experience. For instance, Mike T. had gone into sport primarily to cover up the fact that he was gay. Through his athletic accomplishments, he was able to construct a public heterosexual identity. He loved sport, but he certainly did not experience the athletic world as a comforting womb. It was for him an oppressive closet that forced him to live a double life. "It's *so uncomfortable,* so *hot* in the closet. It's a terrible thing to live with." Mike's athletic career was winding down in the early 1970s, which was also the take-off point for the gay liberation movement, and he considered coming out: "My friends always discouraged me from coming out—you know, 'That'll create problems for you.' Well, I already *had* problems, and the problems had to do with hiding. And I was willing to face those new problems." Finally, well after his athletic career had ended, he came out in an article in a national magazine: "I didn't do it in any small way! And I just felt like a *huge* weight had been lifted from my shoulders. I didn't have to *lie* anymore! The whole world was gonna know that I was gay, and I didn't care, and I was *glad,* because suddenly I was *me.* I suddenly felt that I had a real identity: This is me, I'm a gay man, and this is what I do."

Whereas Chris H. and David P. needed to be "back in sport" in order to reconstruct their identities, and Mike T. needed to be out of sport in order to express his authentic identity publicly, Willy S. had little choice in starting over in a "nonsport career." Willy found sport to be a central part of the prison culture, and despite his injured knee, he could still dominate most of his peers in basketball. But athletic competition became less and less meaningful to him: "I was a little kid when I walked in here—I mean, I was a *big* kid, but in my mind, I was no better than a five-year-old. I've learned now that you don't win everything. We don't always win everything. I think we have to learn to accept that, learn to handle defeat. And, in sports, I *never learned how to accept that!*" As we have seen, Willy also had never learned academic skills. Given a "free ride" through school because of his athletic prowess, he was the perfect example of the social construction of the "dumb jock." His intellectual growth after he was incarcerated underscores the tragically racist assumptions that stunt the intellectual potential of young black males like Willy. Though only semiliterate when he entered prison, he began to educate himself. By the time I interviewed him, at age thirty-three, he had earned a masters degree. Though he was frustrated at having recently been denied parole, he had dreams of becoming a medical doctor, and he used sport imagery to describe the challenges and the frustrations that he now faced:

> *I'm trying now to become something, to develop somewhere else. It's like preparing for a football game: training, working out, getting your uniform and pads on, sitting on the bench, and then the coach won't let you play. Now that I'm where I am, it's frustrating, because I have all this new fantastic knowledge that I want to try, but I'm still doing my time.* [Chuckling]—*You know, I'm through with this,* mentally, *but* physically, *it's still happening. It's not through with me.*[2]

Willy S., like David P. and Chris H., was experiencing a "surge of masculine strivings" to "become something" in his early-to-mid thirties. Yet his sudden and dramatic break with athletic stardom thirteen years earlier had forced him to reassess the basis of his identity in ways that successful pro athletes like David and Chris never did: "Now I'm finding that it's not so much the crowd anymore, it's more or less a personal thing. Like with my work, you know, I have to do it *well*. It's a *personal* satisfaction, you know? I really don't *care* about what anybody is saying. It's just something I've created inside of me, because it's just a personal choice now, you know? If you're gonna do it, you may as well do it right."

Unlike Willy, most of the men I interviewed, especially those in their thirties, were still very "other directed," still seeing themselves and defining their success in terms of the crowd. As Chris H. said, "People run the world, and when they say you're successful, then you know you're successful."

Class Differences and Public Success

We have seen in previous chapters that largely because of different socioeconomic and educational opportunities, boys and men from lower-class backgrounds were likely to become highly committed to sport careers, while boys and young men from middle-class backgrounds were likely to make an early shift away from sport. A very small proportion of those who committed themselves to athletic careers, like Thomas M., David P., and Gene H., actually did "make it" in sport in ways that set them up for postathletic careers in public life. Having been a successful pro athlete, Gene told me, allowed him to earn the "respect" of others, and "opened doors" for him in later years. This certainly appears to be true for David and Thomas as well.

Most athletes, though, don't "make it" through sport. Some, like Chris H., become "almost a famous person" and spend their energies after athletic retirement continuing to grab for the elusive ring of public success.[3] A few athletes from lower-class backgrounds, like Calvin H. and Larry W., do manage to take advantage of the opportunities afforded them through athletic scholarships and get a college degree that moves them into a profession. The majority of athletes from lower-class backgrounds, however, end up with a difficult, sometimes traumatic period of disengagement, which is commonly characterized by identity crises, interpersonal problems, and financial instability. Those that avoid the disastrous crash that Willy S. experienced eventually manage to settle into service-sector or blue-collar jobs, which afford them some stability as family breadwinners.

In short, the athletic career appears to men like Ricardo R., Ray J., and Willy S. as the key to upward mobility. The fact that it did not work out that way may be interpreted by them as a personal failure. But in fact, their experiences are typical of the vast majority of athletes from lower-class backgrounds, as revealed in a 1989 study conducted by Don Sabo, Merrill Melnick, and Beth Vanfossen, which compared the experiences of ethnic minority and white athletes and nonathletes. The researchers followed a national sample of 14,000 high school sophomores through high school and four years beyond to determine what, if any, effect sport participation had on their lives. The study found that, independent of race or socioeconomic status, athletic participation yielded various benefits while the athlete was still in school, including higher popularity among peers. But among racial and ethnic minorities, four years after high school there was no correlation between high school athletic participation and greater success either in college or in the work world. "Contrary to popular sentiment, high school sport *exerted no significant positive influence* on the success or aspirations of minorities. [Sport's] long-range impacts on adult success have been *oversold*."[4] The researchers go on to note that high school sport participation does appear to benefit one group in terms of future mobility:

white males from suburban schools. In short, they argue, the idea that sport participation, in and of itself, will lead to upward mobility (a common hope of males from lower-class backgrounds) is a myth. But sport participation appears to reinforce the already existing advantages of those from privileged backgrounds. Compared to their minority counterparts, middle-class white males reap a "cumulative advantage" from having been athletes.

Sabo, Melnick, and Vanfossen's research demonstrates that there is a very different relationship between sport participation and later economic mobility for men from different racial and socioeconomic groups. My research demonstrates the process through which these differences are constructed. We have seen that many successful male athletes from middle-class backgrounds came to view a sport career as "pissing in the wind" or as "small potatoes," and that they made an early choice to concentrate on other educational and professional goals. I have argued that the white, middle-class institutional context, with its emphasis on education and income, made it clear to them that choices existed and that the pursuit of an athletic career was not a particularly good choice to make. Where the boy once found sport to be a means of achieving masculine status, the postadolescent and young adult male from a middle-class background simply transfers his strivings to education and career.

To compare the very different roles that past athletic careers play in one's present public status and identity, let's look once again at former high school teammates Ray J. and Jim P. As we have seen, Ray J. returned from Vietnam missing several fingers, yet still determined to make his mark as an athlete. But his disabilities limited him, and he ended up facing several years of insecurity in his work and in his relationships. Eventually, he got a job driving a city bus, which gave him some stability, but not the public recognition that he had always wanted. In 1973, a friend introduced him to tennis, which he had previously thought of as a "girl's game." The first time he played, he was beaten badly, but he became determined to learn the game and to be one of the best at it. He recalls thinking, "I am *still* somebody—even if I've got no arms and legs, I'm *still somebody!* I told them, 'No problem—I'm right handed, I've gotta learn to hit the ball with my left hand; I've gotta learn to hit with two hands on this side and serve with two fingers on this hand—I got a lot of work to do, you know what I mean?' But I told them, 'I'm gonna be *good!*' I just set my mind to it, man, and I got good at it. Now I'm well-respected." Ray is very clear about what it means to be respected: "It means that people look at you and they can say, 'Hey, he's a tennis player.' People ride my bus, you know, and kids who come to tournaments with their parents say, 'Hey, man, you're good—it's great to see you out there playing.' A lot of people see me play. That's the respect, that I'm not just considered a nobody. I'm gonna keep pushin', man. I'm gonna be *good*. I'm *always* gonna be respected, man, no matter where I go."

On the other hand, gaining public respect does not appear to be problematic for Jim P. His present and past athletic accomplishments are not the major basis of his adult public status. He does play some city-league basketball, but his description of what playing sport today means to him contrasts sharply with how important tennis is to Ray J. When I asked him how he felt when he missed three important free throws in a recent basketball game, Jim laughed: "[I was] embarrassed, but it wasn't the end of the world, either. I mean, what the hell, I tried . . . You know, now, it still bothers me, but in the past couple of years it isn't that same motivation anymore. I think, 'I'm thirty-two years old, and so what if I'm out of shape?' I mean, it's not the Super Bowl, or something!" It's not that Jim is unconcerned with being respected. It's just that unlike Ray's job as a bus driver, Jim's profession as a dentist is accorded high public status. His former accomplishments as a high school athlete do continue to add to his public status, as evidenced by his description of a recent community golf tournament he played in. After the tournament, at a barbecue where there were "a lot of drinks," and "you put your arm around guys that were your coaches," he recalls being "flattered" by being told that he had been the best basketball guard his coach ever had. It was, he said, "the ultimate compliment."

For the middle-class men like Jim P. who had chosen careers outside the field, sport clearly remained important. Having been a successful high school or college athlete enhances one's adult status among other men in the community—but only as a badge of masculinity that is *added* to one's current occupational status. In fact, several professional-class men chose to be interviewed in their offices, where they publicly displayed the trophies and plaques that attested to their youthful athletic accomplishments. Their high school and college athletic careers may have appeared to them as "small potatoes," but many successful men spoke of their earlier status as athletes as having "opened doors" for them in their present professions and in community affairs. Sociologist Kathryn Ann Farr's research on what she calls "good old boys' sociability groups" shows how sport, as part of the glue of masculine culture, continues to facilitate "dominance bonding" among privileged men long after active sport careers end. This dominance bonding is based largely upon ritual forms of sociability (comaraderie, competition), "the superiority of which was first affirmed in the exclusionary play activities of young boys in groups."[5] In effect, this athletics-based dominance bonding benefits athletic men over nonathletic men, and excludes women from some of the key informal mechanisms of power within professional and managerial cultures.

SUCCESS, THE BREADWINNER ETHIC, AND CARE

It is common for men, especially in early adulthood, to define themselves primarily in terms of their work. Men's socially defined need to establish themselves as "somebody" in the public world is often accompanied by their physical absence from the home. While these heterosexual, married men are "out there" constructing identities in the world of men, their wives are usually home caring for the day-to-day and moment-to-moment needs of the family.[6] This is often true, as we saw with Chris H., even when the woman also has a job in the paid labor force, thus contributing to the oft-noted double workday of "working mothers."[7]

The powerful drive to be somebody in the public world, which for the men I interviewed was learned largely through athletic careers, clearly helps to maintain men's control over public life and contributes to the subordination and economic dependence of women as mothers and housekeepers.[8] But it is not simply the reconstruction of masculine privilege that we see operating here. When I asked these men to define what success means to them, many of them, like Chris H., spoke of public recognition and status, but nearly all of them went on to discuss their responsibilities as family breadwinners and their hopes to provide security and care for their children.[9] For instance, David P., whose own father left his family when David was young, described his very strong sense of commitment to be a responsible provider for his own family: "I'm working an awful lot these days, and trying not to take time away from my family, and a lot of times putting the family to sleep, and working late hours and going to bed and getting up early and so forth. I've tried to tell my family this a lot of times: The work I'm doing now is gonna make it easier in a few years. That's the reason I'm working now, to get that financial security, and I feel like it's coming very soon." David would like to spend more time with his children. But the demands of work cut into his "quality time" with them: "It's just—it's, you know, you go a long day and you come home, and it's just not the quality time that you'd like to have. And I think when that financial security comes in, then I'm gonna be able to forget about everything."

When I asked Jim P. what success means to him today, he also spoke of security for his family. He is comfortably established as a dentist, but he worries that "the bottom could drop out" if he were to "get injured or disabled," and lose his ability to provide for his wife and children: "I have beaucoups disability insurance—to me, that's security. That's the biggest concern of my life right now, in terms of individual efforts or concerns: being head of the family." Similarly, Ricardo R. expresses his breadwinning responsibility in terms of care. When I asked him what had motivated him to continue working in the same factory, forty hours a week for the past ten years, he replied: "Security. I want to always be secure in the things that I have and the things I do. I'm always fighting for that." By "security," Ricardo means more than simply job security: "family life comes first in that respect, though: Security and family, a good family life. Because when I talk about security, I'm talking about everyone around me. I'm not just talking about myself, you know."

It is likely that these men's strivings for success in the world of work are rooted in their psychological need to establish a separate identity, but their ambitions are also quite often couched in an ethic of care. It is a care that differs markedly from that described by Carol Gilligan and Lillian Rubin.[10] To Gilligan and Rubin, "care" is the kind of empathy and nurturance that women commonly give to their loved ones. A woman's care usually involves direct daily contact with one's family's physical, psychological, and emotional needs. A man's care is usually expressed more abstractly, indirectly, through deeds. What is salient and sometimes tragic about this form of care is that it too often removes men from their families. What are the costs, both to men and to their families, of this physical and emotional separation?

Men, Families, and Intimacy

A common psychological thread can be followed through these men's lives: Always, they have sought to establish connection with others through their public accomplishments. This observation coincides with Daniel Levinson's and Carol Gilligan's contention that in adult male development, individuation (the development of a separate, positional identity) precedes generativity (the ability to care for and nurture others). I have qualified this generalization, though, with my observation that men's strivings for success in the public world of work are often couched in terms of care for their families. Lillian Rubin explains this simultaneous existence of male separation and male care for others by making a distinction between "nurturance" and "intimacy":

> Nurturance is caretaking. Intimacy is some kind of reciprocal expression of feeling and thought, not out of fear or dependent need, but out of a wish to know another's inner life and to be able to share one's own. . . . Commitment itself is not a problem for a man; he's good at that. . . . But ask him to express his sadness, his fear, his dependency—all those feelings that would expose his vulnerability to himself or to another—and he's likely to close down as if under some compulsion to protect himself.[11]

Rubin suggests that men's "emotionally impoverished" state—their split between thought and feelings, their difficulty in empathizing with others' feelings, and their tendency to establish and maintain psychological boundaries, all constitute major barriers to intimacy. But a man also has a powerful need for connection and unity with others, which he can more comfortably express in the care he can provide through his (emotionally safe and distant) role as family breadwinner. For example, when I asked Ricardo R. what success means to him now, I could feel the love for his family in his response: "Well, there's limits to what I can do—but, for me to be successful is to get [my daughter] through school, and to be married, to still be married. Someday I'd like to put a nice down payment on a house. To me, it's kind of a bummer not to have one now, while [my daughter's] still young, you know, something [of] your own, [so] that she knows: 'there's security.'" But when I asked him to describe how he expresses his feelings to the people he is close to, he replied, "Outside I try to play it cool. Inside sometimes I'm boiling, but outside I'm, you know, I feel like I'm almost dead [laughs]—I just don't seem that emotional, I guess . . . [I hold] back, I guess. I don't know. But then if I didn't hold back, I don't know how wild and crazy I would be [laughs]—I'd rather hold back, just for myself, you know. Maybe it keeps me better at bay that way, you know?"

How do these two factors—the man's commitment and care for his family and his need for separation and keeping his emotions "at bay"— affect his primary relationships? First, men have a tendency to be poor verbal communicators and to "let their actions speak for themselves." As a result, a child may much later in life come to realize and appreciate that all of the "sacrifices" her father made were his major way of expressing his love. But the child's experience of her father is of an emotionally distant, even "cold" person.[12] Second, since the sustained verbal expression of the inner life is likely to make a man feel awkward and vulnerable, he'd rather "hold back, just for [him]self," than open up too much with his spouse or children. The fact that men have such a difficult time making sense of the reasons behind their own emotional reticence with their wives and children suggests how deeply rooted in the unconscious fears of intimacy are. For instance, at the end of my interview with David P., he expressed surprise at how open he had been with me about his life, his motivations, fears, and hopes: "You know what? I've told you more in these four-and-a-half hours [laughs]—seriously—than I've ever told any one person. I wish that I could sit down with my wife, say the things to her that I have said here. And maybe by giving her a copy [of the taped interview transcript], it would be like, 'Hey, this is, you know, this is what I think.'" He couldn't really explain why it was hard for him to speak to his wife openly: "I don't know. You know, it's—when you go home, it's—you've got a couple of kids, and you've got to worry about this, and this, and it's just very tough to sit down with your spouse and talk. I've found it very difficult."

What is happening here, in part, is that the repression of feelings and the instrumental personalities that these men have developed to be successful in their athletic and postathletic careers have reinforced their already existing difficulties with emotional connection with others. The man's quest for economic independence thus puts him into a position of increased emotional dependence on his wife, who becomes the "emotional manager" of the family.[13] Despite the changes of the past twenty years—feminism, the continued movement of women into the labor force—most men appear to retain the same psychological and emotional vulnerabilities and needs, and they expect women to take care of those needs, whether they work outside the home or not. A few of the men I interviewed expressed these needs in very "traditional" ways. Gene H. for instance, thirty-six years old and single, clings stubbornly to the image of the woman he will fall in love with and marry:

The main reason I've never been married is because the things I would need, as far as a woman goes, I won't compromise on. I mean I have certain principles and morals about what a woman should be, what a man should be also. I believe a man should be the provider for his family, should be the king of his castle. But the way society's going now, who's to say that a woman's work is housework? Who's to say that a man's work is in the yard? When we're fighting for equal rights and all this crap? I'm to say in my relationship that my woman's work is in the house. And if I need something to eat—I can cook as well as any woman—but I think that that's part of her being a woman, fixing meals and all. I believe that. I could be wrong, but I believe that. I believe in her being a mother—it's a position that's all by itself—there isn't any in-between being a mother. [But] a lot of women are not like that—I just haven't come across the right one.

Of the men in my sample, several did have marriages that approximated the kind of division of labor that Gene describes as his ideal. A few, such as Jon P. and Brent F., were in dual career relationships in which an egalitarian division of household labor was the goal.[14] Several felt ambivalent about the relationship between their own work, their wives' work, and family work. David P., for instance, expressed a great deal of admiration for his wife's having held the family together during the difficult transition time after he retired from baseball. When I interviewed David, his wife had recently resumed teaching on a substitute basis, and though he was pleased with this, it still appeared to him that her career should be subordinate to his:

She would very honestly like to get back into the working world. And I'd love her to. But yet—you know, I want her to, but yet I don't want to deprive some of the things that I'm involved in. I guess in a sense I'm selfish. See, we have an agreement that when she goes out to teach, I take care of the baby. And that's frustrating because I know in business you have to have these meetings whenever those people are available. Yet I would like for her to go out a couple of days a week.

These men, as they negotiate their way into and through their post-athletic careers and early adulthood, are caught between various contradictions. They want to "be somebody," but there's a troubling sense that time is running short for them. They want to express their love for their families, but they often don't feel comfortable doing so in direct ways. So it appears to many of them that working very hard to "be somebody" *is* the way to express their love for their families. If a man becomes a very successful provider of income and stability for his family, then, in Chris H.'s words, "one day they'll respect [him]." But there are internal tensions in this kind of life that several of the men I spoke with were starting to feel. The major tension stemmed from the contradiction between the responsibility of being the family breadwinner and the growing perception that it is desirable for men to be more involved with their children than their fathers were with them. Jim P., for instance, said that he learned from a mentor about the importance of being involved with his children now:

> *We had some nice talks, and he said that his only regret is that he missed the boat with his daughter. He was so involved in community affairs and dental society affairs and his practice, he was never home. He says, "She grew up right before my eyes, and I didn't even realize it." When I heard that from Joe, I'd just had [my own daughter], and I kind of made a vow to myself. I said, "That's not gonna happen to me." And at the time, I was heavily involved with J.C.'s, and I was playing basketball, softball, and this and that—and I could see that kind of happening and it was gonna get worse. And so at that point I just kind of drew back.*

Although Jim is still the family breadwinner, and his wife is primarily the homemaker and mother, his attitude about the importance of spending time with his children while they are young does represent a partial shift from the previous generation of fathers.[15] For most men, this new ideology concerning the importance of fathering exists alongside the traditional values and expectations of the "natural" roles of the male as breadwinner and the female as mother/homemaker. The clash between these traditional and emergent values is reflected in the ambiguous and contradictory statements that most fathers made to me concerning the relationship of their work with their obligations and desires to participate in the family. Recall David P.'s statement that he "wants" to stay with his children when his wife works as a substitute teacher, but that it is sometimes "frustrating" because it impinges upon his ability to be flexible in his business dealings. A man may want, even crave, more connection with his children, but the time that it takes to maintain that connection may cause him to lose the competitive edge he needs to win in the world of work—and that is the arena in which he feels he will ultimately be judged in terms of his success or failure as a man.

FULL CIRCLE: MEN, CHILDREN, AND SPORT

Men's attitudes about their roles in childrearing are changing, but thus far, behavioral changes have been minimal. The job of caring for infants and young children is still left primarily to women, and we can expect that this will result in the perpetuation of gender inequalities.[16] Social scientific research indicates that even among fathers who are more involved with their children, traditional treatment of boys and girls persists. For instance, fathers tend to state a preference for male offspring, touch and vocalize more with their infant sons than with their infant daughters, encourage gender-stereotyped toys, pay more attention to male children than to female children, speak more often and longer with their sons than with their daughters, keep in touch with sons more than with daughters after a divorce. Furthermore, men spend far more time playing games and sports with their sons than with their daughters.[17]

Sixteen of the thirty men I interviewed were fathers, and most of them seemed to view sport for their children as an opportunity to learn social values and as an arena in which to have fun. Most stated that they did not intend to put pressure on their children but wanted to give them the "opportunity and exposure" to be involved in sport. Jim P., who has a son and a daughter, said that he sees sport largely as a common activity that can hold the family together now and in the future, but he also appears to have some hopes that his children might excel: "I want to expose my kids to as many sports as I can—you know, certainly encourage them. I really don't think I'm gonna be a dad that's a pusher. [But] I think genetically our kids are going to be blessed, more because of [my wife's] side of the family than mine. I really feel that, because her two brothers are really good athletes." Jon P., the father of two-year-old twin boys, expressed a similar ambivalence: He wants to "expose" his kids to sport and is aware of not wanting to pressure his sons to be stars, but he also fears that since sport has always been so important to him, he might find himself putting too much emphasis on athletic success, which will "take the fun out of it" for the children: "That just kind of scares me, because I don't know that I'll handle it very well. I don't want to push them very hard, but I don't know—I can see myself putting pressure on the kids, but I don't want to do that. But I want to give them the chance to be exposed and learn the right way to do things. But it can be bad, ruining the enjoyment of the game."

The negative cultural stereotype of the "frustrated jock" father who destroys his son's life with pressure to be a star appears to have permeated the awareness of most of the fathers I interviewed. They say that they don't want to hurt their sons that way. But just below the surface of this verbalized awareness, there often looms a deeply felt dream: "*My* son is going to be *good!*" Listen to Ray J. speak of his two-year-old son's sport future:

> *It's up to him. If he enjoys playing it, that's his choice. I'm not gonna pressure him to do anything. The only thing I want is to use his mind. If he's gonna do something, be the best you can be. Do like I did. I learned to do it.*

[Will you feel disappointed if he doesn't get into sport?]

> *No. I feel he's gonna be good at something, anyway, man. It's really up to him. You know, I'd enjoy him playing sports. If he's good, like at tennis, if he's good by the time he's ten, then he has a chance to make some money. Past that—ten, twelve—you're not going anywhere. So, you know, you've gotta start young. So he plays at two years old, and he enjoys hitting the ball for hours. He just came in with four blisters on his hands! As long as he enjoys it, fine. He'll go out and watch me play tennis for hours, so I imagine he'll learn to play, man, I imagine he'll play [thoughtful pause]—I think he's gonna be good. I think he'll be kicking ass! Yeah. First of all, he's gonna walk on the court, and they're gonna say, "That's Ray's son." That's gonna be one point in his favor—[laughs]. Well, look for your advantage, guy! Your dad is somebody, you know. He is good!*

Clearly, alongside some changes in fathers' attitudes concerning children and sport, some very conventional values and behaviors persist. After talking with Ray for nearly two hours, during which he spoke enthusiastically about his son several times, I asked him if his daughter is at all into sport, and he replied, "Not really. I never really spent much time. She's a girl, man, you know? She comes out to hit the ball against the wall—basically I think it's just to be with me—I don't really see her that much."

Nevertheless, there appears to be a growing acceptance among many fathers that their daughters can be athletes also. Jim P. and Ricardo R. felt it would be healthy for their daughters to be involved in sport. Steve L. also expressed support for his daughter's involvement in athletics. But when he spoke of his son, there was more enthusiasm in his voice—it just seemed more "natural" for his son to go into sport:

My daughter could train to be a professional athlete, but I'm not so sure how happy she would be, and that's most important. I want her to enjoy the sports she plays, to learn from it, and to play as well as she can. But I don't think she has to be better than everybody else at all costs. Now, [my son], I'm sure, will be an athlete because he goes to the ballpark with me. [He] is three, and he goes to the games and stays. Well, it's just natural because he sees Dad playing and he wants to emulate Dad. So I'm sure he'll get involved with it. I'd very much like him to be good at it.

When I asked him why his feelings about sport participation for his son and daughter were so different, he replied:

I'm a bit of a sexist. I shouldn't say this, but I was raised that boys do this and girls do that. And although I don't necessarily believe that now—I like the women's movement type thing—I can't just throw out what I've been taught all my life either. It just seems more natural for me for a boy to play than it does a girl. I wouldn't be surprised if I pushed [him] more. He has that desire that [my daughter] didn't have. The first word he learned was "ball." And I swear I didn't push it on him or anything. Of course, people would get him balls because of me, and he would throw them around and enjoy it. So I get the feeling that he'll probably be like I was—when I was a kid, I wanted to play. I can see [him] being that way. I'll make it available to him and I will work with him and make him as good as he can be, but I'll try to do all that I can to keep sports in its proper perspective.

Sport seems especially important for fathers like Steve to forge a bond with their sons. Sport becomes the link between the generations. Notice how both Ray J. and Steve L., without being prompted, spoke of their sons' present and future athletic interests, desires, and accomplishments as continuous with their own: "I get the feeling that he'll probably be like I was." None of the fathers discussed their daughters' involvement in sport in terms of personal identification. It's fine, maybe even "healthy," for daughters to be "exposed" to sport. But "it just seems more natural" for sons to have that athletic "desire."

WORK AND FAMILY AT MIDLIFE

The kinds of tensions between work and family that Chris H., David P., and others were experiencing commonly lead to changes—even crises—in the life structures of men as they approach middle adulthood. The fading or the loss of the early adulthood dream of success can become an opportunity for expansion, where the man becomes more open to new experiences, new relationships, and new dreams. Some men in midlife begin to experience what Daniel Levinson calls "detribalization." Here, the man "becomes more critical of the tribe—the particular groups, institutions, and traditions which have the greatest significance for him, the social matrix to which he is most attached. He is less dependent upon tribal rewards, more questioning of tribal values. . . . The result of this shift is not normally a marked disengagement from the external world, but a greater integration of attachment and separateness."[18]

This detribalization—putting less emphasis on how one is defined by others and becoming more self-motivated and self-generating—is often accompanied by a growing sense of "flawed" or "qualified" success. A man's early dream of success begins to tarnish, appears increasingly illusory, or the success that a man has achieved begins to appear more and more hollow and meaningless, possibly because it has not delivered the closeness with others that he craves. For example, we have seen that in his youth, Eldon C.'s self-image was based on very narrow definitions of athletic success, and this resulted in a sense of himself as a "failure." A large part of his problem was that he had been a "racer" who focused more on winning, not a "runner" who could compete according to his own internal clock. When I interviewed him, he was forty-eight years old, and had recently experienced a "midlife crisis," where he came to the realization that he "was never going to be on the cover of *Time*." Out of that period of crisis and several years of reading Eastern philosophy, Eldon came to a new level of understanding about his relationship to work and success. He told me that he is still "competitive," but now "it's about being very good, but not being in the headlines":

> I made up this little aphorism: "Dare to be average"—can you feel that for yourself emotionally? It doesn't really mean dare to be average, it means dare to take the pressure off yourself, you know? Dare to

be a normal person. My wife had it made up as a T-shirt for me. It says, "Dare to be average," and it gets funny reactions from people. I think it gets at that place where somehow we all think that we're going to wind up on the cover of Time, *or something, you know? Do you have that? That some day, you're gonna be* great, *and everyone will* know, *everyone will recognize it. And I think I used that to somehow disengage from that, because that's part of the competitor, the racer, the vicious person. And it's a* disease! *It's hard! I'd rather be great now because I'm* good, *and maybe that'll turn into something that's acknowledged, but not at the headline level. I'm not racing so much; I'm concerned that my feet are planted on the ground and that I'm good.*

When I suggested that Eldon was running now, as opposed to racing, he laughed and said that "running and racing have the same goals." But then he continued more thoughtfully, "But maybe you're right—that's a wonderful analogy. Pacing myself. Running is more intelligent—more familiarity with your abilities, your patterns of workouts, who you're running against, the nature of the track, your position, alertness. You have more of an internal clock."

Cole's midlife detribalization—his transition from a "racer" to a "runner"—has left him more comfortable with himself, with his abilities and his limitations. It is no accident that once he disengaged from the narrow definition of public success that he had learned largely through sport, he also experienced an expansion of his ability to develop intimate relationships. He had never been very comfortable with the "typical jock attitude" toward women and sex, but, he said,

I generally maintained a performance attitude about sex for a long time, which was not as enjoyable as it became after I learned to be more like what I thought a woman was like. In other words, when I let myself experience my own body, in a delicious and receptive way rather than in a power, overwhelming way. That was wonderful! [Laughs]—To experience my body as someone desired and given to. That's one of the better things. I think I only achieved that very profound intimacy that's found between people, really quite extraordinarily, quite recently. [Long pause]—It's quite something, quite something. And I feel more fully inducted into the human race by knowing about that.

Eldon's story illustrates how the construction of a masculine identity based on narrow definitions of public athletic success is often closely

linked to—even premised upon—a "performance attitude about sex."
As I argued in earlier chapters, this attitude views women as objects to
be manipulated and conquered. But it also has its costs for men: in
learning to relate to women primarily as subordinate sexual objects,
men also learn to relate to their own bodies simply as sexual performance machines, and they are ultimately dehumanized. Eldon C.'s description of his own transformation in his mid forties suggests that to
the extent that men can transcend their socially learned need to define
their success through the roar of the crowd, they can learn to relate to
women as full human beings and ultimately experience a "delicious"
and "profound intimacy" with women.

But Eldon's transformation is not necessarily typical. There are several possible directions that a man can move if and when he hits a "midlife crisis." Sociological research on men at midlife suggests that only a
portion of them experience a midlife crisis that results in the transcend-
ence of their instrumental personalities and an expansion of their relational capacities. Many men simply continue to pursue public success
at any cost, thus making even more unlikely any meaningful relationships with other people. The midlife discovery that the achievement
game is an unfulfilling rat race can as easily lead to cynical detachment
and greater alienation as it can to detribalization and deeper intimacy.[19]
In other words, there is no assurance that Chris H., as he ages, will
transform himself from a "racer" into a "runner," as Eldon C. has. Even
if he does change in this way, it is likely that he will have missed participating in the formative years of his children's lives. Moreover, while he
has been out there struggling to "be somebody" in public life, his wife
will have spent years working a double workday, with her job in the
paid labor force and her second shift of housework and childcare at
home.

How might we move toward a world where men develop more intimate and egalitarian relationships? My research suggests that simply
encouraging personal changes in boys and young men will have little
impact, since masculine identities and relationships develop within and
through social institutions such as sport. In the final chapter, I will return to some of the questions I laid out in chapter 1 about sport's role
in the overall construction of the gender order. In particular, I will evaluate the extent to which women's recent movement into sport represents a challenge to dominant perceptions of masculinity, femininity,
and power.

8 : Sport and Gender Relations: Continuity, Contradiction, and Change

> *The closer we come to uncovering some form of exemplary masculinity, a masculinity which is solid and sure of itself, the clearer it becomes that masculinity is structured through contradiction: the more it asserts itself, the more it calls itself into question.*
>
> —LYNN SEGAL
> *Slow Motion*

In 1973, conservative writer George Gilder, later to become a central theorist of the antifeminist family policies of the Reagan administration, was among the first to sound the alarm that the contemporary explosion of female athletic participation might threaten the very fabric of civilization. "Sports," Gilder wrote, "are possibly the single most important male rite in modern society." The woman athlete "reduces the game from a religious male rite to a mere physical exercise, with some treacherous danger of psychic effect." Athletic performance, for males, embodies "an ideal of beauty and truth," while women's participation represents a "disgusting perversion" of this truth.[1] In 1986, over a decade later, a similar view was expressed by John Carroll in a respected academic journal. Carroll lauded the masculine "virtue and grace" of sport, and defended it against its critics, especially feminists.

149

He concluded that in order to preserve sport's "naturally conserving and creating" tendencies, especially in the realms of "the moral and the religious, . . . women should once again be prohibited from sport: they are the true defenders of the humanist values that emanate from the household, the values of tenderness, nurture and compassion, and this most important role must not be confused by the military and political values inherent in sport. Likewise, sport should not be muzzled by humanist values: it is the living arena for the great virtue of manliness."[2]

The key to Gilder's and Carroll's chest-beating about the importance of maintaining sport as a "male rite" is their neo-Victorian belief that male-female biological differences predispose men to aggressively dominate public life, while females are naturally suited to serve as the nurturant guardians of home and hearth. As Gilder put it, "The tendency to bond with other males in intensely purposeful and dangerous activity is said to come from the collective demands of pursuing large animals. The female body, on the other hand, more closely resembles the body of nonhunting primates. A woman throws, for example, very like a male chimpanzee."[3] This perspective ignores a wealth of historical, anthropological, and biological data that suggest that the equation of males with domination of public life and females with the care of the domestic sphere is a cultural and historical construction.[4] In fact, Gilder's and Carroll's belief that sport, *a socially constructed institution*, is needed to sustain male-female difference contradicts their assumption that these differences are "natural." As R. W. Connell has argued, social practices that exaggerate male-female difference (such as dress, adornment, and sport) "are part of a continuing effort to sustain a social definition of gender, an effort that is necessary precisely *because the biological logic . . . cannot sustain the gender categories*."[5]

Indeed, throughout this book I have argued against the view that sees sport as a natural realm within which some essence of masculinity unfolds. Rather, sport is a social institution that, in its dominant forms, was created by and for men. It should not be surprising, then, that my research with male athletes reveals an affinity between the institution of sport and men's developing identities. As the young males in this study became committed to athletic careers, the gendered values of the institution of sport made it extremely unlikely that they would construct anything but the kinds of personalities and relationships that were consistent with the dominant values and power relations of the larger gender order. The competitive hierarchy of athletic careers encouraged the development of masculine identities based on very narrow definitions of public success. Homophobia and misogyny were the key bonding agents among male athletes, serving to construct a masculine personality that disparaged anything considered "feminine" in women, in other men, or in oneself. The fact that winning was premised on physical power, strength, discipline, and willingness to take, ignore, or deaden pain inclined men to experience their own bodies as machines, as instruments of power and domination—and to see other peoples' bodies as objects of their power and domination.

In short, my research findings are largely consistent with previous feminist analyses of sport.[6] Whether men continue to pursue athletic careers (as many lower-class males do), or whether they shift away from sport toward education and nonathletic careers (as many middle-class males do), they are likely to continue to feel most comfortable, at least into middle adulthood, constructing identities and relationships primarily through their public achievements. As adults, these men will in all likelihood continue to need women (and may even use their power to keep women) in their "feminine" roles as nurturers, emotion-workers, and mothers, even when these women also have jobs or careers of their own. The result is not only that different "masculine" and "feminine" personality structures are perpetuated, but also that institutional inequities (men's control of public life, women's double workday, etc.) persist.

What my research adds to existing feminist analyses of sport is the recognition that sport does not simply and unambiguously reproduce men's existing power and privilege. Though sport clearly helps to produce culturally dominant conceptions of masculinity, my interviews reveal several strains within the sport/masculinity relationship. Most obviously, men's experiences of athletic careers are not entirely positive, nor are they the same for all men. These facts strongly suggest that sport is not a smoothly functioning, seamless institution, nor is masculinity a monolithic category. There are three factors that undermine sport's ability to construct a single dominant conception of masculinity: (1) the "costs" of athletic masculinity to men; (2) men's different experiences with athletic careers, according to social class, race, and sexual orientation; and (3) current challenges to the equation of sport and heterosexual masculinity, as posed by the rise of women's athletics. To what extent do these tendencies pose fundamental challenges to the institution of sport or to our dominant conceptions of sex and gender?

THE COSTS OF ATHLETIC MASCULINITY

As boys, the men in my study were initially attracted to playing sport because it was a primary means to connect with other people—especially fathers, brothers, and male peers. But as these young males became committed to athletic careers, their identities became directly tied to continued public success. Increasingly, it was not just "being there with the guys" but beating the other guys that that mattered most. As their need for connection with others became defined more abstractly, through their relationships with "the crowd," their actual relationships with other people tended to become distorted. Other individuals were increasingly likely to be viewed as (male) objects to be defeated or (female) objects to be manipulated and sexually conquered. As a result, the socially learned means through which they constructed their identities (public achievement within competitive hierarchies) did not deliver what was most craved and needed: intimate connection and unity with other people. More often than not, athletic careers have exacerbated existing insecurities and ambivalences in young men's developing identities, thus further diminishing their capacity for intimate relationships with others.

In addition to relational costs, many athletes—especially those in "combat sports" such as football—paid a heavy price in terms of health. As I outlined in chapter 4, the successful operation of the male body-as-weapon may have led, for a time, to victories on the athletic field, but it also led to injuries and other health problems that lasted far beyond the end of the athletic career.

It is extremely unlikely that a public illumination of the relational and health costs paid by male athletes will lead to a widespread rejection of sport by young males. There are three reasons for this. First, the continued affinity between sport and developing masculine identities suggests that many boys will continue to be attracted to athletic careers for the same reasons they have in the past. Second, since the successful athlete often basks in the limelight of public adoration, the relational costs of athletic masculinity are often not apparent until after the athletic career ends, and he suddenly loses his connection to the crowd. Third, though athletes may recognize the present and future health costs of their athletic careers, they are likely to view them as dues willingly paid. In short, there is a neat enough fit between the psychological and emotional tendencies of young males and the institution of sport that these costs—if they are recognized at all—will be considered "necessary evils," the price men pay for the promise of "being on top." [7]

COMPETING MASCULINITIES

As I have demonstrated throughout this book, boys' emerging identities may influence them to be attracted to sport, but they nevertheless tend to experience athletic careers differently, based upon variations in class, race, and sexual orientation. Despite their similarities, boys and young men bring different problems, anxieties, hopes, and dreams to their athletic experiences, and thus tend to draw different meanings from, and make different choices about, their athletic careers.

Race, Class, and the Construction of Athletic Masculinity

My interviews reveal that within a social context stratified by class and by race, the choice to pursue—or not to pursue—an athletic career is determined by the individual's rational assessment of the available means to construct a respected masculine identity. White middle-class men were likely to reject athletic careers and shift their masculine strivings to education and nonsport careers. Conversely, men from poor and blue-collar backgrounds, especially blacks, often perceived athletic careers to be their best chance for success in the public sphere. For nearly all of the men from lower class backgrounds, the status and respect that they received through sport was temporary—it did not translate into upward mobility.

One might conclude from this that the United States should adopt a public policy of encouraging young lower-class black males to "just say no" to sport. This strategy would be doomed to failure, because poor young black men's decisions to pursue athletic careers can be viewed as rational, given the constraints that they continue to face. Despite the increased number of black role models in nonsport professions, employment opportunities for young black males actually deteriorated in the 1980s, and nonathletic opportunities in higher education also declined. By 1985, blacks constituted 14 percent of the college-aged (18–24 years) U.S. population, but as a proportion of students in four-year colleges and universities, they had dropped to 8 percent. By contrast, black men constituted 49 percent of male college basketball players, and 61 percent of male basketball players in institutions that grant athletic scholarships.[8] For young black men, then, organized sport appears to be more likely to get them to college than their own efforts in nonathletic activities.

In addition to viewing athletic careers as an arena for career success, there is considerable evidence that black male athletes have used sport as a cultural space within which to forge a uniquely expressive style of masculinity, a "cool pose." As Majors puts it,

Due to structural limitations, a black man may be impotent in the intellectual, political, and corporate world, but he can nevertheless display a potent personal style from the pulpit, in entertainment, and in athletic competition, with a verve that borders on the spectacular. Through the virtuosity of a performance, he tips the socially imbalanced scales in his favor and sends the subliminal message: "See me, touch me, hear me, but, white man, you can't copy me!"[9]

In particular, black men have put their "stamp" on the game of basketball. There is considerable pride in U.S. black communities in the fact that black men have come to dominate the higher levels of basketball—and in the expressive style with which they have come to do so. The often aggressive "cool pose" of black male athletes can thus be interpreted as a form of masculinity that symbolically challenges the class constraints and the institutionalized racism that so many young black males face.

Sexual Orientation and the Construction of Athletic Masculinity

Until very recently, it was widely believed that gay men did not play organized sports. Nongay people tended to stereotype gay men as "too effeminate" to be athletic. This belief revealed a confusion between sexual orientation and gender. We now know that there is no neat fit between how "masculine" or "feminine" a man is, and whether or not he is sexually attracted to women, to men, to both, or to neither.[10] Interestingly, some gay writers also believed that gay men were not active in sport. For instance, Dennis Altman wrote in 1982 that most gay men were not interested in sport, since they tended to reject the sexual repression, homophobia, and misogyny that are built into the sportsworld.[11]

The belief that gay men are not interested or involved in sport has proven to be wrong. People who made this assumption were observing the overtly masculine and heterosexual culture of sport and then falsely concluding that all of the people within that culture must be heterosexual. My interview with Mike T., and biographies of gay athletes such as David Kopay suggest that young gay males are often attracted to sport because they are just as concerned as heterosexual boys and young men with constructing masculine identities.[12] Indeed, a young closeted gay male like Mike T. may view the projection of an unambiguous masculinity as even more critical than his nongay counterparts do. As Mike told me, "There are a *lot* of gay men in sports," but they are almost all closeted and thus not visible to public view.

As Mike's story illustrates, gay male athletes often share similar motivations and experiences with nongay athletes. This suggests that as long as gay athletes stay closeted, they are contributing to the construction of culturally dominant conceptions of masculinity. However, Brian Pronger's recent research suggests that many gay male athletes experience organized sport in unique ways. In particular, Pronger's interviews with gay male athletes indicate that they have a "paradoxical" relationship to the male athletic culture. Though the institution itself is built largely on the denial (or sublimation) of any erotic bond between men, Pronger argues, many (but not all) gay athletes experience life in the locker room, as well as the excitement of athletic competition, as highly erotic. Since their secret desires (and, at times, secret actions) run counter to the heterosexist culture of the male locker room, closeted gay male athletes develop ironic sensibilities about themselves, their bodies, and the sporting activity itself.[13] Gay men are sexually oppressed through sport, Pronger argues, but the ironic ways they often redefine the athletic context can be interpreted as a form of resistance with the potential to undermine and transform the heterosexist culture of sport.

The Limits of Masculine Resistances

Men's experience of athletic careers—and the meanings they assign to these experiences—are contextualized by class, race, and sexual orientation. My research, and that of other social scientists, suggests that black male athletes construct and draw on an expressive and "cool" masculinity in order to resist racial oppression. Gay male athletes sometimes construct and draw on an "ironic" masculinity in order to resist sexual oppression. In other words, poor, black, and gay men have often found sport to be an arena in which they can build a masculinity that is, in some ways, resistant to the oppressions they face within hierarchies of intermale dominance.

But how real is the challenge these resistant masculinities pose to the role that sport has historically played in perpetuating existing differences and inequalities? A feminist perspective reveals the limited extent to which we can interpret black and gay athletic masculinities as liberating. Through a feminist lens, we can see that in adopting as their expressive vehicle many of the dominant aspects of athletic masculinity (narrow definitions of public success; aggressive, sometimes violent competition; glorification of the athletic male body-as-machine; verbal misogyny and homophobia), poor black and gay male athletes contribute to the continued subordination of women, as well as to the circumscription of their own relationships and development.

Tim Carrigan, Bob Connell, and John Lee assert that rather than undermining social inequality, men's struggles within class, racial, and sexual hierarchies of intermale dominance serve to reinforce men's global subordination of women. Although strains caused by differences and inequalities among men represent potential avenues for social change, ultimately, "the fissuring of the categories 'men' and 'women' is one of the central facts about a patriarchal power and the way it works. In the case of men, the crucial division is between hegemonic masculinity and various subordinated masculinities."[14] Hegemonic masculinity is thus defined in relation to various subordinated masculinities as well as in relation to femininities. This is a key insight for the contemporary meaning of sport. Utilizing the concept of "multiple masculinities," we can begin to understand how race, class, age, and sexual hierarchies among men help to construct and legitimize men's overall power and privilege over women. In addition, the false promise of sharing in the fruits of hegemonic masculinity often ties black, working-class, or gay men into their marginalized and subordinate status. For instance, my research suggests that while black men's development of "cool pose" within sport can be interpreted as creative resistance against one form of social domination (racism), it also demonstrates the limits of an agency that adopts other forms of social domination (athletic masculinity) as its vehicle.

My research also suggests how homophobia within athletic masculine cultures tends to lock men—whether gay or not—into narrowly defined heterosexual identities and relationships. Within the athletic context, homophobia is closely linked with misogyny in ways that ultimately serve to bond men together as superior to women. Given the extremely oppressive levels of homophobia within organized sport, it is understandable why the vast majority of gay male athletes would decide to remain closeted. But the public construction of a heterosexual/masculine status requires that a closeted gay athlete actively participate in (or at the very least, tolerate) the ongoing group expressions of homophobia and misogyny—what Mike T. called "locker room garbage." Thus, though he may feel a sense of irony, and may even confidentially express that sense of irony to gay male friends or to researchers, the public face that the closeted gay male athlete presents to the world is really no different from that of his nongay teammates. As long as he is successful in this public presentation-of-self as heterosexual/masculine, he will continue to contribute to (and benefit from) men's power over women.

Sport in Gay Communities

The fissuring of the category "men," then, as it is played out within the dominant institution of sport, does little to threaten—indeed, may be a central mechanism in—the reconstruction of existing class, racial, sexual, and gender inequalities.[15] Nevertheless, since the outset of the gay liberation movement in the early 1970s, organized sport has become an integral part of developing gay and lesbian communities. The ways that "gay" sports have been defined and organized are sometimes different—even radically different—than the dominant institution of sport in society.

The most public sign of the growing interest in athletics in gay communities was the rapid growth and popularity of bodybuilding among many young, urban gay men in the 1970s and early 1980s. The meanings of gay male bodybuilding are multiple and contradictory.[16] On the one hand, gay male bodybuilding overtly eroticizes the muscular male body, thus potentially disrupting the tendency of sport to eroticize male bodies under the guise of aggression and competition. On the other hand, the building of muscular bodies is often motivated by a conscious need by gay men to prove to the world that they are "real men." Gay bodybuilding thus undermines cultural stereotypes of homosexual men as "nelly," effeminate, and womanlike. But it also tends to adopt and promote a very conventional equation of masculinity with physical

strength and muscularity.[17] In effect, then, as gay bodybuilders attempt
to sever the cultural link between masculinity and heterosexuality, they
uncritically affirm a conventional dichotomization of masculinity/male
vs. femininity/female.

By contrast, some gay athletes have initiated alternative athletic institutions that aim to challenge conventional views of sexuality and gender. As we saw in earlier chapters, Mike T. had originally gone into
sport to prove that he was "male," to cover up the fact that he was gay.
When his career as an Olympic athlete finally ended, he came out publicly, and soon was a very active member of the San Francisco Bay Area
gay community. He rekindled his interest in the arts and dance. He also
remained very active in athletics, and he increasingly imagined how
wonderful it would be to blend the beauty and exhilaration of sport, as
he had experienced it, with the emergent, liberating values of the feminist, gay, and lesbian communities of which he was a part. In 1982, his
dream became a reality, as 1,300 athletes from twelve different nations
gathered in San Francisco to participate in the first ever Gay Games.[18]

Though many of the events in the Gay Games are "conventional"
sports (track and field, swimming, etc.), and a number of "serious athletes" compete in the events, overall the Games reflect a value system
and a vision based on feminist and gay liberationist ideals of equality
and universal participation. As Mike T. said,

> You don't win by beating someone else. We defined winning as doing
> your very best. That way, everyone is a winner. And we have age-
> group competition, so all ages are involved. We have parity: If there's
> a men's sport, there's a women's sport to complement it. And we go out
> and recruit in Third World and minority areas. All of these people are
> gonna get together for a week, they're gonna march in together, they're
> gonna hold hands, and they'll say, "Jesus Christ! This is wonderful!"
> There's this discovery: "I had no idea women were such fun!" and,
> "God! Blacks are okay—I didn't do anything to offend him, and we
> became friends!" and, "God, that guy over there is in his sixties, and
> I had no idea they were so sexually active!"—[laughs].

This emphasis on bridging differences, overcoming prejudices, and
building relationships definitely enhanced the athletic experience for
one participant I interviewed. This man said that he loved to swim, and
even loved to compete, because it "pushed" him to swim "a whole lot
better." Yet in past competitions, he had always come in last place. As

he put it, "The Gay Games were just wonderful in many respects. One of them was that people who came in second, or third, and *last* got standing ovations from the crowd—the crowd genuinely recognized the thrill of giving a damn good shot, regardless of where you came in, and gave support to that. Among the competitors, there was a whole lot of joking and supportiveness."

In 1986, 3,482 athletes participated in Gay Games II in San Francisco. In 1990, at Gay Games III in Vancouver, 7,200 athletes continued the vision of building, partly through sport, an "exemplary community" that eliminates sexism, homophobia, and racism. Mike T. described what the Gay Games mean to him:

To me, it's one of those steps in a thousand-mile journey to try and raise consciousness and enlighten people—not just people outside the gay community, but within the gay community as well, [because] we're just as racist, ageist, nationalistic, and chauvinistic as anybody else. Maybe it's simplistic to some people, you know, but why does it have to be complicated? Put people in a position where they can experience this process of discovery, and here it is! I just hope that this is something that'll take hold and a lot of people will get the idea.

The Gay Games represent a radical break from past and current conceptions of the role of sport in society. But they do not represent a major challenge to sport as an institution. Alternative athletic venues like the Gay Games, since they exist outside of the dominant sports institution, do not directly confront or change the dominant structure. On the other hand, these experiments are valuable in terms of demonstrating the fact that alternative value systems and structures are possible.[19]

THE CHALLENGE OF FEMALE ATHLETICISM

Organized sport, as we know it, emerged largely as a masculinist response to a crisis in the gender order of the late nineteenth and early twentieth centuries. The world of sport gave men a retreat from what they feared was a "feminized" modern culture, and it gave white upper-class men (initially), and working-class and minority men (eventually) a means of "naturalizing" dominant forms of masculinity. Throughout most of the twentieth century, this masculine institution of sport existed alongside a vibrant but much less visible tradition of women's sport. In the early 1970s, there emerged what Stephanie Twin has called a "second wave of athletic feminism."[20] The explosion of girls' and women's athletics in the next two decades served notice that female athletes could no longer be ignored to the extent that they once were.

How have men responded to women's recent movement into sport? There is some evidence that increasing female athleticism has caused many boys and men to adjust—and sometimes radically alter—their preconceptions of what women are capable of. Personally confronting the reality of female athleticism has caused some boys and men to question what sociologist Nancy Theberge has called "the myth of female frailty."[21] On the other hand, there is also considerable evidence that women's sport has been institutionally contained, and thus its potential challenge to sport's construction of hegemonic masculinity has been largely defused.

Individual Responses to Female Athleticism

Men have not responded in a singular manner to women's increased athleticism. Some men continue to ignore or denigrate female athletes. But it appears that when men are personally confronted with female athletes, they are forced to reevaluate some of their preconceived notions about gender difference. For instance, Adam A. had in recent years made the transition from coaching high school boys' football and baseball to coed cross country and girls' softball. His decision to make this shift resulted from changes in his values (wanting to get out of the high-visibility, high-pressure "major sports") and, in turn, led to further changes in his perspective on the meaning of sport for males and for females. I asked him what kinds of changes he sees resulting from the increase in girls' sport participation at his school, and he described institutional strains, as well as shifts in his own beliefs and values:

> I think now there's some competition [between boys' and girls' athletic teams] for things like the number of baseballs, the number of bats, the number of facilities. And it's important how that's handled by coaches and administrators. The Boosters Club still seems to have that old stigma about "minor sports." Football, of course, is the macho one. So the boys feel that the girls really don't belong, and they're getting short-sheeted because there should be more room to play, but there's not because they have to share it with the girls. But one thing that I would like to interject here is that before I coached girls, I felt the same way. And I feel that now I'm not that way too much. I feel I'm pretty fair.

Yet I still had that idea until I began coaching girls' track and had an appreciation for the amount of work that girls put into their sport. And now there's no difference in my mind. But I shared the assumption, initially, that they're just out there to primp and powder their noses and they're not gonna put out too much. Which of course is not true. I had no other evidence to base it on but my own bias.

As girls and women gain more athletic opportunities than in the past, they become more highly skilled, more serious athletes. This, in turn, often challenges—even undermines—the kinds of "biases" that Adam A. used to have. A few of the men in my study said that they experienced dramatic personal transformations as a result of being confronted by feminism, and especially by strong, assertive, athletic women. For instance, Clarence T. had been a better-than-average high school student-athlete, yet behind the glow of success was a feeling of unease, unhappiness, and loneliness. As we have seen, Clarence eventually came to reject the pressure of athletic competition during his college years, yet he still felt unhappy and lonely, and his weight ballooned from 160 to 190 pounds. After college, he moved to Colorado where he got involved in noncompetitive physical activities such as hiking, cycling, and climbing. For the first time in his life, he started to feel good about himself, and even "exhilarated" with physical activity. During his three years in Colorado, Clarence taught at an alternative school with some feminist women and "began to develop an understanding of sexism." But his budding feminist consciousness existed mostly on an abstract level, until he had a transformative athletic experience with a female colleague who was "a real strong feminist":

The turning point in my understanding of feminism was the day that [she] and I decided to teach a class in rock climbing. So we said, fine, why don't we just go out and do some climbing, just to check ourselves out. So I'm assuming that I'm the better climber and that I'm stronger than she is—and we get to these rocks, and we're climbing up, and I start to get a little sense that she's a little bit better climber than I am. And we go up to the top, make this move, and I can't make the move! She's gone ahead of me and protected it, and I can't make it up there! And that just sort of broke through some stuff in my relationship with her, and we began to communicate about the fact that I had been putting her down a lot and assuming she wasn't very competent, and assuming I was better than her. And then I began to learn a lot from her about feminism, and the way women are treated by men. And that really made a difference to me.

Now, Clarence T.'s work is specifically aimed at developing antisexist curriculum in schools. The political nature of his change of heart, sparked largely by the challenge of an "athletic feminist" woman, was not common among the men I studied. But a more general theme in his life was shared by some of the men I interviewed. Clearly, the masculine structure and values of athletic careers had left many of these men feeling empty, especially in terms of the kinds of relationships they developed with other people. A few of these men were very conscious of the fact that sport had not delivered what they most craved; worse, the athletic career had been primarily a source of pain and anxiety. Recall that Bill S. had been an extremely aggressive high school competitor, but when he was injured and refused to "play hurt," his teammates, his coach, and the community called him a "pussy" and blamed him for the team's loss. Bill was emotionally hurt by this, and dropped out of sport for years. He told me, though, that he had recently taken up playground basketball again, and though he felt ambivalent about how his old competitive aggressions seemed to reemerge in this context, he felt good about playing again. But most satisfying were his weekly raquetball games with his wife. She had never been very athletic, he said, so they decided to adjust the situation in order to make the game more "fair": "I enjoy playing raquetball with her. I play with my left hand, and with an eye-patch on, which is really hard [laughs]—But I do it to make things fair. That's the way we play. And she beats me sometimes, and I beat her sometimes. I feel really good about how I play, what kind of attitude I play with." Bill said that he feels "okay" when he loses to his wife; and while one interpretation of this might be that playing left-handed and with an eye-patch is a patronizing gesture that allows him to know, even in defeat, that he is the superior athlete, I would argue that there is something else going on here. In changing the rules to make them more "equal," Bill and his wife have broken with the dominant masculine athletic value system. First, they are redefining "fairness," not as "equal opportunity" within a rigid rule structure, but rather, as "equality" within a negotiated and fluid rule structure.[22] Most important, the foundation for their game is a value-system that elevates the quality of their relationship to a position of prominence over winning.

Similarly, Rick J.'s disengagement from his basketball career had left him feeling empty, alone, and struggling. He was considering abandoning even playground ball, since he "didn't get the strokes" from it that he wanted. But in the past year, he said, he had begun practicing with a women's basketball team, and he had eventually played in some mixed male-female games. These games were "exhilarating" for him, as he saw men and women at very different skill levels play, develop, and improve:

> [*By the end of the season*], *every woman was playing at such a high level, and I've never seen improvement like that. The point is, it was an exhilarating basketball experience for me, but it wasn't necessarily basketball that drew me to this group of people at this point in my life. It felt like a little bit more, which is different in my experience. There was a different quality of relationships. There was probably more of a feeling of togetherness, you know, of natural support. And there's a difference that I notice* after *the game, at the bar. The game gets talked about some at the bar afterward. But it's left, you know, when enough talking has been done about it.*

Since he's tall and quite skilled, Rick said that in the mixed-sex games he sometimes had to "hold back" a bit and not play up to his skill level. When I asked him if he did not at times miss playing "at a higher level," with bigger, more skilled players, he responded, "Yeah, I really miss that. [But] I think I have to make a choice for myself what I want: a high-skill level sort of team, where my relationships with the men are limited, or whether I want a team where the relationships are solid and can grow, and where that takes precedence over the level of skill. I think I'm ready to go in that direction for a while."

Rick J.'s response to my question echoed Bill S.'s and Clarence T.'s emergent value system, which, though somewhat ambivalent, elevates relationships above competition and winning, thus inverting the priorities that govern the dominant forms of sport. Each of these men's personal transformations took place within a similar social context. First, each of them had had less than successful and less than happy experiences with their own athletic careers. Second, each of these men came to understand the meanings of their negative athletic experiences through their interactions with athletic women.

Perhaps millions of boys and men have loved playing sport, but—like Clarence, Rick, and Bill—have experienced athletic careers as problematic, even painful and traumatic. Some may simply reject sport, but throw themselves wholeheartedly into some nonathletic activity structured according to the same masculine value system and power relations. Others might develop low self-images and view themselves as less than masculine, as personal failures. Feminism offers men an alternative way in which to view their negative experiences with athletic careers. Relationships with feminist and athletic women have given some men a context within which to transform their relationship with sport, rather than blindly accepting—or rejecting—sport altogether.

SPORT AS PUBLIC SPECTACLE: GENDERED MEANINGS

Does female athleticism pose a fundamental challenge to male power in society? We have seen that individual men who are confronted by female athletes are often challenged to change their conceptions of male/female difference. These kinds of changes can contribute to the development of more egalitarian relationships with women. But though profeminist personal transformations in men can be seen as a positive sign, they are also quite rare. Moreover, it appears that individual changes do not necessarily challenge the social role that sport continues to play in the construction of gender difference and inequality.

Why is this? To begin to answer this question, we need to recognize that in addition to being composed of "gendered structures" and "gendered personalities," the social organization of gender is also constructed by symbols and ideologies.[23] My study, in focusing on the relationship between masculine identities and the social structure of sport (and to a lesser extent, other social institutions), has largely ignored the third element of the gender order, symbolism and ideology. Clearly, any analysis of the broader social meanings of contemporary sport must take into account the fact that for millions of people, their dominant experience of sport is not as athletes, but as spectators of a mediated public spectacle.

Thus, a key to whether or not increasing female athleticism will amount to a real challenge to sport's role in a system of masculine domination is whether and how the media covers girls' and women's sport. Research from the late 1970s and through the 1980s reveals that the sport media have not accurately or fairly reflected the boom in female athletic participation.[24] Two recent studies of sport media which I conducted with Margaret Carlisle Duncan, Kerry Jensen, and Linda Williams confirm that this is still the case. First, we compared televised coverage of women's and men's sport. In our examination of TV sport news over a six-week period in 1989, we found that men's sport received 92 percent of the coverage, women's sport 5 percent, and gender-neutral topics, 3 percent. Rather than appearing on TV sport news as athletes, women more commonly appeared as comical targets of the newscasters' jokes or as sexual objects (e.g., as bikini-clad spectators at men's baseball games). We also found that in televised coverage of college basketball and professional tennis, commentators tended to talk about women's sport and women athletes very differently than the ways they talk of men. For example, women athletes were commonly referred to as "girls," while men athletes (who are of the same age) were never called "boys," but always "men." We concluded that this difference, along with others, tended to infantilize women athletes, while granting male athletes adult status.[25]

Our second study, which examined four of the top-selling newspapers in the United States over a three-month period in 1990, revealed that stories on men's sport outnumbered those on women's sport by a 23 to 1 ratio. Moreover, stories on women's sport accounted for only 3.2 percent of front-page sport stories, tended to be shorter in length than stories on men's sport, and were less likely to be accompanied by a photograph than were stories on men's sport. In short, newspaper and TV news still tend to ignore or trivialize women's sport in ways that render it less visible and less legitimate than men's sport. The message is clear: "sport news" still means *men's* sport news.[26]

In recent years, though, especially with the expansion of cable television, there has been a significant, if modest, increase in women's sport programming on television.[27] But the continued lack of quality coverage of women's sport still tends to reflect and reinforce the lower status of women athletes. Moreover, the very different ways that women's sport is presented on television—the lower production quality, the gender-biased language of commentators—are likely to reinforce existing negative attitudes or ambivalences about women's sport and women athletes. As a result, it appears that the challenge to masculine hegemony posed by the expansion of girls' and women's sport has been ideologically contained by the sport media. The "men" have been separated from the "girls."

However, this containment is not total. As I have noted above, the simple existence of girls' and women's sport may stretch, if not absolutely transform, our taken-for-granted assumptions about natural male-female difference. For instance, Ricardo R. told me that he sees his nine-year-old daughter's involvement in softball as a "very positive thing," while also noting that there are still certain aspects of the sports-world that separate males and females:

> *There are situations where women are a lot better—in gymnastics and other situations where they can stretch their bodies—it seems like men are limited in that respect. But in a game that's rough and tumble, basically unless it's an all-women league, I'd say that women really can't be accepted in those situations, you know. But I really enjoy the progress they're making now, having bobby-sox baseball for little girls, even flag football. And in high school they have whole leagues now like for the boys. I think that's great. You used to watch women's games in the 60s and 70s, and you could just watch all these mistakes—I mean routine grounders, a little bobble, or an error on the first base-man, things like that. They wouldn't know how to do a double play. But now they're really sharp—I mean, they can play a man's game as far as mental sharpness. But I think physically they're limited to their own sex. There is still the male part of the game. That is, males have better physical equipment for sports, as far as what they can do and what they can't do.*

There is more to Ricardo's words than a stubbornly persistent need to assert natural male superiority. On the one hand, he expresses a new respect for what girls and women can accomplish when given the orga-nizational opportunities to play sport. But his statement also exempli-fies the built-in limits and ambiguities of a liberal strategy of "equal opportunity for women" within the present institution of sport. Imbed-ded in the liberal ideal of equal opportunity is a strong belief that in-equality is part of the natural order. Thus it's only "fair" that women get an equal chance to compete, but it's really such a relief to find that, once given the opportunity, they just don't have the "physical equipment" to measure up to the men. "They're [still] limited to their own sex."

Increased athletic participation for girls and for women does par-tially undermine sexist attitudes and assumptions among some men. Yet as long as we are simply attempting to incorporate women within an institution that is, in its dominant structure and values, a masculine construction, "equal opportunity" for females will ultimately serve to affirm and naturalize masculine superiority. The reason is this: Today's sport media—and, indeed, liberal feminists who are intent on gaining equal opportunities for female athletes—often ignore the fact that male and female bodies do tend to differ in potential physical strength, endurance, agility, and grace. Despite considerable overlap, the average adult male is about five inches taller than the average female. Can women really hope to compete with men at the highest levels of basketball or volleyball? Males average 40 percent muscle and 15 percent body fat, while females average 23 percent muscle and 25 percent body fat. Can women possibly compete at the highest levels with men in football, track and field, hockey, or baseball? On the other hand, women have some physical differences from men that can be translated into athletic superiority. For instance, as Ricardo R. acknowledged, women's different skeletal structures and greater flexibility make for superior performances on a balance beam. In addition, women's higher body fat ratio gives them greater buoyancy in water and greater insulation against heat loss, which has translated into women's times in distance swimming, especially in cold water, being considerably faster than men's.[28]

In other words, as long as we are intent on measuring the highest levels of physical performance, males are likely to excel in some activities, females in others. Yet given our present values and institutional arrangements, these average physiological differences between the sexes nearly always end up being translated into female physical "inferiority." The reason for this is simple: The most highly valued sports in the U.S. (especially the "money sports" like football) are at present organized according to the most extreme possibilities of the male body. "Equal opportunity" for women within these masculine-defined sports puts women at a decided disadvantage.

Significantly, though coverage of women's sport lags far behind coverage of men's sport, the sport media increasingly appear to be employing liberal conceptions of equal opportunity in their presentations of the athletic performances of women.[29] With women competing in male-defined sports, the media can employ statistics as "objective measures of performance." Spectators can see for themselves that, for instance, though the women competitors in the Olympics are impressive athletes, the medal winners' performances would rarely be good enough to qualify them for the finals in the men's events.[30] Equal opportunity within this system thus provides support for the ideology of meritocracy, while subtly supplying incontrovertible evidence of the "natural superiority" of males over females. Clearly, if equal opportunity for women is not to serve simply as the basis for a reconstituted ideology of male superiority, the institution of sport itself must be transformed from a masculine construction to a human construction.

Watching Men's Sport, Constructing Masculinities

What does televised sport mean to male viewers? The mythology and symbolism of today's most popular spectator sports are probably meaningful to viewers on a number of levels: patriotism, militarism, violence, and meritocracy are all dominant themes. But it is reasonable to speculate that gender is a salient organizing theme in the construction of meanings, especially with respect to the more aggressive and violent aspects of sport. For example, when I was interviewing a thirty-two-year-old white professional-class male, and I asked him how he felt about the fact that recently a woman had been promoted to a position of authority in his workplace, he replied, "A woman can do the same job as I can do—maybe even be my boss. But I'll be *damned* if she can go out on the [football] field and take a hit from Ronnie Lott."[31]

At the most obvious level, we can read this man's statement as an indication that he is identifying with Ronnie Lott as a man, and the basis of the identification is the violent male body. Football, based as it is on the fullest potential of the male body (muscular bulk, explosive power) is clearly a world apart from women, who are relegated to the roles of sex objects on the sidelines, rooting their men on. In contrast to the bare and vulnerable bodies of the cheerleaders, the armored male bodies of the football players are elevated to mythical status and thus give testimony to the undeniable "fact" that here is at least one place where men are clearly superior to women. Yet it is also significant that this man was quite aware that he (and perhaps 99 percent of the rest of the male population of the United States) was probably equally incapable of taking a "hit" from the likes of Ronnie Lott and living to tell of it. I would speculate that by recognizing the simultaneous construction of identification and difference among men, we may begin to understand the major role that televised sport plays in the current gender order.

IDENTIFICATION. With the twentieth-century decline of the practical relevance of physical strength in work and in warfare, representations of the male body as strong, virile, and powerful have taken on increasingly important ideological and symbolic significance in gender relations.[32] Indeed, the body plays such a central role in the contemporary gender order because it is so closely associated with the "natural." Yet, as we have seen, though the body is popularly equated with nature, it is nevertheless an object of social practice: The development of men's bodies for athletic competition takes a tremendous amount of time, exercise, weight-training, and even use of illegal and dangerous drugs such as steroids. But the sport media tend to obscure the reality of this social construction, weaving a cloak of symbol and interpretation around these gendered bodies that naturalizes them.[33]

Some recent theorists have suggested that the true significance of sport as mediated spectacle lies in male spectators having the opportunity to identify narcissistically with the muscular male body. Media analyst Margaret Morse, for instance, in a fascinating examination of the use of slow-motion instant replays in football, argues that the visual representation of violence is transformed by slow motion replays into "gracefulness." The salience of the image of male power and grace lies not in identification with violence, Morse argues, but rather, in the opportunity to engage in an identificatory male gaze that is both narcissistic and homoerotic.[34] An additional interpretation is possible. Rather than concluding that televised sport violence has no meaning, it is reasonable to speculate that if men are using sport spectatorship to identify with the male body as a thing of beauty and power, perhaps the violence is an important aspect of the denial of the homoerotic element of that identification.

DIFFERENCE. It is also possible that the media's framing of sport violence plays another important role: the construction of difference among men. As we have seen, it is disproportionately males from lower socioeconomic and ethnic minority backgrounds who commit themselves to athletic careers, and who end up participating at the higher levels of aggressive, violent sports. Privileged men might, as Woody Guthrie once suggested, commit violence against others "with fountain pens," but with the exception of domestic violence against women and children, physical violence is rarely a part of the everyday lives of these men. Yet violence among men may still have important ideological and psychological meaning for men from privileged backgrounds. There is a curious preoccupation among middle-class males with movie characters who are "working-class tough guys," with athletes who are fearsome "hitters" and who heroically "play hurt."[35] These violent "tough guys" of the culture industry—the Rambos, the Ronnie Lotts—are at once the heroes who "prove" that "we men" are superior to women and the "other" against whom privileged men define themselves as "modern."

TV sport commentators, probably unwittingly, tend to contribute to the construction of black male athletes as "other." A 1977 study revealed that white players received more praise and less criticism from pro football commentators than comparable black players. And in 1989, *Boston Globe* reporter Derrick Jackson reported that white male football and basketball players were much more likely to be credited with "intelligence and hard work," while the successes of their black male counterparts were more likely to be attributed to "natural athleticism."[36] It is indeed ironic that so many young poor black males are attracted to sport as an arena in which to become "respected," yet once there, to be successful, they must become intimidating, aggressive, even violent in order to survive. Then the media images of, for instance, Nathan C. or Ronnie Lott "destroying" an opposing player become symbolic "proof" of the racist stereotype that black males are indeed "naturally more violent and aggressive." Thus, though on one level athletes may represent power to the viewer, these men are, in fact, mere "surrogates of power."[37] The reins of power in modern U.S. society lie not in the hands of men who have pursued athletic careers, though media images of the more successful of these men are often used to sell products or political candidates. Rather, the dominant positions of economic and social power lie outside the world of sport, and these positions are occupied by men who may have left their own athletic careers behind in the schoolyard. But these men speak a language of power learned on playgrounds and playing fields, and the media's presentation of sport contributes to the ideological legitimation and naturalization of their power and privilege over women and over marginalized and subordinated men.

TRANSFORMING SPORT AND MASCULINITY

Since the institution of sport is both constructed by, and in turn helps to construct, the overall gender order, it makes no sense to speak of transforming sport in the abstract.[38] Any fundamental changes in the values and structure of organized sport necessarily must take place within a larger movement to transform other social institutions (economy, politics, family, education, etc.). But this does not mean that attempts to change sport have no worth. I have argued here that sport is a key component of our current gender order. Further, though sport's major impact appears to support the status quo of hegemonic masculinity, there are also internal contradictions in men's experiences with athletic careers. These problems have been given potential new meaning by women's recent challenge to sport as a masculine institution.

It would be foolhardy to reject sport outright, as some radicals in the past have done. For instance, in the late 1960s and early 1970s, the U.S. counterculture denounced organized competitive sport as inherently destructive. Instead, they encouraged the implementation of "New Games," which emphasized universal participation (in place of a star system), a focus upon enjoyment (instead of upon winning), and spontaneity (instead of rigid rules). Essentially, the counterculture attempted to replace "sport" with "play," and in so doing, threw the baby out with the bath water.[39] Their mistake was to assume that competitive sport is in itself oppressive, instead of developing a critique of the specific manifestations of sport, as it has been shaped by commercial interests, by racism, and by sexism.

For better or for worse, vast numbers of boys and men (and increasing numbers of girls and women) today have found sport to be a major context in which they experience fun, where they relax and build friendships with others, where they can push their bodies toward excellence, where they may learn to cooperate toward a shared goal, and where they may get a sense of identification and community in an otherwise privatized and alienating society. Rather than ignoring this reality, a radical critique of sport should emphasize how difficult it is for people to experience these positive aspects of sport participation so long as they are constructing identities within athletic careers.

It is possible for sport to be reorganized in such a way that its positive potentialities—which all of the men I interviewed experienced to a degree, but which, for many of them, were eclipsed by anxiety and pain—can rise to the surface. But if, as I have suggested, the current affinity between boys' and men's developing masculine identities and the institution of sport continues, then simply attempting to reorganize sport will be an exercise in futility. There are two fundamental requisites for the humanization of sport: First, boys and girls should be brought up and nurtured in an equal manner, and this work must be shared equally by men and women. Second, all of our social institutions—schools, workplaces, families, the state—must be reorganized in ways that maximize equality for all people. Girls and boys, women and men who are raised in such an egalitarian world might finally be able to enjoy sport for all that it really has to offer.

Appendixes
Notes
Bibliography
Index

Appendix I: Individual Data on Interviewees

PSEUDONYM	SPORT(S)/LEVEL	INTERVIEW DATE/ TIME (MIN)	AGE	SOCIAL CLASS (OF ORIGIN)	RACE	EDUCATION	CURRENT
Adam A.	HS: FB, BB, BS C: FB, BS	1–84/ 140	42	wk	White	B.S.	HS teacher/coach
Barry B.	HS: FB, BB, TF C: FB PRO:FB (7 yrs)	2–84, 3–84/ 150	31	wk	Black	B.S.	Director, nonprofit organization
Nathan C.	HS: FB, BB, TF C: FB PRO: FB (8 yrs)	5–84/ 90	35	poor/wk	Black	B.S.	Sport camp organizer
Eldon C.	HS: FB, BS, TF C: TF	6–83, 7–83/ 180	48	wk	Black	Ph.D.	college teacher
Mark C.	HS: BB CC: BB	1–84/ 90	33	m	White	A.A.	driver/distributor
Sam D.	HS: FB, BB	2–84/100	33	m	White	B.A.	social worker
Frank E.	HS: BB, T	2–84/ 120	21	wk	Latino	Student	college student
Jack F.	HS: FB C: FB	2–84/ 90	22	wk	Black	Student	college student
Brent F.	HS: BB	5–83/ 90	24	m	White	M.A.	graduate student
Chris H.	HS: BB C: BB PRO: BB (4 yrs)	10–83/ 150	34	poor/wk	Black	B.A.	parole officer/ assistant college coach

Name	Athletic background	Draft	Age	Marital	Race	Education	Occupation
Gene H.	HS: FB, BS C: FB PRO: FB (9 yrs)	9–83/ 120	36	wk	Black	B.A.	small business owner
Calvin H.	HS: BB, BS, TF C: BB	4–84/ 90	42	wk	Black	Ph.D.	college teacher
Ray J.	HS: FB, BB, BS CC: BB	7–84/ 90	34	wk	Black	HS	bus driver
Rick J.	HS: BB, BS	8–83/ 90	26	m	White	M.A.	unemployed
Neal K.	HS: FB, WL	1–84/ 100	21	wk	Black	Student	college student
Steve L.	HS: BS, SW C: BS	8–83/ 90	32	wk	White	B.S.	college athletic director
Thomas M.	HS: FB, BB, BS C: FB PRO: FB (7 yrs)	9–83/ 90	41	poor/wk	Black	B.A.	small business owner
Gerald M.	HS: BB	6–84/ 100	32	m	Black	HS	fast food worker
David P.	HS: FB, BB, BS PRO: BS (11 yrs)	10–83, 11–83/ 210	36	poor/wk	White	HS	pro baseball office job
Jon P.	HS: BB, CC	3–84/ 90	31	m	White	M.S.	college teacher
Jim P.	HS: FB, BB, BS	1–84/ 180	32	m	White	D.D.S.	dentist
Ricardo R.	HS: FB, BB, BS CC: FB	7–83, 8–83/ 110	32	poor/wk	Latino	H.S.	factory worker
Willy S.	HS: FB, BB, TF C: FB PRO: FB (1/2 yr)	4–83, 5–83/190	33	poor/wk	Black	M.A.	prison inmate
Terry S.	HS: BS C: BS	2–84/ 90	22	m	White	Student	college student

Appendix I—*continued*

PSEUDONYM	SPORT(S)/LEVEL	INTERVIEW DATE/ TIME (MIN)	AGE	SOCIAL CLASS (OF ORIGIN)	RACE	EDUCATION	CURRENT
Bill S.	HS: FB, TN, BB	8–83/90	30	wk	White	H.S.	oil rig worker
Clarence T.	HS: FB	3–83/120	33	wk	White	B.A.	HS teacher
Mike T.	HS: FB, TF, GM C: TF OLY: TF	5–84/100	46	m	White	M.D.	medical doctor
Larry W.	HS: FB C: FB	9–83, 10–83/100	46	poor/wk	Black	Ed.D.	Jr. HS teacher/ coach
Ralph W.	HS: FB	2–84/90	28	wk	Black	Student	college student
Don W.	HS: FB, BB, BS	9–83/90	32	m	White	A.A.	truck driver/ delivery

Key

Sport(s)/Level: HS = high school. **CC** = community college. **C** = four-year college. **OLY** = Olympics. **PRO** = professional. **FB** = football. **BB** = basketball. **BS** = baseball. **TF** = track and field. **WL** = weight lifting. **SW** = swimming. **CC** = cross country. **TN** = tennis. **GM** = gymnastics.
Social Class of Origin: poor/wk = poor working class. **wk** = working class (blue-, pink-collar jobs). **m** = middle class (professional/white-collar/managerial jobs).

176

Appendix 2

Interviewing Male Former Athletes

Subjects for this study were selected in a number of ways. The first three former professional athletes were selected through my contacts in the National Football League Players' Association and in a major league baseball team. Subsequent former professionals were identified through "snowballing" (i.e., the first few men I interviewed referred me to others). Former high school and college athletes were identified through my personal memory of individuals, contacts made on playgrounds, suggestions made by friends and colleagues, and then through snowballing. Though the sample was not scientifically selected, an effort was made to see that the sample was representative in terms of race and social class background (see appendix 3 for more discussion of race and class), and that there was some variety in terms of age, types of sport played, and levels of success in athletic careers. Without exception, each man contacted agreed to be interviewed.

The Interview Process

As I began the research for this book, my decision as to how to go about interviewing men was influenced by a lively debate among feminist social scientists as to whether or not there is such a thing as a "feminist methodology." On the one side of the debate are those, like sociologist Ann Oakley, who claim that there is something very different about feminist research: Feminists aim to break down the traditional relationship of interviewer-subject/interviewee-object by relating to those they interview in egalitarian and reciprocal ways. They argue that both interviewer and interviewee should benefit in feminist research.[1] Others, such as sociologist Judith Stacey, have argued that the idea of a non-hierarchical relationship between researchers and the researched is an unobtainable fantasy. Power and status inequities—and even betrayal—are built into the relationship between the researchers and those they are researching. Since researchers are building professional careers and (even in the case of long-term participant-observation and ethnography) will nearly always eventually leave the community they are researching, they always have a different stake in the research process.[2]

As I conducted my interviews, I was aware that I had a "professional" purpose: The intimate information I received from interviewees would help me complete my Ph.D. degree, write a book, and launch my career as a sociologist. This purpose gave me a stake in the interviews that was not shared by the interviewees. By contrast, they apparently had little to gain, and possibly even something to lose if they revealed information that was painful, embarrassing, or damaging to their reputations. Despite these differences, I tried as much as possible to create an interview process that would be of benefit to the interviewee. Since I was interested in exploring how men construct and define meaning in their lives, I allowed each man to direct the interviews to a certain extent. I found most men relished this opportunity (especially since, in recent years, "out of the spotlight," they had received very little of this kind of attention.)

I eventually discovered that there were pitfalls in this method. These men did love to "talk sports." But I began to find that their willingness to talk contributed to my illusion that this process was "easy." Men tend to be good at talking about events, big games or seasons, but not so willing, comfortable, or practiced at talking about inner feelings—especially hurt, sadness, fear, or vulnerability. I began to realize that most interviewees had a tendency to abstract their feelings, even to the extent of talking of themselves in the third person. After the first few interviews, once I identified my own collusion in this masculine communication pattern, I employed a strategy of asking directly, "How did that make you feel?" or "How do you feel about that now?" In effect, this interview strategy amounted to breaking what sociologist Arlie Hochschild calls the "feeling rules" of male-male interactions.[3] The fact is, I realized, most men are rarely asked, especially by other men, to talk about their feelings as a valid part of their existence. I found that when they were given the opportunity, most of the men I interviewed were very open about their feelings. At the end of each interview, I would ask each interviewee to evaluate the interview, to tell me how it made him feel. Almost all of the men said that they had enjoyed the interview.

Many relished the chance to recall "the good old days." For most of the men, there was more to it than that, though. For instance, David P. said, "I think I've told you more in four-and-a-half hours than I've told any one person at any time. I wish I could sit down with my wife and say the things to her that I have said here." For David, and for several others that I interviewed, the interview process had clearly been a learning experience, as it offered them the opportunity to think about, and speak about, their lives in ways that they previously had not. In these cases, I was certain that the interview had not simply been a one-way process, with me taking from them.

Race, Class, and Social Distance

I was not always certain that the interview was going to be seen as a "positive experience." I was more confident that the interview was a learning (or a therapeutic) experience when I interviewed the white, middle-class men. I was not so sure when I interviewed the poor, working class, black, and Latino men. There are two reasons for this. First, though my shared background as a former athlete created a bond of sorts between myself and the men I interviewed, there was clearly less social distance between me and my white, professional class interviewees than there was with poor, working-class and minority interviewees.

Sociologists Bob Blauner and David Wellman have argued that the methods commonly used by white, privileged researchers to study blacks in the United States amount to an intellectual "colonization" of the latter by the former.[4] Indeed, whether we like it or not, white sociologists are likely to be viewed by our working-class and ethnic minority subjects as representatives of the "professional-college-educated world" toward which they are likely to hold ambivalent feelings. Moreover, our own social class, race, and professional training tends to color our definitions of working-class and minority men, perhaps leading us to expect them to be more "traditional" (i.e., inexpressive, authoritarian) than their white, middle-class male counterparts. The working-class or minority interviewee's response to this expectation may be self-fulfilling, for as Barbara Ehrenreich has pointed out, the interviewer's middle-class gaze "can be an uncomfortable one—associated in lower classes with workplace supervision and with negative judgements by teachers and other authorities. What appears to be a lack of 'interpersonal skills' can be a withdrawal from middle class discourse."[5]

Indeed, I found that a few black former athletes seemed especially wary of being interviewed by a white sociologist. For instance, Gene H., a former professional football player, was at first very reluctant to "open up," giving mostly short, clipped, prepackaged answers to my questions. Gradually, after an hour or so, he began to talk more freely, even to the point of reciting some poetry that was especially meaningful to him. At the conclusion of the interview, he explained why he took some time before deciding to open up: "Well, other guys that interviewed me, the one that asks me, 'Is this black or is this white?'—any *dummy* can answer. That doesn't mean hell. He can *see* what's black and what's white, you know? But ask me a question that leaves the door open for me to go with it—*then* I will have a chance to express myself. But don't ask me questions that you already know the answer to, and you only want one answer." This man, it turned out, was more than willing to express his thoughts and feelings about many topics, but with a traditional ("colonizing") interview format, it is likely that he would have withdrawn from this middle-class discourse, and perhaps reinforced the popular image of the inexpressive, inarticulate "dumb jock."

With some working-class and minority men who were not so experienced with being interviewed, I had to deal with an opposite problem. Especially with those who had not been greatly successful at sport, who had not attended or completed college, the major barrier to openness in the interview did not appear to be withdrawal due to lack of trust, but was more grounded in what sociologists Richard Sennett and Jonathan Cobb have called the "hidden injuries of class": Working-class men's tendency to wonder, "Just what have I got to say to this person that might matter?" or a tendency to doubt one's ability to be "articulate enough" to make any sense at all.[6] I found that the open-ended, semi-structured interview format, along with an attitude of respect and acceptance on my part toward the man I was interviewing eventually led to a very free discussion. Such was the case with Ricardo R., a Latino factory worker, a married father of two, who was a star high school football and baseball player. At the end of our second interview, Ricardo revealed that he had initially been worried, but he now seemed almost startled at how open he had been, and how good it had felt:

> I really didn't think I was gonna—I was kind of doubting that I was going to be able to bring out, you know, what I really wanted to say.

[But] I think I've done really good at expressing myself, what I really feel. It's almost like opening up something that I've never really had to. You know, it's almost like taking a—having a shower come over your head, kind of like cleansing yourself. You know, I never really talked to anyone about my sports days in this kind of detail. I could always relate something that happened in a game or something like that, but I never actually have had to analyze why I did certain things. So—I really feel a whole lot better about it. I feel like it helped, feel like I got a lot out [slightly embarrassed laugh]—*If it feels good, do it, right?*

Arlie Hochschild has argued that working-class men like Ricardo R. are likely to have been raised to believe that "your feelings don't count because you aren't (or won't be) considered important by others."[7] It follows from this, then, that the decolonization of interviews with working-class men requires that the interviewer actively encourage the interviewee to express his thoughts and feelings and then constantly validate those expressions. For Ricardo, the fact that the interview felt like a "cleansing shower" served to highlight just how few such moments have been for him. Yet his words, and his tone of voice—"If it feels good, do it, right?"—suggest an openness, even an aching, for more such expression.

Encouraging men to "talk about their feelings" is, of course, a step away from asking them to actually express those feelings. Yet the simple fact of asking men to describe and discuss their feelings (in addition to their thoughts and actions) can be a subtly subversive act that begins to break through the very limiting rules that normally govern interactions between men. This method can provide a gentle, yet profound, nudge against men's barriers to self-disclosure in ways that benefit the interviewee. Furthermore, the new kinds of "data" that we receive through our interactions with our interviewees can be given back to them in the form of a gift: A critical examination of the limits of masculinity that holds within it the potential emergence of a world in which men can enjoy more humane, egalitarian, and intimate relationships, friendships, and workplaces.

Appendix 3

Social Class and Race of Interviewees

Though my sample was not scientifically or randomly selected, I consciously chose to interview men from diverse social class and racial backgrounds. Neither social class nor race are easy to define, and thus people are often difficult to categorize. In cases where the race of an interviewee was not self-apparent, I categorized him according to his own definition. For instance, one man who identified himself as "black" actually had African, Mexican, Native American, and European ancestors. Just as with the category "Asian," "Latino" is an umbrella category that encompasses people from many different national and cultural backgrounds. One of the two "Latinos" I interviewed identified himself as "Chicano," and the other, born in Mexico, called himself a "Mexican." Similarly, the whites I interviewed came from varying national and ethnic backgrounds. Given these complexities, generalizations based on "race" should always be taken with a grain of salt.

The complexity of the concept of race is compounded even more when we consider social class differences. Most people in the United States tend to describe themselves as "middle class," despite huge disparities in income, wealth ownership, status, and power. Thus I categorized interviewees by social class of origin largely by inference, based on what kinds of work their parents did, what kinds of living conditions they experienced growing up, what kinds of schools they went to, and so on. Three social class categories emerged. Middle-class interviewees came from families where parents performed college-educated professional, or managerial, or middle-to-upper-level white-collar jobs, where the standards of living were comfortable to affluent, and where children went to high-quality public or private schools with college-preparatory curricula. Working-class men came from families where the parents performed blue-collar or pink-collar work, where the standard of living was relatively stable, but neither affluent nor poor, and where children went primarily to public schools. Poor working-class men came from families where parents (sometimes single parents) were employed sporadically in low-paying blue-collar or pink-collar work, where the standard of living was continually at or near the poverty level, and where children attended public schools that inadequately prepared them for college.

Though some differences existed between men from working-class and poor working-class families, the major differences that emerged in my interviews were between men from middle-class families and those from working-class or poor working-class backgrounds. Thus, for the sake of comparison with the middle-class group, I combined the working-class and poor working-class groups to form a single category which I refer to as "lower class" throughout this book.

The Class/Race Relationship

Sorting through the relationship between social class and race is extremely complicated, even with a large survey or a large sample of interviewees. This task is further complicated in my study by my small sample size, and by the fact that, as table 1 indicates, almost all (fifteen of sixteen) of the black and Latino interviewees came from poor working-class or working-class backgrounds, while the majority (nine of fourteen) of the white men I interviewed came from middle-class backgrounds. To a great extent, then, class and race are confounded in my sample.

Table 1. Race and Social Class of Origin of Interviewees

	Poor/Wk Class	Working Class	Middle Class
Black	5	8	1
Latino	1	1	0
White	1	4	9

As I began to analyze my data, a dilemma emerged. I wanted to discover the commonalities of men's experiences in sport, but I also wanted to sort through the differences, especially by race and social class. Clear distinctions emerged between the men from different backgrounds. Whether these differences were due to race, or to social class, or to some combination of the two was difficult to say, given the fact that I had very few poor or working-class whites, and only one ethnic minority male from a middle-class background in my sample.

I finally chose to speak of the differences primarily in terms of social class, though I knew that in doing this I risked glossing over racial dynamics. My choice to utilize a class analysis emerged largely from my reading of the literature on race and class, and to a lesser extent from my own data. Sociologist William Julius Wilson argued in his controversial 1978 book, *The Declining Significance of Race,* that at least since the early 1960s, the life chances of black youths have been determined more by their class position than by race.[1] Social demographer Michael Hout's research supports Wilson's claims that social class is increasingly important in the occupational placement of blacks.[2] Research in sport sociology supports the argument for the salience of class. For instance, sociologist William Rudman, in comparing blacks' and whites' orientations to sport, initially found profound differences. Blacks were found to be more likely than whites to view sport favorably, to incorporate sport into their daily lives, and to be affected by the outcome of sporting events. However, when age, education, and social class were factored into the analysis, Rudman found that race did not explain whites' and blacks' different orientations. Blacks' affinity to sport is best explained by their tendency to be clustered disproportionately in lower income groups. My data offer at least anecdotal evidence in support of the contention that social class is more significant than race in explaining boys' and men's differing relationships to sport. David P., the only white man I interviewed who came from a poor working-class family clearly had much more in common with poor blacks and Latinos (in terms of the structure of opportunity he faced and his particular insecurities and motivations in pursuing an athletic career) than he did with middle-class whites. The one middle-class black man I interviewed, Gerald M., had a very similar background to the white, middle-class interviewees and significant differences with the poor working-class blacks I interviewed. Gerald told me that as a youth he idolized Wilt Chamberlain and dreamed of being a pro basketball player, yet his father, an educated professional, discouraged his athletic strivings: "He knew I liked the game. I *loved* the game. But basketball was not recommended; my dad would say that's a stereotyped image for a black youth. When your basketball is gone and finished, what are you gonna be able to do? One day you might get injured. What are you gonna look forward to? Those are the things that he said. If you look around, the majority of the players don't have anything, and the majority are black, and it's a sad thing. He stressed education."

My decision to utilize social class as the primary mode of comparison in my study of athletes should not be taken as a statement that race is unimportant or irrelevant. I am fully aware that in my decision to focus primarily on social class, I risk glossing over the ways that race and class intersect to form particular social spaces, identities, and problems.[3] Sociologist Bob Blauner, who in 1989 completed a three-decade study of the lives of U.S. blacks and whites, agrees that class is increasingly definitive, but he also warns that

> *Race and class have always been closely connected in American life, and their separate influences cannot be easily unraveled. The black underclass is not simply a product of shifts in the economy and changes in the type and location of jobs, as Wilson has argued. That blacks without marketable skills live in inner-city ghettos is also the result of centuries of overt discrimination and today's more institutional racism. Social class does loom more fateful in racial stratification, but the significance of race has not declined correspondingly. The separation between blacks and whites, and the racism that feeds on this division, remains a powerful force in American life.*[4]

Similarly, sociologist Milton Gordon has argued that it is impossible analytically to separate race or ethnicity from social class. But he goes on to argue that social class is probably more important in explaining cultural behavior, lifestyle, and taste, while race is more important in explaining a sense of collective identity.[5] Given this, I think that the emergence of social class as the critical variable in my research is due largely to my focus in the interviews on motivations for becoming committed to athletic careers (or for deciding to pursue nonathletic careers). Indeed, when I did focus on issues of collective identity, my interviews with black former athletes provided several examples that suggest that the existence of famous black athletes as role models were key factors in their coming to view themselves as "athletes." Moreover, interviews with black and Latino men revealed the persistence of racist attitudes and (at times) a racial division of labor within sport. I point out these instances in the text when appropriate.

Notes

INTRODUCTION

1. These statistics are compiled yearly by the National Federation of State High School Associations in Kansas City, Mo. The 1989–90 statistics were received via a phone interview with the NFSHSA. For a discussion of the implications of this continuing trend of increasing high school athletic participation by girls, see D. F. Sabo "Title IX and Athletics: Sex Equity in Schools," in *Updating School Board Policies* 19 (1988): 1–3.

2. *The Wilson Report: Moms, Dads, Daughters, and Sports*, (New York: Wilson Sporting Goods Co. and the Women's Sports Foundation, 1988).

3. See A. Crittenden, "Closing the Muscle Gap," in S. Twin, ed., *Out of the Bleachers: Writings on Women and Sport* (Old Westbury, N.Y.: Feminist Press, (1979) and K. Dyer, pp. 5–10; *Challenging the Men: The Social Biology of Female Sport Achievement* (St. Lucia: University of Queensland, 1983).

4. Most prominent in this shift in control of women's collegiate sport into men's hands was the fact that the NCAA took control over most women's athletic programs, while the formerly female-controlled AIAW all but disappeared. "In 1972, virtually all athletic programs for women were directed by women, with only 6 percent of Division I programs merged into single athletic departments. By 1979–80, over 80 percent of all collegiate athletic administrations were merged, and 90 percent of the merged administrations had men at the helm. . . . over 300 women disappeared from women's athletic decision-making positions during the period between 1975 and 1985" (G. A. Uhler, "Athletics and the University: The Post-Woman's Era," in *Adademe* 73 [1987]: 25–29). Between 1974 and 1979, as the status and the funding for women's college sport increased, 724 of the 768 new coaching jobs on women's collegiate teams went to men—a staggering 95 percent. See G. H. Sage, *Power and Ideology in American Sport: A Critical Perspective* (Champaign, Ill.: Human Kinetics Publishers, 1990), p. 52. As a result, from 1974 to 1986, the percentage of women's college sport coached by women dropped from 81 percent to 51 percent. For an excellent overview of the present state of women's collegiate athletics, see S. Birrell, "The Woman Athlete's College Experience: Knowns and Unknowns," *Journal of Sport and Social Issues* 11 (1987/88): 82–96. See also Birrell, "Discourses on the Gender/Sport Relationship: From Women in Sport to Gender Relations," *Exercise and Sport Science Review* 16 (1988): 159–200; A. Knoppers, B. B. Meyer, M. Ewing and L. Forrest, "Gender and the Salaries of Coaches,"*Sociology of Sport Journal* 6 (1989): 348–61; N. Theberge, "Gender, Work, and Power: The Case of Women in Coaching," *Canadian Journal of Sociology* 15 (1990): 59–75.

5. Uhler, "Athletics and the University." See also Knoppers et al., "Gender and the Salaries of Coaches."

6. A number of "radical critics" of sport included some treatment of gender issues in their overall class or racial analysis: Paul Hoch labeled sport a "school for sexism," while Naison saw it as an institutional source of the "ideology of male domination." See P. Hoch, *Rip Off the Big Game* (Garden City, N.Y.: Doubleday, 1972); and P. Naison, "Sports, Women, and the Ideology of Domination," *Radical America*, July/August, 1972, p. 96. The writings of Jack Scott and Harry Edwards focused on unraveling the links between sport ideology, class relations, and race inequality, yet they also discussed sex segregation and inequality in sport. See J. Scott, *The Athletic Revolution* (London: Free Press, 1971), and H. Edwards, *Sociology of Sport* (Homewood, Ill.: Dorsey, 1973).

7. Harry Brod makes this point more generally about the study of men in the introduction to his *The Making of Masculinities: The New Men's Studies* (Winchester, Mass.: Allen and Unwin, 1987).

8. A few of the works that came out of the emergent "men's liberation movement" of the 1970s, though they did not constitute full-scale studies of masculinity and sport, began to acknowledge the masculinity-sport relationship as problematic. However, these works were not written by former athletes, but by men who had not been successful in sport, and who therefore were inclined to emphasize its negative side. See, for instance, *Unbecoming Men* (Washington, N.J.: Times Change Press, 1971). See also W. Farrell, *The Liberated Man* (New York: Bantam Books, 1975); M-F. Fasteau, *The Male Machine* (New York: McGraw-Hill, 1974).

9. Important collections of "men's studies" works can be found in Brod, *The Making of Masculinities;* M. Kaufman, ed., *Beyond Patriarchy: Essays by Men on Pleasure, Power, and Change* (Toronto: Oxford University Press, 1987); and M. S. Kimmel, ed., *Changing Men: New Directions in Research on Men and Masculinity* (Beverly Hills: Sage, 1987). Of special theoretical importance in conceptualizing men and masculinity are T. Carrigan, B. Connell, and J. Lee, "Hard and Heavy: Toward a New Sociology of Masculinity," *Theory and Society* 14 (1985): 551–603; R. W. Connell, *Gender and Power* (Stanford: Stanford University Press, 1987); and J. H. Pleck, *The Myth of Masculinity* (Cambridge: MIT Press, 1982).

10. See also B. Kidd, "Sports and Masculinity," in Kaufman, *Beyond Patriarchy*, pp. 250–65; M. A. Messner, "The Meaning of Success: The Athletic Experience and the Development of Male Identity," in Brod, *The Making of Masculinities*, pp. 193–209; Messner, "The Life of a Man's Seasons: Male Identity in the Lifecourse of the Athlete," in Kimmel, *Changing Men*, 53–67; D. F. Sabo, "Sport, Patriarchy, and Male Identity: New Questions about Men and Sport," *Arena Review* 9 (1985): 1–30. For the most recent collection of theory and research on sport and masculinity, see M. A. Messner and D. F. Sabo, eds., *Sport, Men, and the Gender Order: Critical Feminist Perspectives* (Champaign, Ill.: Human Kinetics Press, 1990).

CHAPTER 1. SPORT, MEN, AND GENDER

1. See R. Raphael, *The Men from the Boys: Rites of Passage in Male America* (Lincoln: University of Nebraska Press, 1988). Raphael praises initiation rites mainly because "they work" to make men feel more secure about who they are.

He sidesteps the question of whether or not men's "need" for initiation is biological or cultural, but the reader is left to assume that there must be some "male essence" buried in each man that needs to be uncovered and liberated through ritual, a questionable assumption at best. The idea that men need initiation rites into manhood is apparently very attractive to a number of middle-aged, mostly white and professional-class men in the United States today, as attested by the popular, well-attended "Mythopoetic" men's initiation rites, which include drumming, body-painting, chanting, dancing, and mask-making. This notion rests on an overgeneralized and romanticized view of traditional tribal cultures. For the quintessential mythopoetic statement, see R. Bly, *Iron John: A Book about Men* (Reading, Mass.: Addison-Wesley, 1990). For a critical discussion of a mythopoetic men's weekend retreat, see J. Tevlin, "Of Hawks and Men: A Weekend in the Male Wilderness," *Utne Reader*, November/December 1989; pp. 50–59.

2. It has been argued by some anthropologists and historians that "play" is an essential aspect of all human culture. For instance, Dutch historian J. Huizinga defined "play" as "free activity standing quite consciously outside 'ordinary' life as being 'not serious,' but at the same time absorbing the player intensely and utterly. It is an activity connected with no material interest, and no profit can be gained by it" (see J. Huizinga, *Homo Ludens: A Study of the Play Element in Culture* [Boston: Beacon Press, 1955]). As sociologist Jay J. Coakley notes, by this definition, "play" is primarily "an activity engaged in *for its own sake,* and it "proceeds according to *informally emergent norms.*" By contrast, sport is characterized by formal club, team, league, national, and even international organizations, by patterned and regularized systems of rules that are enforced by official regulatory bodies, and often by the presence of spectators. As Coakley defines it, "sport is an institutionalized competitive activity that involves vigorous physical exertion or the use of relatively complex skills by individuals whose participation is motivated by a combination of the intrinsic satisfaction associated with the activity itself and the external rewards earned through participation" (J. J. Coakley, *Sport in Society: Issues and Controversies* [St. Louis: C. V. Mosby, 1978, p. 13]). Thus, although "play" and "sport" are related, they are not the same thing. Significantly—and this becomes increasingly true at the higher levels of college and professional sport—the intrinsic satisfactions of "the play element" often become submerged as the extrinsic rewards of winning games, matches, or championships take on greater and greater importance. My focus in this book is on boys' and men's involvement in this institutionalized system of sport.

3. For a general discussion of the social constructionist view of masculine identity, see the introduction to M. S. Kimmel and M. A. Messner, eds., *Men's Lives* (New York: Macmillan, 1989); pp. 1–13.

4. C. W. Mills, *The Sociological Imagination* (London: Oxford University Press, 1959).

5. D. Levinson et. al., *The Seasons of a Man's Life* (New York: Ballantine Books, 1978). As R. W. Connell has argued, "The theorised life history can be a powerful tool for the study of social structures and their dynamics as they impinge upon (and are reconstituted in) personal life" ("An Iron Man: The Body and Some

Contradictions of Hegemonic Masculinity," in Messner and Sabo, *Sport, Men, and the Gender Order*, p. 84).

6. For an excellent overview of U.S. sport as a social institution, see G. H. Sage, *Power and Ideology in American Sport: A Critical Perspective* (Champaign, Ill.: Human Kinetics Publishers, 1990). Sage points out, among other things, that sport is a major economic force, generating a "gross national sport product" of approximately $50 billion in 1987.

7. Sociologist Bruce Kidd notes that the ancient Olympics, often idealized in the modern era, were in fact inextricably bound up with the prevailing system of power. The Games began with a direct connection to military skill and celebrated the subjection of women and slaves by excluding them from eligibility and the glory of victory. See B. Kidd, "The Myth of the Ancient Olympic Games," in A. Tomlinson and G. Whannel eds., *Five Ring Circus: Money, Power, and Politics at the Olympic Games* (London: Pluto, 1984), pp. 71–83. For a discussion of the ways that U.S. sport has been intertwined with power in the larger society, see H. Edwards, *Sociology of Sport* (Homewood, Ill: Dorsey, 1973); D. S. Eitzen and G. Sage, "Racism in Sports," in D. S. Eitzen and G. Sage, Eds., *Sociology of American Sport* (Dubuque: Brown, 1978), pp. 235–59.

8. J. A. Mangan, *The Games Ethic and Imperialism: Aspects of the Diffusion of an Ideal* (New York: Viking Penguin, 1986).

9. Quoted in ibid., pp. 35–36.

10. C. R. L. James, *Beyond a Boundary* (New York: Pantheon Books, 1983), p. 72.

11. Ibid., p. 71.

12. Ibid., p. 72.

13. See J. M. Brohm, *Sport: A Prison of Measured Time* (London: Ink Links, 1978); R. Goldman, "We Make Weekends: Leisure and the Commodity Form," in *Social Text* 8 (1983/84): 84–103; R. Gruneau, *Class, Sports, and Social Development* (Amherst: University of Massachusetts, 1983); B. Rigauer, *Sport and Work* (New York: Columbia University Press, 1981).

14. E. Gustkey, "Eighty Years Ago, the Truth Hurt," *Los Angeles Times*, July 8, 1990, p. C1.

15. See Edwards's essay on Paul Robeson in H. Edwards, *The Struggle that Must Be* (New York: Macmillan, 1980); and J. Tygiel, *Baseball's Great Experiment: Jackie Robinson and His Legacy* (New York: Vintage Books, 1984). The meaning of "black domination" of certain sports is still hotly contested in the United States, with biological determinists arguing against those who believe that blacks are largely socially channeled into athletic careers because of an otherwise limited structure of opportunity. For a discussion of the historical development of this debate, see D. K. Wiggins, "Great Speed but Little Stamina: The Historical Debate over Black Athletic Superiority," *Journal of Sport History* 16 (1989): 158–85. For an excellent analysis of this debate as it has manifested itself in the media, see L. R. Davis, "The Articulation of Difference: White Preoccupation with the

Question of Racially Linked Genetic Differences among Athletes," *Sociology of Sport Journal* 7 (1990): 179–87.

16. Instead of simply viewing the institution of sport as a "reflection" of capitalist domination, Gruneau insisted instead on viewing sport as a cultural arena in which capitalist class domination "constrains," but does not fully "determine" social and ideological outcomes. Through sport, ruling-class "hegemony"—domination that is never total, that is continuously negotiated—is constructed. This view of sport leaves room for seeing working class participants as conscious human agents, who can themselves define, even sometimes critically transform, the athletic experience in oppositional ways. See Gruneau, *Class, Sports, and Social Development*, and Je. Hargreaves, ed., *Sport, Culture, and Ideology* (London: Routledge and Kegan Paul, 1982).

17. See H. Lenskyj, *Out of Bounds: Women, Sport, and Sexuality* (Toronto: Women's Press, 1986); and S. L. Twin, ed., *Out of the Bleachers: Writings on Women and Sport* (Old Westbury, N.Y.: Feminist Press, 1979).

18. R. W. Connell, *Gender and Power* (Stanford: Stanford University Press, 1987).

19. P. Filene, *Him/Her/Self: Sex Roles in Modern America* (New York: Harcourt Brace Jovanovich, 1975). Michael Kimmel identifies three categories of organized responses to this crisis of masculinity: antifeminist backlash, masculinism, and profeminism. The construction of organized sport as a homosocial institution can be seen as a combination of the first two responses. See M. S. Kimmel, "Men's Responses to Feminism at the Turn of the Century," *Gender and Society* 1 (1987):517–30.

20. H. Hartmann, "Capitalism, Patriarchy, and Job Segregation," *Signs* 1 (1976):137–69; E. Zaretsky, *Capitalism, the Family, and Personal Life* (New York: Harper Colophon, 1973).

21. E. A. Rotundo, "Body and Soul: Changing Ideals of American Middle Class Manhood, 1770–1920," *Journal of Social History* 16 (1983): 23–38.

22. A. Tolson, *The Limits of Masculinity: Male Identity and Women's Liberation* (New York: Harper and Row, 1977).

23. See Kimmel, "Men's Responses to Feminism at the Turn of the Century"; Filene, *Him/Her/Self;* J. Hantover, "The Boy Scouts and the Validation of Masculinity," *Journal of Social Issues* 34 (1978): 184–95; and D. Macleod, *Building Character in the American Boy: The Boy Scouts, YMCA, and Their Forerunners, 1870–1920* (Madison: University of Wisconsin Press, 1983). M. A. Clawson has argued that the Masonic fraternal order emerged in this same period as a response to feminism and to the destruction of traditional male craft work, brought about by industrialization and the rise of factory work: "Through its construction of ties based upon images of masculinity and craftsmanship, the mixed-class, all-male American fraternal order worked to deny the significance of class difference and to offer gender and race as appropriate categories for the organization of collective identity" (*Constructing Brotherhood: Class, Gender, and Fraternalism* [Princeton: Princeton University Press, 1989], p. 15). See also M. S. Kimmel, "Baseball and the Reconstitution of American Masculinity: 1880–1920," in Messner and Sabo, *Sport, Men, and the Gender Order,* pp. 55–66.

24. C. Smith-Rosenberg, *Disorderly Conduct: Visions of Gender in Victorian America* (New York: Oxford University Press, 1985); p. 245.

25. Ibid., p. 244.

26. See S. Brownmiller, *Against Our Will: Men, Women, and Rape* (New York: Simon and Schuster, 1975).

27. E. Dunning, "Sport as a Male Preserve: Notes on the Social Sources of Masculine Identity and Its Transformations," *Theory Culture & Society* 3 (1986):79–90.

28. See E. J. Gorn, *The Manly Art: Bare-Knuckle Prize Fighting in America* (Ithaca: Cornell University Press, 1986).

29. L. Bryson, "Sport and the Maintenance of Masculine Hegemony" *Women's Studies International Forum 10* (1987): 349.

30. See R. S. Bennett, K. G. Whitaker, N. J. W. Smith, and A. Sablove, "Changing the Rules of the Game: Reflections towards a Feminist Analysis of Sport," *Women's Studies International Forum* 10 (1987): 369–80; L. Komisar, "Violence and the Masculine Mystique," in D. F. Sabo and R. Runfola, eds., *Jock: Sports and Male Identity,* (Englewood Cliffs, N.J.: Prentice-Hall, 1980), pp. 131–57; N. Theberge, "Sport and Women's Empowerment," *Women's Studies International Forum* 10 (1987): 387–94.

31. See J. Weeks, *Sexuality and Its Discontents: Meanings, Myths, and Modern Sexualities* (London: Routledge and Kegan Paul, 1985); D. F. Greenberg, *The Construction of Homosexuality* (Chicago: University of Chicago Press, 1988); Todd Crossett, "Masculinity, Sexuality, and the Development of Early Modern Sport," in Messner and Sabo, *Sport, Men, and the Gender Order,* pp. 45–54; and Lenskyj, *Out of Bounds.*

32. Recent feminist theories of the historical and contemporary meanings of organized sport have benefited from a dialogue with neo-Marxist theories of sport, especially that of Richard Gruneau. Though important, Gruneau's analysis continues the Marxist error of economic reductionism. Since the economy is always viewed as primary and causal, other forms of inequality and oppression are viewed as secondary to class oppression. Marxism thus tends to render invisible the specific ways that sport (and other institutions) contributes to the oppression of women, as well as of racial, ethnic, and sexual minorities. Despite this limitation, feminist theorists of the mid-to-late 1980s began to appropriate the concept of hegemony as a means of understanding gender relations and sport. See, for instance, M. A. Hall, ed., "The Gendering of Sport, Leisure, and Physical Education," a special issue of *Women's Studies International Forum* 10 no. 4 (1987); and M. A. Messner, "Sports and Male Domination: The Female Athlete as Contested Ideological Terrain," *Sociology of Sport Journal* 3 (1988): 197–211.

33. See Twin, *Out of the Bleachers.* See also R. A. Smith, "The Rise of Basketball for Women in College," *Canadian Journal of History of Sport and Physical*

Education 1: (1970) 21–23; H. Lefkowitz-Horowitz, "Before Title IX" (paper presented at Stanford Humanities Center Sport and Culture Meetings, April, 1986); and Lenskyj, *Out of Bounds.*

34. Cited in Lenskyj, *Out of Bounds,* p. 19.

35. Ibid., p. 39.

36. Ibid., p. 71.

37. N. Theberge, "A Critique of Critiques: Radical and Feminist Writings on Sport," *Social Forces* (1981): p. 342. For an overview of the groundbreaking feminist analyses and critiques of sport, see S. Birrell, "Achievement Related Motives and the Woman Athlete," in C. A. Oglesby, ed., *Women and Sport: From Myth to Reality* (Philadelphia: Lea and Farber 1978), pp. 141–59; M. Duquin, "The Androgynous Advantage," in Oglesby, *Women and Sport;* pp. 173–91; S. Greendorfer, "The Role of Socializing Agents in Female Sport Involvement," *Research Quarterly* 48 (1977): 304–10; M. A. Hall, "A 'Feminine Woman' and an 'Athletic Woman' as Viewed by Female Participants and Non-Participants in Sport," *British Journal of Physical Education* 3 (1972), and *Sport and Gender: A Feminist Perspective on the Sociology of Sport* (Ottawa: Canadian Association of Health, Physical Education, and Recreation, Sociology of Sport Monograph Series, 1978); D. V. Harris, *Women and Sport: A National Research Conference* (Proceedings from the National Research Conference, Women and Sport, Penn State HPER Series 2, Pennsylvania State University, August 13–18, (1972); Twin, *Out of the Bleachers.*

38. A major reason behind the reductionism of much Marxist and feminist theory has been the continued insistence, based in Enlightenment thinking, that there must be a fundamental dynamic (class, gender, etc.) driving history, and thus one fundamental historical subject (the working-class, women, etc.). In contrast, Sandra Harding argues that the fractured nature of social reality—and indeed, the fractured nature of contemporary identity even among feminists (black women, Asian women, Native American women, working class women, lesbian women, black lesbian women, etc.)—should serve as a warning against the development of theories that automatically view one form of social domination (and identity) as fundamental. See S. Harding, *The Science Question in Feminism* (Ithaca: Cornell University Press, 1986).

Thus in the 1970s and 1980s, feminist women of color argued that white, middle-class feminists in the Western world had tended to universalize their own issues and interests as "women's issues." This contributed to feminism's marginalization and alienation of women of color, working-class, and Third World women. Women of color, in particular, have often argued that their experiences and life-chances are at least as much shaped and limited by class and race domination as they are by gender. Thus they call for conceptual schemes that theorize varied and shifting manifestations of masculine domination as they interact with other forms of social domination. For major statements, see M. Baca Zinn, L. W. Cannon, E. Higgenbotham, & B. Thornton Dill, "The Costs of Exclusionary Practices in Women's Studies," *Signs* 11 (1986): 290–303; P. H. Collins, *Black Feminist Thought: Knowledge, Consciousness, and the Politics of Empowerment* (Boston: Unwin Hyman (1990); A. Davis, *Woman, Race, and Class* (New York: Vintage; 1981); M. Frye, "The Possibility of Feminist Theory," in D. L. Rhode, ed., *Theoretical Differences on Sexual Difference* (New Haven: Yale University Press 1990), pp. 174–84; B. Hooks, *Feminist Theory: From Margin to Center* (Boston: South End Press, 1984). The development of a nonhierarchical, nonreductionist theory does not mean accepting a watered-down relativism or theoretical anarchy. Rather, it means developing theories that allow us to conceptualize varied and shifting forms of domination in such a way that we do not elevate one as primary, distorting or ignoring the others. With respect to the study of sport, this line of theoretical inquiry is developed more fully in S. Birrell, "Women of Color, Critical Autobiography, and Sport," in Messner and Sabo, *Sport, Men, and the Gender Order*, pp. 185–200; M. A. Messner, "Men Studying Masculinity: Some Epistemological Questions in Sport Sociology," *Sociology of Sport Journal* 7 (1990): 136–53; and in Messner and Sabo's introduction to *Sport, Men, and the Gender Order*, pp. 1–18.

39. Connell, *Gender and Power*.

40. See Hantover, "The Boy Scouts and the Validation of Masculinity." Gorn's history of bare-knuckle prize fighting and Kimmel's examination of the rise of U.S. baseball both demonstrate that the growth in popularity in these sports was initially related to the increasingly problematic construction of "manhood" among middle-class men in the face of the "feminization" of society and in response to perceived threats from immigrant men and men of other races and social classes. See Gorn, *The Manly Art*, and Kimmel, "Baseball and the Reconstitution of American Masculinity."

41. Helen Lefkowitz-Horowitz, *Campus Life: Undergraduate Cultures from the End of the Eighteenth Century to the Present* (New York: Alfred A. Knopf, 1987), p. 42.

42. B. Kidd, "The Men's Cultural Centre: Sports and the Dynamic of Women's Oppression/Men's Repression," in Messner and Sabo, *Sport, Men, and the Gender Order*, pp. 31–44.

43. See D. Whitson, "Sport and the Social Construction of Masculinity," in Messner and Sabo, *Sport, Men, and the Gender Order*, pp. 19–30.

44. J. Lever, "Sex Differences in the Games Children Play," *Social Problems* 23 (1976): 478–87, and "Sex Differences in the Complexity of Children's Play and Games," *American Sociological Review* 43 (1978): 471–83.

45. Sabo and Runfola, *Jock*, p. xi.

46. The emphasis on the costs to men of the male sex role echoed the men's liberation literature of the 1970s. With respect to sport, it was probably Walter Schafer who first made this argument. See W. E. Schafer, "Sport and Male Sex Role Socialization," *Sport Sociology Bulletin* 4 (1975): 47–54.

47. For excellent feminist critiques of the limits of sex role theory, see T. Carrigan, B. Connell, and J. Lee, "Hard and Heavy: Toward a New Sociology of Masculinity," *Theory and Society* 14 (1985): 551–603; J. Stacey and B. Thorne, "The Missing Feminist Revolution in Sociology," *Social Problems* 32 (1985): 301–16; and Connell, *Gender and Power*.

48. N. Chodorow, *The Reproduction of Mothering* (Berkeley: University of California Press (1978); D. Dinnerstein, *The Mermaid and the Minotaur: Sexual Arrangements and Human Malaise* (New York: Harper Colophon, 1976).

49. L. B. Rubin, *Intimate Strangers: Men and Women Together* (New York: Harper and Row, 1983); C. Gilligan, *In a Different Voice: Psychological Theory and Women's Development* (Cambridge: Harvard University Press, 1982).

50. Psychologists such as Joseph Pleck have been especially critical of feminist psychoanalytic theory and have defended a version of sex role theory. See J. H. Pleck, *The Myth of Masculinity* (Cambridge: MIT Press, 1982). Many sociologists, interestingly, have been more receptive to feminist psychoanalytic thought. Sociologists are more likely to criticize the reductionist uses of psychoanalytic theory than to defend sex role theories, which are seen as of limited utility. Some critics, though, have argued that feminist psychoanalysis tends to ignore the ways that gender identity is shaped by gendered power relations built into social institutions. See, for instance, I. M. Young, "Is Male Gender Identity the Cause of Male Domination?" in J. Trebilcott, ed., *Mothering: Essays in Feminist Theory* (Roman and Allanheld, 1983), pp. 129–46.

51. A number of feminist social scientists have made this argument. See, for instance, Connell, *Gender and Power;* J. Flax, "Political Philosophy and the Patriarchal Unconscious: A Psychoanalytic Perspective on Epistemology and Metaphysics," in S. Harding and M. B. Hintikka, eds., *Discovering Reality: Feminist Perspectives on Epistemology, Metaphysics, Methodology, and Philosophy of Science* (Boston: D. Reidel, 1983), pp. 245–82; S. Harding, "What Is the Real Material Base of Patriarchy and Capital?" in L. Sargent , ed., *Women and Revolution* (Boston: South End Press 1981); N. C. M. Hartsock, "The Feminist Standpoint: Developing the Ground for a Specifically Feminist Historical Materialism," in Harding and Hintikka, *Discovering Reality,* pp. 283–310.

52. I. Craib, "Masculinity and Male Dominance," *Sociological Review* 38 (1987): 737.

53. The images of the onion and the tapestry are suggested by Lillian Rubin, though she still tends to see core gender identity as causal. See L. B. Rubin, *Just Friends: The Role of Friendship in Our Lives* (New York: Harper and Row, 1985).

54. See J. Benjamin, *The Bonds of Love: Psychoanalysis, Feminism, and the Problem of Domination* (New York: Pantheon, 1988); and F. Haug, *Female Sexualization* (London: Verso Books, 1987).

55. This line of reasoning is demonstrated in P. G. White and A. B. Vagi, "Rugby in the Nineteenth-Century British Boarding School System: A Feminist Psychoanalytic Perspective," in Messner and Sabo, *Sport, Men, and the Gender Order,* pp. 67–78.

56. C. L. Williams, *Gender Differences at Work: Women and Men in Nontraditional Occupations* (Berkeley: University of California Press 1989), pp. 12–13.

57. Daniel Levinson takes this approach, but in his search for a single male lifecourse, he tends to over-emphasize the psychological, and de-emphasize the

very different institutional contexts in which boys and men from different social classes and ethnic groups develop. See Levinson et. al., *The Seasons of a Man's Life.*

CHAPTER 2. BOYHOOD

1. Cited in M. S. Kimmel, "Baseball and the Reconstitution of American Masculinity, 1880–1920," in M. A. Messner and D. F. Sabo, eds., *Sport, Men, and the Gender Order: Critical Feminist Perspectives* (Champaign, Ill.: Human Kinetics Publishers, 1990), PP. 55–66.

2. D. S. Eitzen, "Athletics in the Status System of Male Adolescents: A Replication of Coleman's *The Adolescent Society*," *Adolescence* 10 (1975): 268–76; D. F. Sabo, "Sport, Patriarchy, and Male Identity: New Questions about Men and Sport," *Arena Review* 9 (1985): 1–30; D. F. Sabo and Women's Sports Foundation, *The Women's Sports Foundation Report: Minorities in Sports*, August 15, 1989.

3. R. W. Connell, "An Iron Man: The Body and Some Contradictions of Hegemonic Masculinity," in Messner and Sabo, *Sport, Men, and the Gender Order*, pp. 83–96.

4. See F. Rebelsky and C. Hanks, "Fathers' Verbal Interaction with Infants in the First Three Months of Life," *Child Development* 42 (1971): 63–68; and F. A. Petersen and K. S. Robson, "Father Participation in Infancy," *American Journal of Orthopsychiatry* 39 (1969): 466–72.

5. S. Osherson, *Finding Our Fathers: How a Man's Life Is Shaped by His Relationship with His Father* (New York: Fawcett Columbine, 1986), p. 20.

6. Z. Rubin, "Fathers and Sons: The Search for Reunion," *Psychology Today*, June 1982, p. 23.

7. Osherson, *Finding Our Fathers*, p. 27.

8. Barrie Thorne, "Girls and Boys Together . . . but Mostly Apart: Gender Arrangements in Elementary Schools," in W. W. Hartup and Z. Rubin, eds., *Relationships and Development* (Hillside, N.J.: Lawrence Earlbaum, 1986), p. 70. Similarly, Barbara Humberstone's research explores the implications of physical education programs that are constructed with the goal of breaking down gender divisions and distinctions. See B. Humberstone, "Warriors or Wimps? Creating Alternative Forms of Physical Education," in Messner and Sabo, *Sport, Men, and the Gender Order*, pp. 201–10.

9. B. Thorne, "Children and Gender: Constructions of Difference," in D. L. Rhode, ed., *Theoretical Perspectives on Sexual Difference* (New Haven: Yale University Press, 1990), 100–113.

10. Jean H. Piaget, *The Moral Judgment of the Child* (New York: Free Press, 1965); J. Lever, "Sex Differences in the Games Children Play," *Social Problems* 23 (1976): 478–87.

11. C. Gilligan, *In A Different Voice: Psychological Theory and Women's Development* (Cambridge: Harvard University Press, 1982). For a discussion of how these gendered moral developmental tendencies continue to be reflected among contemporary college athletes, see M. E. Duquin, "Power and Authority: Moral Consensus and Conformity in Sport," *International Review for Sociology of Sport* 19 (1984): 295–304.

12. Carol Gilligan has observed that when adult females are asked to describe who they are, they almost always begin by talking about their relationships with other people. Women thus have "relational identities" that are constructed in a "web of care." Men, on the other hand, describe themselves primarily in terms of accomplishments and achievements that set them apart from others. Thus, Gilligan describes men's identities as "positional," being defined and articulated within competitive hierarchies. See Gilligan, *In a Different Voice*.

13. Jessica Benjamin has argued that individuation is accomplished, paradoxically, only through relationships with other people in the social world. So though the major task of masculinity is the development of a "positional identity" that clarifies the boundaries between self and other, this separation must be accomplished through some form of connection with others. See J. Benjamin, *The Bonds of Love: Psychoanalysis, Feminism, and the Problem of Domination* (New York: Pantheon Books, 1988).

14. W. E. Schafer, "Sport and Male Sex Role Socialization," *Sport Sociology Bulletin* 4 (1975): 47–54.

15. G. K. Lehne, "Homophobia among Men: Supporting and Defining the Male Role," in M. S. Kimmel and M. A. Messner, eds., *Men's Lives* (New York: Macmillan, 1989), 416–29.

16. See D. Kopay and P. D. Young, *The Dave Kopay Story* (New York: Arbor House, 1977), p. 12; and B. Pronger, "Gay Jocks: A Phenomenology of Gay Men in Athletics," in Messner and Sabo, *Sport, Men and the Gender Order*, pp. 141–52.

17. Brian Pronger has written that "because gay men grow up in a predominantly heterosexual world, they have learned the standard language of masculinity." However, gay men also know that they do not conform to the heterosexual standards that are the cornerstone of hegemonic masculinity. They thus tend to develop a sense of "irony" about their own "masculinity" in public arenas such as organized sport (Pronger, "Gay Jocks," p. 145).

18. J. H. Pleck, "Men's Power with Women, Other Men, and in Society," in E. H. Pleck and J. H. Pleck, eds., *The American Man* (Englewood Cliffs, N.J.: Prentice-Hall, 1980), pp. 417–33.

19. See especially chapter 5 of Gary Alan Fine, *With the Boys: Little League Baseball and Preadolescent Culture* (Chicago: University of Chicago Press, 1987). Though Fine utilizes a symbolic interactionist perspective, his observations concerning homophobia and misogyny among young boys are consistent with Chodorow's observation that the devaluation of women and the "feminine" in boys and men is part of the establishment of male identity and the construction of men's power and privilege over women. For a "relational" conception of the role of sexuality in children's culture, see B. Thorne and Z. Luria, "Sexuality and Gender in Children's Daily Worlds," *Social Problems* 33 (1986): 176–190.

20. Fine, *With the Boys*, p. 109.

21. *Ibid.*, p. 107.

22. R. W. Connell, "'A Whole New World': Remaking Masculinity in the Context of the Environmental Movement," *Gender and Society* 4 (1990): 459.

CHAPTER 3. THE MEANING OF SUCCESS

1 C. Neff, "Return of the Hero," *Sports Illustrated*, October 10, 1988): p. 63.

2. See G. A. Fine, *With the Boys: Little League Baseball and Preadolescent Culture* (Chicago: University of Chicago Press, 1987); E. W. Vaz, "The Culture of Young Hockey Players: Some Initial Observations," in D. F. Sabo and R. Runfola, eds., *Jock: Sports and Male Identity* (Englewood Cliffs, N.J.: Prentice-Hall, 1980); pp. 142–57. For a more general discussion of the negative outcomes of young people being socialized toward a view of sport that emphasizes winning, see J. H. Goldstein and B. J. Bredemeier "Socialization: Some Basic Issues," *Journal of Communication* 27 (1977): 154–59.

3. J. Coakley, *Sports in Society* (St. Louis: C. V. Mosby, 1978), p. 49.

4. W. M. Leonard and J. M. Reyman, "The Odds of Attaining Professional Athlete Status: Redefining the Computations," *Sociology of Sport Journal* 5 (1988): 162–69.

5. See H. Edwards, "The Collegiate Athletic Arms Race: Origins and Implications of the 'Rule 48' Controversy," *Journal of Sport and Social Issues* 8 (1984): 4–22; D. S. Harris and D. S. Eitzen, "The Consequences of Failure in Sport," *Urban Life* 7 (1978): 177–88; and P. Hill and B. Lowe, "The Inevitable Metathesis of the Retiring Athlete," *International Review of Sport Sociology* 9 (1979): 5–32.

6. A great deal of evidence supporting this contention emerged in studies performed in the mid-to-late 1970s. See, for instance, D. W. Ball, "Failure in Sport," *American Sociological Review* 41 (1976): 726–39; Harris and Eitzen, "The Consequences of Failure in Sport"; G. B. Leonard, "Winning Isn't Everything: It's Nothing," in Sabo and Runfola, *Jock*, pp. 259–66; R. C. Townsend, "The Competitive Male as Loser," in Sabo and Runfola, *Jock*, pp. 266–79; T. Tutko and W. Bruns, *Winning Is Everything and Other American Myths* (New York: Macmillan, 1976). Many of these studies come to conclusions about men and sport which are similar to more general studies of blue collar men, which suggested that low self-images as well as interpersonal problems result from the discontinuity between the ideological belief that "hard work will result in success" and the reality that many know that they have worked hard yet have not been upwardly mobile. See R. Sennett and J. Cobb, *The Hidden Injuries of Class* (New York: Random House, 1973); L. B. Rubin, *Worlds of Pain: Life in the Working Class Family* (New York: Basic Books, 1976).

7. As it is used here, the term "career" is defined more broadly than "occupation." Most of these men never became professional athletes and thus never received an income directly from athletic activities. So to say that they had athletic "careers" is to say that, at least for a time, sport served as the major organizing principle of their public lives and their identities.

8. W. E. Schafer, "Sport and Male Sex Role Socialization," *Sport Sociology Bulletin* 4 (1975): 50.

9. This insight—that young men come to view their family relationships instrumentally—coincides with Levinson's argument that for men, successful individuation precedes intimacy, in other words, that men must establish their place in the world before they are capable of intimate personal relationships. It also coincides with Gilligan's argument that men's identities tend to be positional, while women's tend to be relational. Yet while this appears often to be true of men's relationship to their family of origin, it does not necessarily extend to their relationships with wives, lovers, and children. As I will show in chapter 7, gender differences in terms of instrumental success versus attachment and intimacy are not always as dichotomous as Gilligan and others have suggested. Adult men—especially those who are fathers—tend to describe their strivings in public life using a language of care and responsibility for their families. See C. Gilligan, *In A Different Voice: Psychological Theory and Women's Development* (Cambridge: Harvard University, 1982); and D. J. Levinson et al. *The Seasons of a Man's Life* (New York: Ballantine Books, 1978).

10. This sort of adult male fantasy has become commercialized in recent years. Many major league baseball teams now hold adult "fantasy camps," where middle-aged stock brokers, lawyers, and car salesmen can, for a hefty fee, play ball with former professional stars. There are also "fantasy tapes" that one can buy, such as the one made by Los Angeles Lakers' announcer Chick Hern, where he announces (again, for a fee) an entire "game" where *you* turn out to be the star player.

11. See M. E. Duquin, "Power and Authority: Moral Consensus and Conformity in Sport," *International Review for Sociology of Sport* 19 (1984): 295–304. This difference might also explain why female athletes are more likely to attribute the causes of their successes to factors "external" to themselves (coaches, teammates, family, luck) while males are more comfortable taking individual credit for their successes. See M. C. McHugh, M. E. Duquin, and I. H. Frieze, "Beliefs about Success and Failure: Attribution and the Female Athlete," in C. A. Oglesby, ed., *Women and Sport: From Myth to Reality* (Philadelphia: Lea and Farber, 1978), pp. 173–91.

12. P. A. Adler and P. Adler, "The Gloried Self: The Aggrandizement and the Constriction of Self," *Social Psychology Quarterly* 52 (1989): 299–310.

13. Eitzen's study of adolescent culture found that athletic prowess was still the single most important factor for status in high school male peer groups in the mid 1970s, and this was especially true of boys from less educated backgrounds. See D. S. Eitzen, "Athletics in the Status System of Male Adolescents: A Replication of Coleman's *The Adolescent Society*," *Adolescence* 10 (1975): 268–276. Thirer and Wright's more recent study indicates that sport, in the mid 1980s was still very important in male peer status systems, but not so important among female adolescents. See J. Thirer and S. D. Wright, "Sport and Social Status for Adolescent Males and Females," *Sociology of Sport Journal* 2 (1985): 164–71.

14. See F. J. Berghorn et. al., (1988) "Racial Participation in Men's and Women's Intercollegiate Basketball: Continuity and Change, 1958–1985," *Sociology of*

Sport Journal 5 (1988): 107–24; S. Bowles and H. Gintis, *Schooling in Capitalist America* (New York: Basic Books, 1976); C. Jencks, *Inequality* (New York: Harper Colophon, 1972).

15. D. A. Purdy, D. S. Eitzen, and R. Hufnagel, (1984) "Are Athletes Also Students? The Educational Attainment of College Athletes," *Social Problems* 29 (1984): 439–48.

16. Edwards, "The Collegiate Athletic Arms Race," p. 7.

17. Ibid.

18. P. Adler and P. A. Adler, "From Idealism to Pragmatic Detachment: The Academic Performance of College Athletes," *Sociology of Education* 58 (1985): 241–50. See also Adler and Adler, "Role Conflict and Identity Salience: College Athletes and the Academic Role," *Social Science Journal* 24 (1987): 443–55.

19. M. Dunkle, "Minority and Low-Income Girls and Young Women in Athletics," *Equal Play* 5 (1985): 12–13.

20. C. W. Franklin, "Surviving the Institutional Decimation of Black Males: Causes, Consequences, and Intervention." in H. Brod, ed., *The Making of Masculinities: The New Men's Studies* (Winchester, Mass.: Allen and Unwin, 1987), pp. 155–70.

21. M. Baca Zinn, "Chicano Men and Masculinity," *Journal of Ethnic Studies* 10 (1982): 29–44. R. Majors, "Cool Pose: The Proud Signature of Black Survival," *Changing Men: Issues in Gender, Sex, and Politics* 17 (1986): 5–6, "Cool Pose: Black Masculinity and Sports," in M. A. Messner and D. F. Sabo, *Sport, Men, and the Gender Order: Critical Feminist Perspectives* (Champaign, Ill.: Human Kinetics Publisher, 1990), pp. 109–14.

CHAPTER 4. THE EMBODIMENT OF MASCULINITY

1. R. W. Connell, "An Iron Man: The Body and Some Contradictions of Hegemonic Masculinity," in M. A. Messner and D. F. Sabo, eds., *Sport, Men, and the Gender Order: Critical Feminist Perspectives* (Champaign, Ill.: Human Kinetics Publishers, 1990), p. 90. An "Iron Man" is an athlete who competes in an event that includes swimming, running, and surf craft riding. Champion Iron Men have very high status in Australia. Connell analyzes gender and the body on a more theoretical level in the chapter "Men's Bodies," in his *Which Way Is Up? Essays on Sex, Class, and Culture* (Boston: Allen and Unwin, 1983), pp. 17–32; and in *Gender and Power* (Stanford: Stanford University Press, 1987).

2. Under advanced capitalism, the continuing rationalization of the workplace and the permeation of "personal life" with the logic of technical efficiency have led to what Winter and Robert call "an emerging male self exemplifying the logic of instrumental reason" (M. F. Winter and E. R. Robert, "Male Dominance, Late Capitalism, and the Growth of Instrumental Reason," *Berkeley Journal of Sociology* 25 [1980]: 259). Hoch and Brohm have argued that the sportsworld increasingly resembles this rationalized capitalist economy. See P. Hoch, *Rip Off the Big Game* (Garden City, N.Y.: Doubleday, 1972); and J. M. Brohm, *Sport: A Prison of Measured Time* (London: Ink Links, 1978).

3. For a discussion of gender and "emotion work," see A. R. Hochschild, *The Managed Heart: Commercialization and Human Feeling* (Berkeley: University of California Press, 1983). See also Hochschild's "Emotion Work, Feeling Rules, and Social Structure," *American Journal of Sociology* 85 (1979): 551–75. Within the athletic context, emotion work is discussed in C. P. Gallmeier, "Putting on the Game Face: The Staging of Emotions in Professional Hockey," *Sociology of Sport Journal* 4 (1987): 347–62.

4. Connell, "An Iron Man," p. 95.

5. Nash and Lerner found that in pee wee hockey, despite adult supervision aimed at minimizing violent behavior, young players were influenced by violent role models in professional hockey. J. E. Nash and E. Lerner, "Learning from the Pros: Violence in Youth Hockey," *Youth and Society* 13 (1981): 112–23. Other studies have reached similar conclusions. See, for instance, M. D. Smith, "Significant Others Influence on the Assaultive Behavior of Young Hockey Players," *International Review of Sport Sociology* 3/4 (1974): 217–27; and D. A. Mugno and D. L. Felz, "The Social Learning of Aggression in Youth Football in the United States," *Canadian Journal of Applied Sport Sciences* 10 (1985): 26–35.

6. E. W. Vaz; "The Culture of Young Hockey Players: Some Initial Observations," in D. F. Sabo and R. Runfola, eds., *Jock: Sports and Male Identity* (Englewood Cliffs, N.J.: Prentice-Hall, 1980), pp. 142–57.

7. D. F. Foley, "The Great American Football Ritual: Reproducing Race, Class, and Gender Inequality," *Sociology of Sport Journal* 7 (1990): 127.

8. D. Meggyesy, *Out of Their League*. (Berkeley: Ramparts Press, 1970), p. 12.

9. See note 3 above.

10. Violence in sport is widely viewed as a social problem. Some have argued that sport offers a socially acceptable context in which to express a natural aggressive human (or male) instinct—the catharsis thesis. See K. Lorenz, *On Aggression* (New York: Harcourt Brace Jovanovich, 1966); and R. A. Moore, *Sports and Mental Health* (Springfield, Ill.: Charles C. Thomas, 1966). Today, the weight of evidence supports a social-constructionist explanation. Athletic violence is learned behavior. See summaries of the research on sport violence in J. J. Coakley, *Sport and Society: Issues and Controversies* (St. Louis: C. V. Mosby, 1978); J. Schneider, and D. S. Eitzen, "The Structure of Sport and Participant Violence," *Arena Review* 7 (1983): 1–16. Pleck summarizes the biological, psychological and sociological research on the more general topic of men and violence, and concludes that there is no convincing evidence to support the contention that men are genetically or hormonally predisposed to violent behavior. In fact, the weight of evidence suggests that most boys and men are not comfortable committing acts of violence—aggression and violence are learned behavior, and some men learn it better than others. See J. H. Pleck, *The Myth of Masculinity* (Cambridge: MIT Press, 1982); M. Scher and M. Stevens, "Men and Violence," *Journal of Counseling and Development* 65 (1987): 351–55. I will not enter the debate here as to how to define sport violence or whether "violence" needs to be differentiated from "aggression." Instead, I will begin with the assumption that in many of our most popular sports,

the achievement of goals (scoring and winning) is predicated on the successful utilization of violence—that is, these are activities in which the human body is turned into a weapon to be used against other bodies, resulting in pain, serious injury, and even death. See D. Atyeo, *Blood and Guts: Violence in Sports* (New York: Paddington Press, 1979); D. F. Sabo, "Pigskin, Patriarchy, and Pain," *Changing Men: Issues in Gender, Sex, and Politics* 16 (1986): 24–25; and J. Underwood, *The Death of an American Game* (Boston: Little, Brown Co, 1979).

11. Pollack and Gilligan's study of college students revealed that men and women, in writing stories in response to pictures they are shown, tend to perceive danger in different social situations. Men tend to write stories of danger and violence when shown pictures of close personal affiliation (intimacy). Women are more likely to see danger and violence in pictures of impersonal competitive situations. See S. Pollack and C. Gilligan, "Images of Violence in Thematic Apperception Test Stories," *Journal of Personality and Social Psychology* 42 (1982): 159–67.

12. C. Gilligan, *In a Different Voice: Psychological Theory and Women's Development* (Cambridge, Mass.: Harvard University Press, 1982); pp. 43–44.

13. See M. E. Duquin, "Power and Authority: Moral Consensus and Conformity in Sport," *International Review for Sport Sociology* 19 (1984): 295–304; and B. J. Bredemeier, "Athletic Aggression: A Moral Concern," in J. H. Goldstein, ed., *Sports Violence* (New York: Springer-Verlag, 1983), pp. 47–82.

14. Mummendey and Mummendey make a similar point in their description of aggression among soccer players as a form of social interaction. See A. Mummendey and H. D. Mummendey, "Aggressive Behavior of Soccer Players as Social Interaction," in Goldstein, ed., *Sports Violence*, pp. 111–28.

15. P. Lyman, "The Fraternal Bond as a Joking Relationship: A Case Study of Sexist Jokes in Male Group Bonding," in M. S. Kimmel, ed., *Changing Men: New Directions in Research on Men and Masculinity* (Newbury Park: Sage, 1987), pp. 148–63.

16. B. J. Bredemeier and D. L. Shields, "Athletic Aggression: An Issue of Contextual Morality," *Sociology of Sport Journal* 3 (1986): 15–28.

17. Many football players approve of rule changes that would make the game safer for players but state that they must continue to play by the rules until they are changed. See, for instance, J. Tatum, *They Call Me Assassin* (New York: Doubleday, 1972). However, it is not the players who make the rules, nor is player safety always the major concern of the rule-makers. Rules, especially at the professional and major college levels, increasingly reflect commercial interests of owners and of television. See J. J. Sewart, "The Commodification of Sport," *International Journal for Sociology of Sport* 22 (1987): 171–91. Artificial turf, for instance, is widely despised by players as causing shin splints, ankle and knee injuries, and "rug-burns," yet it is attractive to owners because it is less expensive to maintain than natural grass. Even equipment that is intended to protect the player, such as the football helmet, becomes a weapon that increases the number and severity of certain kinds of injuries. Better helmets and padding paradoxically allow players

to hit harder. Helmet blows accounty for 9.4 percent of all NFL injuries. See J. Underwood, *Death of an American Game*.

18. G. Wojciechowski and C. Dufresne, "Football Career Is Taking Its Toll on NFL's Players," *Los Angeles Times*, June 26, 1988, sec. 3, p. 1.

19. David Atyeo points out that each year, in U.S. sport, there are roughly "twenty million injuries serious enough to be treated by a doctor. Of these twenty million, six million leave lasting and permanent reminders, ranging from scars to paraplegia and death." Football in particular, Atyeo says, each year "kills on average twenty-eight players and maims thousands more. It leaves everyone who reaches its higher levels with some form of lasting injury and, according to one medical report, cuts as much as twenty years off a professional player's life-expectancy" (*Blood and Guts*, pp. 11–12, 149).

20. Sabo, "Pigskin, Patriarchy, and Pain," p. 24.

21. I am grateful to Cheryl Cole for this insight.

22. Stone's story also illustrates what Michael Kaufman has called "the triad of men's violence," the three corners of which are violence against women, violence against other men, and violence against oneself. See M. Kaufman, "The Construction of Masculinity and the Triad of Men's Violence," in his *Beyond Patriarchy: Essays by Men on Pleasure, Power, and Change* (Toronto: Oxford University Press, 1987), pp. 1–29.

23. D. Meggyesy, *Out of Their League*, pp. 83–84.

24. Pleck points out that the gap between the average life-expectancy of men and women has been increasing. In 1900, men were expected to live 46.3 years, women, 48.3 years. For those born in 1975, the life-expectancy is now 68.7 years for men, 75.5 years for women. Pleck and others conclude that this gap is due to the "lethal" aspects of masculinity in modern society. (*The Myth of Masculinity*, pp. 150–52). See also J. L. Chapman, "Increased Male Mortality and Male Roles in Industrialized Societies," *M: Gentle Men for Gender Justice* 7 (1981/82): 7–8; S. M. Jourard, "Some Lethal Aspects of the Male Role," in J. H. Pleck and J. Sawyer, eds., *Men and Masculinity* (Englewood Cliffs, N.J.: Prentice-Hall, 1974), pp. 21–29); S. Julty, "Men and Their Health: A Strained Alliance," *M: Gentle Men for Gender Justice* 7 (1981/82): 5–6; J. Harrison, J. Chin, and T. Ficarrotto, "Warning: Masculinity May Be Dangerous to Your Health," in M. S. Kimmel and M. A. Messner, eds., *Men's Lives* (New York: Macmillan, 1989), pp. 296–311.

25. Coakley, *Sport in Society*, p. 26.

26. Meggyesy, *Out of Their League*, p. 231.

27. See M. F. Stuck, ed., "Drugs and Sport," a special issue of *Arena Review* 12 no. 1. (1988).

28. See the discussion of the initial public response to Johnson's steroid use in W. O. Johnson, "Take a Bow! Give South Korea Kudos for the Summer Games," *Sports Illustrated*, October 10, 1988, pp. 36–43.

29. Reported in Atyeo, *Blood and Guts*, p. 250. For personal accounts of drug use in pro football in this era, see also C. Oliver, *High for the Game* (New York: Morrow, 1971); and Meggyesy, *Out of Their League.*

30. T. Chaikin with R. Telander, "The Nightmare of Steroids," *Sports Illustrated*, October 24, 1988, pp. 82–102.

31. "Steroid Guru" Dan Duchaine, a former bodybuilder who now consults with other bodybuilders on steroid use, advocates "moderate" use of the drugs. He claims that the dangers of steroid use are overstated. In discussing the steroid Anadrol, he states, "It is a quite nasty drug towards the liver, however, causing jaundice problems. . . . If you can tolerate large amounts of alcohol, you can probably tolerate Anadrol" (P. Alfano, "A 'Guru' Who Spreads the Gospel of Steroids," *New York Times*, November 19, 1988, p. 1).

32. M. D. Shear, "Pro Football Players Testify against Steroid Use," *Los Angeles Times*, May 10, 1989, sec. 3, p. 3.

33. A frightening finding of this study was that of the young males who had used the drug, 26.7 percent were not athletes: They used the drug to build muscles in order to improve their physical appearance. See R. Tosches, "Steroid Report a Revelation to CIF Hierarchy," *Los Angeles Times*, January 1, 1989, p. 18.

34. J. R. Fuller and M. J. LaFountain, "Illegal Steroid Use among Fifty Weightlifters," *Sociology and Social Research* 73 (1988): 20.

35. Ibid., pp. 19–20.

36. J. M. Hoberman, "Sport and the Technological Image of Man," in W. J. Morgan and K. V. Meier, eds., *Philosophic Inquiry in Sport* (Champaign, Ill.: Human Kinetics Publishers, 1988), p. 319.

37. *Ibid.*, p. 321.

38. Atyeo, *Blood and Guts*, p. 253.

39. C. P. Gallmeier, "Juicing, Burning, and Tooting: Observing Drug Use among Professional Hockey Players," *Arena Review* 12 (1988): 1–12.

40. See J. P. De Mondnard, "For and Against Doping and Its Controls: True and False Arguments," *Olympic Review* 180 (1982): 583–86.

41. See M. P. Koss and T. E. Dinero, "Predictors of Sexual Aggression among a National Sample of Male College Students," in R. A. Prentky and V. Quinsey, eds., *Human Sexual Aggression: Current Perspectives, Annals of the New York Academy of Sciences* 528 (1988): 133–46.

42. See L. B. Rubin, *Intimate Strangers: Men and Women Together* (New York: Harper and Row, 1983), p. 140.

43. J. Leiber, "No Bones about It," *Sports Illustrated*, August 19, 1989, p. 54.

44. Ibid., p. 56.

45. Quoted in Atyeo, *Blood and Guts*, p. 176.

46. See J. C. Phillips, "Toward an Explanation of Racial Variations in Top Level Sports Participation," *International Review of Sport Sociology* 11 (1976): 39–55.

47. Myriad studies on racial "stacking" in sport have been performed. Some of the more important include J. E. Curtis and J. W. Loy, "Positional Segregation in Professional Baseball: Replications, Trend Data, and Critical Observation," *International Review of Sport Sociology* 13(1978): 5–21; J. E. Curtis and J. W. Loy, "Race/Ethnicity and Relative Centrality of Playing Positions in Team Sports," in R. S. Hutton, ed., *Exercise and Sport Sciences Review*, vol. 6 (Philadelphia: Franklin Institute, 1979), pp. 285–313; D. S. Eitzen and N. R. Yetman, "Racial Dynamics in American Sports: Continuity and Change," in R. M. Pankin, ed., *Social Approaches to Sport* (Rutherford: Farleigh-Dickenson University Press, 1982), pp. 235–59; J. W. Loy, Jr. and J. F. McElvogue, "Racial Segregation in American Sport," *International Review of Sport Sociology* 5 (1970): 5–23.

48. R. Majors, "Cool Pose: Black Masculinity and Sports," in Messner and Sabo, *Sport, Men, and the Gender Order*, pp. 97–108.

49. For discussions of the historical and social construction of the myths of black men's "natural" violent tendencies, see A. Davis, *Woman, Race, and Class* (New York: Vintage Books, 1981); and chapter 4 of R. Staples, *Black Masculinity* (San Francisco: Black Scholar Press, 1982).

CHAPTER 5. FRIENDSHIP, INTIMACY, AND SEXUALITY

1. See King, "Curtain Call," in *Sports Illustrated*, October 15, 1990. All quotes are from p. 40.

2. D. Riesman, *The Lonely Crowd: A Study of the Changing American Character* (New Haven: Yale University Press, 1953).

3. C. Lasch, *The Culture of Narcissism* (New York: Warner Books, 1979), p. 209.

4. For an excellent example of a coach successfully (if temporarily) molding a group of individual "stars" into a team, see D. Halberstam, *The Breaks of the Game* (New York: Ballentine Books, 1981).

5. C. R. L. James's description of a painful reunion that he had with a former cricket teammate captures the essense of cross-racial friendships that develop in the athletic context: "We had nothing so say to each other, our social circles were too different, and he never came again. He went to Europe to study medicine and years afterwards, when we were grown men, I met him once or twice. We greeted each other warmly, but I was always embarrassed and I think he was too. There was a guilty feeling that something had gone wrong with us. Something had. The school-tie can be transplanted, but except on annual sporting occasions the old school-tie cannot be. *It is a bond of school only on the surface. The link is between family and friends, between members of the class or caste*" (emphasis added); C. R. L. James, *Beyond a Boundary* (New York: Pantheon Books, 1983), p. 41.

6. For mid 1970s discussions of the shallowness of men's friendships with other men, see W. Farrell, *The Liberated Man* (New York: Bantam Books, 1975); M-F. Fasteau, *The Male Machine* (New York: McGraw-Hill, S. F. Morin and E. M.

Garfinkel, "Male Homophobia," *Journal of Social Issues* 34 (1978): 29–47. J. H. Pleck and J. Sawyer, eds., *Men and Masculinity* (Englewood Cliffs, N.J.: Prentice-Hall, 1974).

7. L. B. Rubin, *Intimate Strangers: Men and Women Together* (New York: Harper and Row, 1983), p. 135. Rubin's definition of "intimacy," while helpful in constructing her typology of gender differences in friendship patterns, is clearly class biased. Her emphasis on verbalization of one's "inner life" is based on a very upper-middle class, therapeutic definition of intimacy, which might ignore or devalue other, nonverbal, forms of expression more common in social groups that are not so immersed in the professional/therapeutic culture. Rubin develops a more complete analysis of gender and friendship in *Just Friends: The Role of Friendship in Our Lives* (New York: Harper and Row, 1985).

8. B. Bradley, *Life on the Run* (New York: Bantam Books, 1977).

9. See F. M. Cancian, *Love in America: Gender and Self-Development* (Cambridge: Cambridge University Press, 1987); and S. Swain, "Covert Intimacy: Closeness in Men's Friendships," in B. J. Risman and P. Schwartz, eds., *Gender in Intimate Relationships: A Microstructural Approach* (Belmont, Cal.: Wadsworth, 1989), pp. 71–86.

10. Swain, "Covert Intimacy," pp. 71, 85.

11. Ibid., p. 78.

12. Ibid., p. 77.

13. P. Lyman, "The Fraternal Bond as a Joking Relationship: A Case Study of Sexist Jokes in Male Group Bonding," in M. S. Kimmel, ed., *Changing Men: New Directions in Research on Men and Masculinity.* (Newbury Park: Sage, 1987), pp. 148–63.

14. Here are some of the roots of the still-popular misconception that male homosexuality is connected to some essential "femininity," a confusion of sexual identity with gender identity. This confusion is clearly a cultural manifestation. See W. L. Williams, *The Spirit and the Flesh: Sexual Diversity in American Indian Culture* (Boston: Beacon Press, 1986).

15. D. J. Mrozek, *Sport and the American Mentality, 1880–1910* (Knoxville: University of Tennessee Press, 1983), p. 20.

16. T. Crosset, "Masculinity, Sexuality, and the Development of Early Modern Sport," in M. A. Messner and D. F. Sabo, eds., *Sport, Men, and the Gender Order: Critical Feminist Perspectives* (Champaign, Ill.: Human Kinetics Publishers, 1990), pp. 45–54.

17. I recall, though, that despite the fact that scientific "sexology" had long-since discredited the notion of the spermatic economy, and despite the fact that Joe Namath had exploded the myth in professional football by showing up for big games, even the Super Bowl, and making thinly veiled statements about whom he had slept with the previous night, I had a community college coach in 1971 who would routinely warn us before every weekend to "save [our] energies for the games . . . stay away from the split-tails" (which of course meant women.)

18. Lyman, "The Fraternal Bond as a Joking Relationship," p. 151.

19. Ibid., p. 156.

20. J. Brown, *Out of Bounds* (New York: Kensington, 1989), pp. 183–84, 190.

21. D. F. Sabo, "The Myth of the Sexual Athlete," in *Changing Men: Issues in Gender, Sex, and Politics* 20 (1989): 38–39.

22. T. J. Curry, "Fraternal Bonding in the Locker Room: A Profeminist Analysis of Talk about Competition and Women" *Sociology of Sport Journal* 8 (1991): 119–135.

23. Sabo, "The Myth of the Sexual Athlete," p. 39.

24. Christine Williams points out in her study of the construction of gender in the Marine Corps and in the nursing profession that homophobia and misogyny are a common part of basic training for male Marines. See C. L. Williams, *Gender Differences at Work: Women and Men in Nontraditional Occupations.* (Berkeley: University of California Press, 1989).

25. A. Brittan, *Masculinity and Power* (Oxford: Basil Blackwell, 1989), p. 41.

26. B. Pronger, *The Arena of Masculinity: Sports, Homosexuality, and the Meaning of Sex* (New York: St. Martin's Press, 1990), pp. 195, 199.

27. See, for instance, D. Herman, "The Rape Culture," in J. Freeman, ed., *Women: A Feminist Perspective*, 3d ed. (Mountain View, Cal.: Mayfield, 1984), pp. 20–38; T. Beneke, *Men on Rape* (New York: St. Martin's Press, 1982).

28. E. J. Kanin, "Date Rape: Differential Sexual Socialization and Relative Deprivation," *Victimology* 9 (1984): 95–108.

29. M. P. Koss, and T. E. Dinero, "Predictors of Sexual Aggression among a National Sample of Male College Students," in R. A. Prentky and V. Quinsey, eds., *Human Sexual Aggression: Current Perspectives, Annals of the New York Academy of Sciences* 528 (1988): 133–46. For a similar argument on how young male homosocial groups can promote rape, see P. Y. Martin and R. A. Hummer, "Fraternities and Rape on Campus," *Gender and Society* 3 (1989): 457–73.

30. Warshaw, R., *I Never Called it Rape* (New York: Harper and Row, 1988), p. 112.

31. Cited in ibid., p. 113.

32. An ethnographic study of a Texas high school football team revealed a lot of what anthropologist Douglas Foley called "rhetorical performance" about sex in the locker room. See D. E. Foley, "The Great American Football Ritual: Reproducing Race, Class, and Gender Inequality," *Sociology of Sport Journal* 7 (1990): 111–35.

33. M. M. Johnson, *Strong Mothers, Weak Wives* (Berkeley: University of California Press, 1988).

34. Dominant cultural conceptions of "the coach," of course, presume coaching to be a male occupation. As a result, women coaches must constantly negotiate

their way within a highly masculine occupation. See N. Theberge, "Gender, Work, and Power: The Case of Women in Coaching," *Canadian Journal of Sociology* 15 (1990): 59–75.

35. D. F. Sabo and J. Panepinto, "Football Ritual and the Social Production of Masculinity," in Messner and Sabo, *Sport, Men, and the Gender Order*, pp. 124, 123.

36. For examples of writings by athletes who were developing antiauthoritarian perspectives in the late 1960s and early 1970s, see D. Meggyesy, *Out of Their League* (Berkeley: Ramparts Press, 1970); C. Oliver, *High for the Game* (New York: Morrow, 1971).

37. See H. Edwards, *The Revolt of the Black Athlete* (New York: Free Press, 1969).

38. Meggyesy, *Out of Their League*, p. 153.

CHAPTER 6. OUT OF THE LIMELIGHT

1. D. J. Levinson et. al., *The Seasons of a Man's Life* (New York: Ballantine Books, 1978); p. 51.

2. B. D. McPherson, "Former Professional Athletes' Adjustment to Retirement," *The Physician and Sports Medicine* 1978, p. 55.

3. Hill and Lowe point out that within athletics, "even minor consequences of aging assume critical importance for the professional athlete. . . . The athlete is obliged to grow old before his time and, although he is in the prime of his life, he carries the stigma of an old man in the eyes of the younger players" (P. Hill and B. Lowe, "The Inevitable Metathesis of the Retiring Athlete," *International Review of Sport Sociology* 9 [1978]: 20).

4. McPherson, "Former Athletes' Adjustment to Retirement," p. 56.

5. See D. S. Harris and D. S. Eitzen, "The Consequences of Failure in Sport," *Urban Life* 7 (1978): 177–88.

6. C. Gilligan, *In a Different Voice: Psychological Theory and Women's Development* (Cambridge, Mass.: Harvard University Press, 1982).

7. C. H. Cooley, *Life and the Student* (New York: Alfred A. Knopf, 1927).

8. S. Terkel, *Working* (New York: Avon Books, 1975), p. 488.

9. This appears to differ by sport. Some sports, such as football and boxing, really are not played recreationally on an organized basis outside of schools and professional sport. Basketball players, baseball players, and runners all have at least the opportunity to play their sport on a recreational or "pick-up" basis if they so choose.

10. Quotation is from E. Kiersh, *Where Have You Gone, Vince DiMaggio?* (New York: Bantam Books, 1983), p. 17.

11. J. Bouton, *Ball Four* (New York: Dell Publishing, 1970), pp. 56, 74, 77.

12. The analogy of athletic retirement and death is discussed in S. Lerch, "Athletic Retirement as Social Death: An Overview," in N. Theberge and P. Donnelly, eds., *Sport and the Sociological Imagination* (Forth Worth: Texas Christian University Press, 1984), pp. 259–72.

13. For a discussion of women, men, and "emotion work," see A. R. Hochschild, "Emotion Work, Feeling Rules, and Social Structure," *American Journal of Sociology* 85 (1979): 551–75, and *The Second Shift: Working Parents and the Revolution at Home* (New York: Viking Press, 1989).

CHAPTER 7. LIFE AFTER SPORT

1. D. J. Levinson et al., *The Seasons of a Man's Life* (New York: Ballantine Books, 1978); p. 140.

2. In the late 1980s, Willy S. was paroled and began a career in occupational therapy.

3. The term "almost a famous person" is taken from the title of a book on basketball player Bob Presley, whose tragic story in many ways epitomizes the ways that talented young black athletes are treated in American society. See H. Michelson, *Almost a Famous Person* (New York: Harcourt Brace Jovanovich, 1980).

4. This research looked at both female and male athletic participation, although I discuss only the findings concerning male athletes here. See D. F. Sabo and the Women's Sports Foundation, *The Women's Sports Foundation Report: Minorities in Sports* (New York: Women's Sports Foundation, 1989), p. 14.

5. K. A. Farr, "Dominance Bonding through the Good Old Boys Sociability Group," *Sex Roles* 18 (1988): 265.

6. For further discussions of work/family dynamics, see L. B. Rubin, *Worlds of Pain: Life in the Working Class Family* (New York: Basic Books, 1976), and *Intimate Strangers: Men and Women Together* (New York: Harper and Row, 1983); R. Sennett and J. Cobb, *The Hidden Injuries of Class* (New York: Random House, 1973); S. Terkel, *Working* (New York: Avon Books, 1975).

7. Research indicates that when a married mother takes a job in the paid labor force, the household division of labor changes very little. Men may "help out" with the housework and the childcare, but these tasks are still viewed primarily as "women's work." See J. Gardiner, "Women's Domestic Labor," in Z. R. Eisenstein, ed., *Capitalist Patriarchy and the Case for Socialist Feminism* (New York: Monthly Review Press, 1979), pp. 173–89; H. Hartmann, "The Family as the Locus of Gender, Class, and Political Struggle: The Case of Housework," *Signs* 6 (1981): 366–94; R. Zussman, "Work and Family in the New Middle Class," in N. Gerstel and H. Gross, eds., *Family and Work* (Philadelphia: Temple University Press, 1987), pp. 338–46. A. R. Hochschild, *The Second Shift: Working Parents and the Revolution at Home* (New York: Viking Press, 1989). Whether a woman works outside the home or not, the family "emotion work" is often still primarily her responsibility. See A. R. Hochschild, "Emotion Work, Feeling Rules, and Social Structure," *American Journal of Sociology* 85 (1979): 551–75.

8. Since the early 1970s, it has been axiomatic within feminist theory to posit the separation or opposition between domestic and public realms as a major basis of women's subordinate social status. For the paradigmatic statement, see M. Z. Rosaldo, "Woman, Culture, and Society: A Theoretical Overview," in M. Z. Rosaldo and L. Lamphere, eds., *Woman, Culture, and Society* (Stanford: Stanford University Press, 1974), pp. 17–42. For recent critiques and revisions of Rosaldo's theory, see J. Sharistanian, ed., *Beyond the Public/Domestic Dichotomy: Contemporary Perspectives on Women's Public Lives* (New York: Greenwood Press, 1987).

9. Barbara Ehrenreich has asserted that since the 1950s, there has been a clear trend of men running away from their responsibilities as breadwinners, thus resulting in the rapidly growing numbers of single-parent families headed by women, the low percentage of divorced fathers who pay adequate child support, and the frighteningly rapid growth of the feminization of poverty. See B. Ehrenreich, *The Hearts of Men* (Garden City, N.Y.: Anchor Press/Doubleday, 1983). Ehrenreich is probably correctly identifying a social trend among educated, white middle-class men. But among poor blacks, the feminization of poverty appears to have as much to do with declining educational and work opportunities for young males as it does with male irresponsibility. See W. J. Wilson and K. M. Neckerman, "Poverty and Family Structure: The Widening Gap between Evidence and Public Policy Issues," in S. H. Danzinger and D. H. Weinberg (eds.) *Fighting Poverty* (Cambridge: Harvard University Press, 1986), pp. 232–59; and R. Sidel, *Women and Children Last: The Plight of Poor Women in Affluent America* (New York: Viking Penguin, 1986).

10. Rubin, *Intimate Strangers;* C. Gilligan, *In a Different Voice: Psychological Theory and Women's Development* (Cambridge: Harvard University Press, 1982).

11. Rubin, *Intimate Strangers*, p. 82.

12. S. Osherson, *Finding Our Fathers: How a Man's Life Is Shaped by his Relationship with His Father* (New York: Fawcett Columbine, 1986).

13. Hochschild, "Emotion Work, Feeling Rules, and Social Structure."

14. Rosanna Hertz, in her study of professional "dual career families," found that the division of labor in family work was in fact becoming more egalitarian. However, women still do more of the housework, and when the first child arrives, it is the woman who attends to more of the childcare, including finding and supervising childcare providers. R. Hertz, *More Equal Than Others: Women and Men in Dual-Career Marriages* (Berkeley: University of California Press, 1986). Hochschild's study of two-job families also illuminates the new housework and childcare problems that have emerged behind the rhetoric of egalitarianism. See *The Second Shift*.

15. Osherson observes in *Finding Our Fathers* that this is a consistent trend among young fathers today: More and more men say that they want to spend more time with their own children than their fathers did with them. Rubin's research corroborates this (see *Intimate Strangers*).

16. Lillian Rubin states that "They may be few in number, but where fathers share primary responsibility for parenting, a father and his infant will show the same evidence of attachment that has, until now, been said to be unique to the mother-infant relationship" *Intimate Strangers*, p. 185. Changes in the social structure of parenting, then, are a necessary (if not fully sufficient) part of the overall transformation required for the development of full equality between men and women.

17. See chapter 6 of M. M. Johnson, *Strong Mothers, Weak Wives* (Berkeley: University of California Press, 1988). Although mothers often exhibit similar "gender differentiating" parenting styles, almost all of the research indicates that fathers do so more consistently, and to greater extremes than mothers do. See C. D. Hoffman, S. E. Tsuneyoshi, M. Ebina, and H. Fite, "A Comparison of Adult Males' and Females' Interactions with Girls and Boys," *Sex Roles* 11 (1984): 799–811; L. W. Hoffman, "Changes in Family Roles, Socialization, and Sex Differences," *American Psychologist* 32 (1977): 644–57; R. D. Parke and B. R. Tinsley, "The Father's Role in Infancy: Determinants of Involvement in Caregiving and Play," in M. E. Lamb, *The Role of the Father in Child Development*, 2d ed. (New York: John Wiley, 1981).

18. Levinson et al., *Seasons of a Man's Life*, p. 242.

19. M. P. Farrell and S. D. Rosenberg, *Men at Midlife*. (Boston: Auburn House, 1981); and A. Tolson, *The Limits of Masculinity: Male Identity and Women's Liberation* (New York: Harper and Row, 1977).

CHAPTER 8. SPORT AND GENDER RELATIONS

1. G. Gilder, *Sexual Suicide* (New York: Bantam Books, 1973), pp. 216, 218.

2. J. Carroll, "Sport: Virtue and Grace," *Theory Culture and Society* 3 (1986), 91–98. Jennifer Hargreaves delivers a brilliant feminist rebuttal to Carroll's masculinist defense of sport in the same issue of the journal. See Je. Hargreaves, "Where's the Virtue? Where's the Grace? A Discussion of the Social Production of Gender through Sport," pp. 109–21.

3. G. Gilder, *Sexual Suicide*, p. 221.

4. For a critical overview of the biological research on male-female difference, see A. Fausto-Sterling, *Myths of Gender: Biological Theories about Men and Women* (New York: Basic Books, 1985). For an overview of the historical basis of male domination, see R. Lee and R. Daly, "Man's Domination and Woman's Oppression: The Question of Origins," in M. Kaufman, ed., *Beyond Patriarchy: Essays by Men on Pleasure, Power, and Change* (Toronto: Oxford University Press, 1987), pp. 30–44.

5. R. W. Connell, *Gender and Power* (Stanford: Stanford University Press, 1987), p. 81. (emphasis in original text).

6. I discuss previous feminist analyses of sport in the Introduction and in chapter 1 of this book.

7. Indeed, "men's liberationists" of the 1970s were overly optimistic in believing that a public illumination of the "costs of masculinity" would induce men to "reject the male role." See, for instance, W. Farrell, *The Liberated Man* (New York:

Bantam Books, 1975); J. Nichols, *Men's Liberation: A New Definition of Masculinity* (New York: Penguin Books, 1975). These men's liberationists underestimated the extent to which the costs of masculinity are linked to the promise of power and privilege. One commentator went so far as to argue that the privileges of masculinity were a "myth" perpetrated by women to keep men in destructive success-object roles. See H. Goldberg, *The Hazards of Being Male: Surviving the Myth of Masculine Privilege* (New York: Signet, 1976). For more recent discussions of the need to analyze both the "costs" and the "privileges" of dominant conceptions of masculinity, see M. E. Kann, "The Costs of Being on Top," *Journal of the National Association for Women Deans, Administrators, and Counselors* 49 (1986): 29–37; and M. A. Messner, "Men Studying Masculinity: Some Epistemological Questions in Sport Sociology," *Sociology of Sport Journal* 7 (1990): 136–53.

8. W. J. Wilson and K. M. Neckerman, "Poverty and Family Structure: The Widening Gap between Evidence and Public Policy Issues," in S. H. Danzinger and D. H. Weinberg, eds., *Fighting Poverty* (Cambridge: Harvard University Press, 1986), pp. 232–59; F. J. Berghorn et al., "Racial Participation in Men's and Women's Intercollegiate Basketball: Continuity and Change, 1958–1985." *Sociology of Sport Journal* 5 (1988), 107–24.

9. R. Majors, "Cool Pose": Black Masculinity and Sports," in M. A. Messner and D. F. Sabo, *Sport, Men, and the Gender Order: Critical Feminist Perspectives.* (Champaign, Ill.: Human Kinetics Publishers, 1990), p. 111.

10. See S. Kleinberg, "The New Masculinity of Gay Men, and Beyond," in Kaufman *Beyond Patriarchy, pp. 120–38.*

11. D. Altman, *The Homosexualization of America* (Boston: Beacon Press, 1982).

12. See D. Kopay and P. D. Young, *The Dave Kopay Story* (New York: Arbor House, 1977).

13. B. Pronger, "Gay Jocks: A Phenomenology of Gay Men in Athletics," in Messner and Sabo, *Sport, Men, and the Gender Order,* pp. 141–52; and *The Arena of Masculinity: Sports, Homosexuality, and the Meaning of Sex* (New York: St. Martin's Press, 1990).

14. T. Carrigan, B. Connell, and J. Lee, "Hard and Heavy: Toward a New Sociology of Masculinity," *Theory and Society* 14 (1985): 551–603.

15. One potentially important, but largely unexplored, fissure among men is that between athletes and nonathletes. There are tens of millions of boys who do *not* pursue athletic careers. Many boys dislike sport. Others may yearn to be athletes, but may not have the body size, strength, physical capabilities, coordination, emotional predisposition, or health that is necessary to successfully compete in sports. What happens to these boys and young men? What kinds of adult masculine identities and relationships do they eventually develop? Does the fact of not having been an athlete play any significant role in their masculine identities, goals, self-images, and relationships? The answers to these questions, of course, lie outside the purview of my study. But they are key to understanding the contemporary role that sport plays in constructions of gender.

16. For interesting discussions of bodybuilding, gender, and sexuality, see B. Glassner, *Bodies: Why We Look the Way We Do (and How We Feel about It)* (New York: G. P. Putnam's Sons; 1988); A. M. Klein, "Little Big Man: Hustling, Gender Narcissism, and Homophobia in Bodybuilding," in Messner and Sabo, *Sport, Men, and the Gender Order*, pp 127–40.

17. Alan Klein's research revealed that nongay male bodybuilders are also commonly motivated by a need to make a public statement with their muscular bodies that they are indeed "masculine." To the nongay bodybuilder, muscles are the ultimate sign of heterosexual masculinity. But, ironically, as one nongay male bodybuilder put it, "We're everything the U.S. is supposed to stand for: strength, determination, everything to be admired. But it's not the girls that like us, it's the fags!" Interestingly, Klein found that many male bodybuilders who defined themselves as "straight" (including the one quoted above) made a living by prostituting themselves to gay men. See Klein, "Little Big Man," p. 135.

For a thought-provoking feminist analysis of the contradictory relationship between gay male sexuality and masculinity, see T. Edwards, "Beyond Sex and Gender: Masculinity, Homosexuality and Social Theory," in J. Hearn and D. Morgan, eds., *Men, Masculinities, and Social Theory* (London: Unwin Hyman, 1990), pp. 110–23.

18. The Gay Games were originally called the "Gay Olympics," but the U. S. Olympic Committee went to court to see that the word "Olympics" was not used to denote this event. Despite the existence of "Police Olympics," "Special Olympics," "Senior Olympics," "Xerox Olympics," "Armenian Olympics," even "Crab Cooking Olympics," the U.S.O.C. chose to enforce their control legally over the term "Olympics" when it came to the "Gay Olympics." For further discussion of the politics of the Gay Games, see M. A. Messner, "Gay Athletes and the Gay Games: An Interview With Tom Waddell," *M: Gentle Men for Gender Justice* 13 (1984): 13–14.

19. During the 1982 Gay Games in San Francisco, the major local newspapers tended to cover the Games mostly in the "lifestyle" sections of the paper, not in the sports pages. Alternative sports demonstrate the difficulties of attempting to change sport in the absence of larger institutional transformations. For instance, the European sport of korfball was developed explicitly as a sex-egalitarian sport. The rules of korfball aim to neutralize male-female biological differences that may translate into different levels of ability. But recent research shows that old patterns show up, even among the relatively "enlightened" korfball players. Korfball league officials are more likely to be male than female. More important, the more "key" roles within the game appear to be dominated by men, while women are partially marginalized. See D. Summerfield and A. White, "Korfball: A Model of Egalitarianism?" *Sociology of Sport Journal* 6 (1989): 144–51.

20. S. L. Twin, ed. *Out of the Bleachers: Writings on Women and Sport* (Old Westbury, N.Y.: Feminist Press, 1979).

21. See N. Theberge, "Women's Athletics and the Myth of Female Frailty," in J. Freeman, *Women: A Feminist Perspective* (Mountain View, Cal.: Mayfield, 1989), pp. 507–22.

22. See Carol Gilligan's discussion of the gendered basis of these two conceptions of "fairness" (*In a Different Voice: Psychological Theory and Women's Development* [Cambridge, Mass.: Harvard University Press, 1982]).

23. Sandra Harding argues that to understand the contemporary gender order, we need to examine how gender identities, a gendered division of labor, and gender symbolism interact with each other. See S. Harding, *The Science Question in Feminism* (Ithaca: Cornell University Press, 1986).

24. For instance, a two-year analysis of two newspapers revealed that only 4.4 percent of total column inches devoted to sport focused on women's sport. See J. Bryant, "A Two-year Selective Investigation of the Female in Sport as Reported in the Paper Media," *Arena Review* 4 (1980): 32–44. In 1986, Theberge and Cronk's research revealed that work routines in newspaper sport departments and values of reporters continued to preclude adequate coverage of women's sport. See N. Theberge and A. Cronk, "Work Routines in Newspaper Sports Departments and the Coverage of Women's Sports," *Sociology of Sport Journal* 3 (1986): 195–203. Research on children's sport magazines revealed that visual images of male athletes in these magazines tend to outnumber those of female athletes by roughly a two-to-one ratio. See J. Rintala and S. Birrell, "Fair Treatment for the Active Female: A Content Analysis of *Young Athlete* magazine," *Sociology of Sport Journal* 1 (1984:) 231–50. Moreover, text and visual images tend to frame female and male athletes "as fundamentally and essentially different" and thus to support stereotypical notions of natural differences between the sexes. See M. C. Duncan and A. Sayaovong, "Photographic Images and Gender in *Sports Illustrated for Kids*," *Play and Culture* 3 (1990): 91–116. When women athletes are shown on television, they are often portrayed "ambivalently." See M. C. Duncan and C. A. Hasbrook, "Denial of Power in Televised Women's Sports," *Sociology of Sport Journal* 5 (1988): 1–21.

25. See M. C. Duncan, M. A. Messner, L. Williams, K. Jensen, and the Amateur Athletic Foundation of Los Angeles, *Gender Stereotyping in Televised Sports* (1990). For a copy of the report, write to AAF, 2141 West Adams Blvd., Los Angeles, Cal. 90018. For further discussion of the qualitative differences in the ways television sport commentators talk about women's and men's sport, see M. A. Messner, M. C. Duncan, and K. Jensen, "Separating the Men from the Girls: The Gendered Language of Televised Sports," *Gender and Society* (forthcoming).

26. See M. C. Duncan, M. A. Messner, L. Williams, and the Amateur Athletic Foundation of Los Angeles, *Coverage of Women's Sports in Four Daily Newspapers* (1991). For a copy of the report, write to AAF; 2141 West Adams Blvd., Los Angeles, Cal. 90018.

27. See S. T. Eastman and T. P. Meyter, "Sports Programming: Scheduling, Costs, and Competition," in L. A. Wenner (ed.) *Media, Sports, and Society* (Newbury Park: Sage, 1989), pp. 97–119.

28. For an excellent analysis and discussion of the extent to which athletic performance differences between the sexes are biologically based or socially constructed, see K. Dyer, *Challenging the Men: The Social Biology of Female Sport Achievement* (St. Lucia: University of Queensland Press, 1983). Susan Brownmiller argues that if cross-sex competition within the present athletic institutions is truly on the agenda, women are going to be "fighting biology all the way" on male-defined turf. See S. Brownmiller, *Femininity* (New York: Fawcett Columbine, 1984).

29. Duncan and Hasbrook's research on gender in the sport media suggests that overtly sexist portrayals of women athletes are becoming more rare, but the verbal commentary as well as visual representations of female athletes tends to be "ambivalent" in ways that symbolically deny power to women. See Duncan and Hasbrook, "Denial of Power in Televised Women's Sports."

30. For instance, Florence Griffith-Joyner's world records in the women's 100 meters sprint, 10.49 seconds, and in the 200 meters sprint, 21.34 seconds, are far behind Carl Lewis's world records in the men's 100- and 200 meters sprints (9.92 seconds and 19.72 seconds). Perhaps more significant is the fact that Griffith-Joyner's world record times in these sprints would place her well back in the pack if she were competing with men runners. In the 1990 TAC National Championships meet, for instance, the eighth place finisher in the men's 100 meters sprint had a time of 10.51. The first place time among the women was 11.20. This pattern generally holds true in all of the running and the field events.

31. Lott is a "Hitter" in the National Football League, akin to the type of player that Nathan C. was.

32. M. E. Mishkind, J. Rodin, L. R. Silberstein, and R. H. Streigel-Moore, "The Embodiment of Masculinity: Cultural, Psychological, and Behavioral Dimensions," *American Behavioral Scientist* 29 (1986): 545–62. See also S. Jeffords, *The Remasculinization of America: Gender and the Vietnam War* (Bloomington: Indiana University Press, 1989).

33. See Hargreaves, "Where's the Virtue? Where's the Grace?" and P. Willis, "Women in Sport in Ideology," in J. Hargreaves, ed., *Sport, Culture, and Ideology* (London: Routledge and Kegan Paul, 1982), pp. 117–35.

34. M. Morse, "Sport on Television: Replay and Display," in E. A. Kaplan, ed., *Regarding Television: Critical Approaches* (Los Angeles: University Publications of America, 1983), pp. 44–66. See also T. McCormack, "Hollywood's Prizefight Films: Violence or 'Jock Appeal'?" *Journal of Sport and Social Issues 8* (1984): 19–29.

35. P. Biskind and B. Ehrenreich, "Machismo and Hollywood's Working Class," *Socialist Review* 10 (1980): 109–30.

36. D. Z. Jackson, "Calling the Plays in Black and White," *Boston Globe*, January 22, 1989, p. A30. See also R. E. Rainville and E. McCormick, "Extent of Covert Prejudice in Pro Football Announcers' Speech," *Journalism Quarterly* 54 (1977): 20–26.

37. As Margaret Morse explains, "While players may represent power within the game-fiction, what they enjoy is not so much power as the exchange value of their bodies and body-images. The actual positions of social and economic power lie elsewhere, invisible. Sport today . . . is but a sign and perhaps a substitute for power rather than power itself" ("Sport on Television," p. 58).

38. For a good discussion of the gender politics of attempting to change Canadian sport, see D. Whitson and D. Macintosh, "Gender and Power: Explanations of Gender Inequalities in Canadian National Sport Organizations," *International Review for the Sociology of Sport* 24 (1989): 137–50.

39. See J. Scott, "A Radical Ethic for Sports," *Intellectual Digest* (1972).

APPENDIX 2

1. See A. Oakley, "Interviewing Women: A Contradiction in Terms," in H. Roberts, ed., *Doing Feminist Research* (London: Routlege and Kegan Paul, 1981).

2. J. Stacey, "Can There Be a Feminist Ethnography?" *Women's Studies International Forum* 11 (1988): 21–27.

3. See A. R. Hochschild, "Emotion Work, Feeling Rules, and Social Structure," *American Journal of Sociology* 85 (1979): 551–75.

4. R. Blauner and D. Wellman, "Toward a Decolonization of Research," in J. A. Ladner, ed., *The Death of White Sociology* (New York: Vintage Books, 1973), pp. 310–30.

5. B. Ehrenreich, *The Hearts of Men* (Garden City, N.Y.: Anchor Press/Doubleday, 1983), p. 135.

6. R. Sennett and J. Cobb, *The Hidden Injuries of Class* (New York: Random House, 1973).

7. A. R. Hochschild, *The Managed Heart: Commercialization and Human Feeling* (Berkeley: University of California Press, 1983), p. 159.

APPENDIX 3

1. W. J. Wilson, *The Declining Significance of Race: Blacks and Changing American Institutions* (Chicago: University of Chicago Press, 1978).

2. M. Hout, "Occupational Mobility of Black Men," *American Sociological Review* 49 (1984): 308–22.

3. See E. Ransford and J. Miller, "Race, Sex, and Feminist Outlooks," *American Sociological Review* 48 (1983): 46–49.

4. B. Blauner, *Black Lives, White Lives: Three Decades of Race Relations in America* (Berkeley: University of California Press, 1989), p. 170.

5. M. Gordon, *Assimilation in American Life* (New York: Oxford University Press, 1964). This point is developed at greater length in E. H. Ransford, *Race and Class in American Society: Black, Chicano, Anglo* (Cambridge, Mass.: Schenkman, 1977).

Bibliography

Adler, P. A., and P. Adler. "From Idealism to Pragmatic Detachment: The Academic Performance of College Athletes." *Sociology of Education* 58 (1985): 241–50.

——. "Role Conflict and Identity Salience: College Athletes and the Academic Role." *Social Science Journal* 24 (1987): 443–55.

Adler, P. A., and P. Adler. "The Gloried Self: The Aggrandizement and the Constriction of Self." *Social Psychology Quarterly* 52 (1989): 299–310.

Alfano, P. "A 'Guru' Who Spreads the Gospel of Steroids." *New York Times*, November 19, 1988.

Altman, D. *The Homosexualization of America*. Boston: Beacon Press, 1982.

Atyeo, D. *Blood and Guts: Violence in Sports*. New York: Paddington Press, 1979.

Baca Zinn, M. "Chicano Men and Masculinity." *Journal of Ethnic Studies* 10 (1982): 29–44.

Baca Zinn, M., L. W. Cannon, E. Higgenbotham, and B. Thornton Dill. "The Costs of Exclusionary Practices in Women's Studies." *Signs: Journal of Women in Culture and Society* 11 (1986): 290–303.

Ball, D. W. "Failure in Sport." *American Sociological Review* 41 (1976): 726–39.

Beneke, T. *Men on Rape*. New York: St. Martin's Press, 1982.

Benjamin, J. *The Bonds of Love: Psychoanalysis, Feminism, and the Problem of Domination*. New York: Pantheon Books, 1988.

Bennett, R. S., K. G. Whitaker, N. J. W. Smith, and A. Sablove. "Changing the Rules of the the Game: Reflections towards a Feminist Analysis of Sport." *Women's Studies International Forum* 10 (1987): 369–80.

Berghorn, F. J., N. R. Yetman, and W. E. Hanna. "Racial Participation in Men's and Women's Intercollegiate Basketball: Continuity and Change, 1958–1985." *Sociology of Sport Journal* 5 (1988): 107–24.

Birrell, S. "Achievement Related Motives and the Woman Athlete." In C. A. Oglesby, ed., *Women and Sport: From Myth to Reality*, pp. 141–59. Philadelphia: Lea and Farber, 1978.

——. "The Woman Athlete's College Experience: Knowns and Unknowns." *Journal of Sport and Social Issues* 11 (1987/88): 82–96.

——. "Discourses on the Gender/Sport Relationship: From Women in Sport to Gender Relations." *Exercise and Sport Science Review* 16 (1988): 159–200.

217

————. "Women of Color, Critical Autobiography, and Sport." In M. A. Messner and D. F. Sabo, eds., *Sport, Men and the Gender Order: Critical Feminist Perspectives*, pp. 185–200. Champaign, Ill.: Human Kinetics Publishers, 1990.

Biskind, B., and B. Ehrenreich. "Machismo and Hollywood's Working Class." *Socialist Review* 10 (1980): 109–30.

Bissinger, H. G. *Friday Night Lights: A Town, a Team, and a Dream*. Reading, Mass.: Addison-Wesley, 1990.

Blauner, B. *Black Lives, White Lives: Three Decades of Race Relations in America*. Berkeley: University of California Press, 1989.

Blauner, R. and D. Wellman. "Toward a Decolonization of Research." In J. A. Ladner, ed., *The Death of White Sociology* pp. 310–30. New York: Vintage Books, 1973.

Bly, R. *Iron John: A Book About Men*. Reading, MA: Addison-Wesley Pub. Co., 1990.

Bouton, J. *Ball Four*. New York: Dell Publishing, 1970.

Bowles, S., and H. Gintis. *Schooling in Capitalist America*. New York: Basic Books, 1976.

Bradley, B. *Life on the Run*. New York: Bantam Books, 1977.

Bredemeier, B. J. "Athletic Aggression: A Moral Concern." In J. H. Goldstein, ed., *Sports Violence*, pp. 47–82. New York: Springer-Verlag, 1983.

Bredemeier, B. J., and D. L. Shields, "Athletic Aggression: An Issue of Contextual Morality," *Sociology of Sport Journal* 3 (1986): 15–28.

Brittan, A. *Masculinity and Power*. New York: Basil Blackwell, 1989.

Brod, H., ed. *The Making of Masculinities: The New Men's Studies*. Winchester, Mass.: Allen and Unwin, 1987.

Brohm, J. M. *Sport: A Prison of Measured Time*. London: Ink Links, 1978.

Brown, J. *Out of Bounds*. New York: Kensington, 1989.

Brownmiller, S. *Against Our Will: Men, Women, and Rape*. New York: Simon and Schuster, 1975.

————. *Femininity*. New York: Fawcett Columbine, 1984.

Bryant, J. "A Two-Year Selective Investigation of the Female in Sport as Reported in the Paper Media." *Arena Review* 4 (1980): 32–44.

Bryson, L. "Sport and the Maintenance of Masculine Hegemony." *Women's Studies International Forum* 10 (1987): 349–60.

Cancian, F. M. *Love in America: Gender and Self-Development*. Cambridge: Cambridge University Press, 1987.

Carrigan, T., B. Connell, and J. Lee. "Hard and Heavy: Toward a New Sociology of Masculinity." *Theory and Society* 14 (1985): 551–603.

Carroll, J. "Sport: Virtue and Grace." *Theory, Culture, and Society* 3 (1986): 91–98.

Chaikin, T., with R. Telander. "The Nightmare of Steroids." *Sports Illustrated,* October 24, 1988, pp. 82–102.

Chapman, J. L. "Increased Male Mortality and Male Roles in Industrialized Societies." *M: Gentle Men for Gender Justice* 7 (1981/82): 7–8.

Chodorow, N. *The Reproduction of Mothering.* Berkeley: University of California Press, 1978.

Clawson, M. A. *Constructing Brotherhood: Class, Gender, and Fraternalism.* Princeton: Princeton University Press, 1989.

Coakley, J. J. *Sport in Society.* St. Louis: C. V. Mosby, 1978.

Collins, P. H. *Black Feminist Thought: Knowledge, Consciousness, and the Politics of Empowerment.* Boston: Unwin Hyman, 1990.

Connell, R. W. *Which Way Is Up? Essays on Sex, Class, and Culture.* Boston: Allen and Unwin, 1983.

———. *Gender and Power.* Stanford: Stanford University Press, 1987.

———. "An Iron Man: The Body and Some Contradictions of Hegemonic Masculinity." In M. A. Messner and D. F. Sabo, eds., *Sport, Men, and the Gender Order: Critical Feminist Perspectives,* pp. 83–96 . Champaign, Ill.: Human Kinetics Publishers, 1990.

———. "'A Whole New World': Remaking Masculinity in the Context of the Environmental Movement." *Gender and Society* 4 (1990): 452–78.

Cooley, C. H. *Life and the Student.* New York: Alfred A. Knopf, 1927.

Craib, I. "Masculinity and Male Dominance." *Sociological Review* 38 (1987): 721–43.

Crittenden, A. "Closing the Muscle Gap." In S. Twin, ed., *Out of the Bleachers: Writings on Women and Sport,* pp. 5–10. Old Westbury, N.Y.: Feminist Press, 1979.

Crossett, T. "Masculinity, Sexuality, and the Development of Early Modern Sport." In M. A. Messner and D. F. Sabo, eds., *Sport, Men, and the Gender Order: Critical Feminist Perspectives,* pp. 45–54. Champaign, Ill.: Human Kinetics Publishers, 1990.

Curry, T. J. "Fraternal Bonding in the Locker Room: A Profeminist Analysis of Talk about Competition and Women." *Sociology of Sport Journal* 8 (1991): 119–35.

Curtis, J. E., and J. W. Loy. "Positional Segregation in Professional Baseball: Replications, Trend Data, and Critical Observation." *International Review of Sport Sociology* 13: (1978): 5–21.

———. "Race/Ethnicity and Relative Centrality of Playing Positions in Team Sports." In R. S. Hutton, ed., *Exercise and Sport Sciences Review,* vol. 6, pp. 285–313. Philadelphia: Franklin Institute, 1979.

Davis, A. *Woman, Race, and Class.* New York: Vintage Books, 1981.

Davis, L. R. "The Articulation of Difference: White Preoccupation with the Question of Racially Linked Genetic Differences among Athletes." *Sociology of Sport Journal* 7 (1990): 179–87.

De Mondnard, J. P. "For and Against Doping and Its Controls: True and False Arguments." *Olympic Review* 180 (1982): 583–86.

Dinnerstein, D. *The Mermaid and the Minotaur: Sexual Arrangements and Human Malaise.* New York: Harper Colophon, 1976.

Duncan, M. C., and C. A. Hasbrook. "Denial of Power in Televised Women's Sports," *Sociology of Sport Journal* 5:(1988): 1–21.

Duncan, M. C., M. A. Messner, L. Williams, K. Jensen, and the Amateur Athletic Foundation of Los Angeles, *Gender Stereotyping in Televised Sports* (1990). AAF, 2141 West Adams Blvd., Los Angeles, Cal. 90018.

Duncan, M. C., M. A. Messner, L. Williams, and the Amateur Athletic Foundation of Los Angeles. *Coverage of Women's Sports in Four Daily Newspapers* (1991). AAF, 2141 West Adams Blvd., Los Angeles, Cal. 90018.

Duncan, M. C. and Sayaovong. "Photographic Images and Gender in *Sports Illustrated for Kids*." *Play and Culture* 3 (1990): 91–116.

Dunkle, M. "Minority and Low-Income Girls and Young Women in Athletics." *Equal Play* 5 (1985): 12–13.

Dunning, E. "Sport as a Male Preserve: Notes on the Social Sources of Masculine Identity and Its Transformations," *Theory Culture and Society* 3 (1986): 79–90.

Duquin, M. E. "The Androgynous Advantage." In C. A. Oglesby, ed., *Women and Sport: From Myth to Reality.* Philadelphia: Lea and Farber, 1978.

———. "Power and Authority: Moral Consensus and Conformity in Sport." *International Review for Sociology of Sport* 19 (1984): 295–304.

Dyer, K. *Challenging the Men: The Social Biology of Female Sport Achievement.* St. Lucia: University of Queensland, 1983.

Eastman, S. T., and T. P. Meyter. "Sports Programming: Scheduling, Costs, and Competition." In L. A. Wenner, ed. *Media, Sports, and Society.* Newbury Park: Sage, 1989.

Edwards, H. *The Revolt of the Black Athlete.* New York: The Free Press, 1969.

———. *Sociology of Sport.* Homewood, Ill.: Dorsey, 1973.

———. *The Struggle that Must Be.* New York: Macmillan, 1980.

———. "The Collegiate Athletic Arms Race: Origins and Implications of the 'Rule 48' Controversy." *Journal of Sport and Social Issues* 8 (1984): 4–22.

Edwards, T. "Beyond Sex and Gender: Masculinity, Homosexuality and Social Theory." In J. Hearn and D. Morgan eds., *Men, Masculinities and Social Theory.* London: Unwin Hyman, 1990.

Ehrenreich, B. *The Hearts of Men*. Garden City, N.Y.: Anchor Press/Doubleday, 1983.

Eitzen, D. S. "Athletics in the Status System of Male Adolescents: A Replication of Coleman's *The Adolescent Society.*" *Adolescence* 10 (1975): 268–76.

Eitzen, D. S., and G. H. Sage. "Racism in Sports." In D. S. Eitzen and G. H. Sage, eds., *Sociology of American Sport*. Dubuque: Brown, 1978.

Eitzen, D. S. and N. R. Yetman. "Racial Dynamics in American Sports: Continuity and Change." In R. M. Pankin, ed., *Social Approaches to Sport*. Rutherford: Farleigh-Dickenson University Press, 1982.

Farr, K. A. "Dominance Bonding through the Good Old Boys Sociability Group." *Sex Roles* 18 (1988): 259–77.

Farrell, M. P., and S. D. Rosenberg. *Men at Midlife*. Boston: Auburn House, 1981.

Farrell, W. *The Liberated Man*. New York: Bantam Books, 1975.

Fasteau, M-F. *The Male Machine*. New York: McGraw-Hill, 1974.

Fausto-Sterling, A. *Myths of Gender: Biological Theories about Men and Women*. New York: Basic Books, 1985.

Filene, P. *Him/Her/Self: Sex Roles in Modern America*. New York: Harcourt Brace Jovanovich, 1975.

Fine, G. A. *With the Boys: Little League Baseball and Preadolescent Culture*. Chicago: University of Chicago Press, 1987.

Flax, J. "Political Philosophy and the Patriarchal Unconscious: A Psychoanalytic Perspective on Epistemology and Metaphysics." In S. Harding and M. B. Hintikka, eds., *Discovering Reality: Feminist Perspectives on Epistemology, Metaphysics, Methodology, and Philosophy of Science*. Boston: D. Reidel, 1983.

Foley, D. E. "The Great American Football Ritual: Reproducing Race, Class, and Gender Inequality." *Sociology of Sport Journal* 7 (1990): 111–35.

Franklin, C. W. "Surviving the Institutional Decimation of Black Males: Causes, Consequences, and Intervention." In H. Brod, ed., *The Making of Masculinities: The New Men's Studies*, pp. 155–70. Winchester, Mass.: Allen and Unwin, 1987.

Frye, M. "The Possibility of Feminist Theory." In D. L. Rhode, ed., *Theoretical Differences on Sexual Difference*. New Haven: Yale University Press, 1990.

Fuller, J. R., and M. J. LaFountain. "Illegal Steroid Use among Fifty Weightlifters." *Sociology and Social Research* 73 (1988): 19–21.

Gallmeier, C. P. "Putting on the Game Face: The Staging of Emotions in Professional Hockey." *Sociology of Sport Journal* 4 (1987): 347–62.

———. "Juicing, Burning, and Tooting: Observing Drug Use among Professional Hockey Players." *Arena Review* 12 (1988): 1–12.

Gardiner, J. "Women's Domestic Labor." In Z. R. Eisenstein, ed., *Capitalist Patriarchy and the Case for Socialist Feminism*, pp. 173–89. New York: Monthly Review Press, 1979.

Gilder, G. *Sexual Suicide*. New York: Bantam Books, 1973.

Gilligan, C. *In a Different Voice: Psychological Theory and Women's Development*. Cambridge: Harvard University Press, 1982.

Glassner, B. *Bodies: Why We Look the Way We Do (and How We Feel about It)*. New York: G. P. Putnam's Sons, 1988.

Goldberg, H. *The Hazards of Being Male: Surviving the Myth of Masculine Privilege*. New York: Signet, 1976.

Goldman, R. "We Make Weekends: Leisure and the Commodity Form." *Social Text* 8 (1983/84): 84–103.

Goldstein, J. H. and B. J. Bredemeier "Socialization: Some Basic Issues," *Journal of Communication* 27 (1977): 154–59.

Gordon, M. *Assimilation in American Life*. New York: Oxford University Press, 1964.

Gorn, E. J. *The Manly Art: Bare-Knuckle Prize Fighting in America*. Ithaca: Cornell University Press, 1986.

Greenberg, D. F. *The Construction of Homosexuality*. Chicago: University of Chicago Press, 1988.

Greendorfer, S. "The Role of Socializing Agents in Female Sport Involvement." *Research Quarterly* 48 (1977): 304–310.

Gruneau, R. *Class, Sports, and Social Development*. Amherst: University of Massachusetts Press, 1983.

Gustkey, E. "Eighty Years Ago, the Truth Hurt." *Los Angeles Times*, July 8, 1990, p. CI.

Halberstam, D. *The Breaks of the Game*. New York: Ballentine Books, 1981.

Hall, M. A. "A 'Feminine Woman' and an 'Athletic Woman' as Viewed by Female Participants and Non-Participants in Sport." *British Journal of Physical Education* 3, (1972).

——. *Sport and Gender: A Feminist Perspective on the Sociology of Sport*. Sociology of Sport Monograph Series. Ottawa: Canadian Association of Health, Physical Education, and Recreation, 1978.

——., ed. "The Gendering of Sport, Leisure, and Physical Education." A special issue of *Women's Studies International Forum* 10, no. 4: (1987).

Hantover, J. "The Boy Scouts and the Validation of Masculinity." *Journal of Social Issues* 34 (1978): 184–95.

Harding, S. "What Is the Real Material Base of Patriarchy and Capital?" In L. Sargent, ed., *Women and Revolution*. Boston: South End Press, 1981.

————. *The Science Question in Feminism*. Ithaca: Cornell University Press, 1986.

Hargreaves, Je. "Where's the Virtue? Where's the Grace? A Discussion of the Social Production of Gender through Sport." *Theory Culture & Society* 3 (1986): 109–21.

————., ed. *Sport, Culture, and Ideology*. London: Routledge and Kegan Paul, 1982.

Hargreaves, Jo. *Sport, Power, and Culture: A Social and Historical Analysis of Sports in Britain*. New York: St. Martin's Press, 1986.

Harris, D. S., and D. S. Eitzen, "The Consequences of Failure in Sport." *Urban Life* 7 (1978): 177–88.

Harris, D. V. *Women and Sport: A National Research Conference*. Proceedings from the National Research Conference, Women and Sport, Penn State HPER Series 2, Pennsylvania State University, August 13–18, 1972.

Harrison, J., J. Chin, and T. Ficarrotto. "Warning: Masculinity May Be Dangerous to Your Health." In M. S. Kimmel and M. A. Messner, eds., *Men's Lives*, pp. 296–311. New York: Macmillan, 1989.

Hartmann, H. "Capitalism, Patriarchy, and Job Segregation." *Signs* 1 (1976): 137–69.

————. "The Family as the Locus of Gender, Class, and Political Struggle: The Case of Housework." *Signs* 6 (1981): 366–94.

Hartsock, N. C. M. "The Feminist Standpoint: Developing the Ground for a Specifically Feminist Historical Materialism." In S. Harding and M. B. Hintikka, eds., *Discovering Reality: Feminist Perspectives on Epistemology, Metaphysics, Methodology, and Philosophy of Science*, pp. 283–310. Boston: D. Reidel, 1983.

Haug, F. *Female Sexualization*. London: Verso Books, 1987.

Henley, N. M. *Body Politics: Power, Sex, and Nonverbal Communication*. Englewood Cliffs, N.J.: Prentice-Hall, 1977.

Herman, D. "The Rape Culture." In J. Freeman, ed., *Women: A Feminist Perspective*, 3rd ed., pp. 20–38. Mountain View, Cal.: Mayfield, 1984.

Hertz, R. *More Equal Than Others: Women and Men in Dual-Career Marriages*. Berkeley: University of California Press, 1986.

Hill, P., and B. Lowe. "The Inevitable Metathesis of the Retiring Athlete." *International Review of Sport Sociology* 9 (1979): 5–32.

Hoberman, J. M. "Sport and the Technological Image of Man." In W. J. Morgan and K. V. Meier, eds., *Philosophic Inquiry in Sport*, pp. 319–28. Champaign, Ill.: Human Kinetics Publishers, 1988.

Hoch, P. *Rip off the Big Game*. Garden City, N.Y.: Doubleday, 1972.

Hochschild, A. R. "Emotion Work, Feeling Rules, and Social Structure." *American Journal of Sociology* 85 (1979): 551–75.

———. *The Managed Heart: Commercialization and Human Feeling*. Berkeley: University of California Press, 1983.

———. *The Second Shift: Working Parents and the Revolution at Home*. New York: Viking Press, 1989.

Hoffman, C. D., S. E. Tsuneyoshi, M. Ebina, and H. Fite. "A Comparison of Adult Males' and Females' Interactions with Girls and Boys." *Sex Roles* 11 (1984): 799–811.

Hoffman, L. W. "Changes in Family Roles, Socialization, and Sex Differences." *American Psychologist* 32 (1977): 644–57.

Hooks, B. *Feminist Theory: From Margin to Center*. Boston: South End Press, 1984.

Hout, M. "Occupational Mobility of Black Men." *American Sociological Review* 49 (1984): 308–22.

Huizingo, J. *Homo Ludens: A Study of the Play Element in Culture*. Boston: Beacon Press, 1955.

Humberstone, B. "Warriors or Wimps? Creating Alternative Forms of Physical Education." In M. A. Messner and D. F. Sabo, eds., *Sport, Men, and the Gender Order: Critical Feminist Perspectives*. Champaign, Ill.: Human Kinetics Publishers, 1990.

Jackson, D. Z. "Calling the Plays in Black and White." *Boston Globe*, January 22, 1989, p. A30.

James, C. R. L. *Beyond a Boundary*. New York: Pantheon Books, 1983.

Jeffords, S. *The Remasculinization of America: Gender and the Vietnam War*. Bloomington: Indiana University Press, 1989.

Jencks, C. *Inequality*. New York: Harper Colophon, 1972.

Johnson, M. M. *Strong Mothers, Weak Wives*. Berkeley: University of California Press, 1988.

Johnson, W. O. "Take a Bow! Give South Korea Kudos for the Summer Games." *Sports Illustrated*, October 10, 1988, pp. 36–43.

Jourard, S. M. "Some Lethal Aspects of the Male Role." In J. H. Pleck and J. Sawyer, eds., *Men and Masculinity*, pp. 21–29. Englewood Cliffs, N.J.: Prentice-Hall, 1974.

Julty, S. "Men and Their Health: A Strained Alliance." *M: Gentle Men for Gender Justice* 7 (1981–82): 5–6.

Kanin, E. J. "Date Rape: Differential Sexual Socialization and Relative Deprivation." *Victimology* 9 (1984): 95–108.

Kann, M. E. "The Costs of Being on Top." *Journal of the National Association for Women Deans, Administrators, and Counselors* 49 (1986): 29–37.

Kaufman, M. "The Construction of Masculinity and the Triad of Men's Violence." In M. Kaufman, ed., *Beyond Patriarchy: Essays by Men on Pleasure, Power, and Change*, pp. 1–29. Toronto: Oxford University Press, 1987.

Kidd, B. "The Myth of the Ancient Olympic Games." In A. Tomlinson and G. Whannel, eds., *Five Ring Circus: Money, Power, and Politics at the Olympic Games*. London: Pluto, 1984.

———. "Sports and Masculinity." In M. Kaufman, ed., *Beyond Patriarchy: Essays by Men on Pleasure, Power, and Change*, pp. 250–65. Toronto: Oxford University Press, 1987.

———. "The Men's Cultural Centre: Sports and the Dynamic of Women's Oppression/Men's Repression." In M. A. Messner and D. F. Sabo, eds., *Sport, Men, and the Gender Order: Critical Feminist Perspectives*, pp. 31–44. Champaign, Ill.: Human Kinetics Publishers, 1990.

Kiersh, E. *Where Have You Gone, Vince DiMaggio?* New York: A Bantam Book, 1983.

Kimmel, M. S. "Men's Responses to Feminism at the Turn of the Century." *Gender and Society* 1 (1987): 517–30.

———. "Baseball and the Reconstitution of American Masculinity, 1880–1920." In M. A. Messner and D. F. Sabo, eds., *Sport, Men, and the Gender Order: Critical Feminist Perspectives*. Champaign, Ill.: Human Kinetics Publishers, 1990.

———., ed. *Changing Men: New Directions in Research on Men and Masculinity*. Beverly Hills: Sage, 1987.

Kimmel, M. S. and M. A. Messner, eds. *Men's Lives*. New York: Macmillan, 1989.

King, P. "Curtain Call." *Sports Illustrated*, October 15, 1990, p. 38.

Klein, A. M. "Little Big Man: Hustling, Gender Narcissism, and Homophobia in Bodybuilding." In M. A. Messner and D. F. Sabo, eds., *Sport, Men, and the Gender Order: Critical Feminist Perspectives*, pp. 127–40. Champaign, Ill.: Human Kinetics Publishers, 1990.

Kleinberg, S. "The New Masculinity of Gay Men, and Beyond." In M. Kaufman, ed., *Beyond Patriarchy: Essays by Men on Pleasure, Power, and Change*, pp. 120–38. Toronto: Oxford University Press, 1987.

Knoppers, A.; B. B. Meyer, M. Ewing, and L. Forrest, "Gender and the Salaries of Coaches." *Sociology of Sport Journal* 6 (1989): 348–61.

Komisar, L. "Violence and the Masculine Mystique." In D. Sabo and R. Runfola, eds., *Jock: Sports and Male Identity*, pp. 131–57. Englewood Cliffs, N.J.: Prentice-Hall, 1980.

Kopay, D. and P. D. Young. *The Dave Kopay Story*. New York: Arbor House, 1977.

Koss, M. P., and T. E. Dinero. "Predictors of Sexual Aggression among a National Sample of Male College Students." in R. A. Prentky and V. Quinsey, eds., *Human Sexual Aggression: Current Perspectives. Annals of the New York Academy of Sciences* 528 (1988): 133–46.

Lasch, C. *The Culture of Narcissism*. New York: Warner Books, 1979.

Lefkowitz-Horowitz, H. "Before Title IX." Paper presented at Stanford Humanities Center Sport and Culture Meetings, April 1986.

————. *Campus Life: Undergraduate Cultures from the End of the Eighteenth Century to the Present.* New York: Alfred A. Knopf, 1987.

Lee, R., and R. Daly. "Man's Domination and Woman's Oppression: The Question of Origins." In M. Kaufman, ed., *Beyond Patriarchy: Essays by Men on Pleasure, Power, and Change,* pp. 30–44. Toronto: Oxford University Press, 1987.

Lehne, G. K. "Homophobia among Men: Supporting and Defining the Male Role." In M. S. Kimmel and M. A. Messner, eds., *Men's Lives,* pp. 416–29. New York: Macmillan, 1989.

Leiber, J. "No Bones about It." *Sports Illustrated,* August 19, 1989, p. 54.

Lenskyj, H. *Out of Bounds: Women, Sport, and Sexuality.* Toronto: The Women's Press, 1986.

Leonard, G. B. "Winning Isn't Everything: It's Nothing," In D. F. Sabo and R. Runfola, eds., *Jock: Sports and Male Identity,* pp. 259–66. Englewood Cliffs, NJ: Prentice-Hall, 1980.

Leonard, W. M., and J. M. Reyman. "The Odds of Attaining Professional Athlete Status: Redefining the Computations." *Sociology of Sport Journal* 5 (1988): 162–69.

Lerch, S. "Athletic Retirement as Social Death: An Overview," In N. Theberge and P. Donnelly, eds., *Sport and the Sociological Imagination,* pp. 259–72. Fort Worth: Texas Christian University Press, 1984.

Lever, J. "Sex Differences in the Games Children Play." *Social Problems* 23 (1976): 478–87.

Lever, J. "Sex Differences in the Complexity of Children's Play and Games." *American Sociological Review* 43 (1978): 471–83.

Levinson, D. J., C. N. Darrow, E. B. Klein, M. H. Levinson, and B. McKee. *The Seasons of a Man's Life.* New York: Ballantine Books, 1978.

Lorenz, K. *On Aggression.* New York: Harcourt Brace Jovanovich, 1966.

Loy, J. W. Jr., and J. F. McElvogue. "Racial Segregation in American Sport." *International Review of Sport Sociology* 5 (1970): 5–23.

Lyman, P. "The Fraternal Bond as a Joking Relationship: A Case Study of Sexist Jokes in Male Group Bonding." In M. S. Kimmel, ed., *Changing Men: New Directions in Research on Men and Masculinity,* pp. 148–63. Newbury Park: Sage, 1987.

Macleod, D. *Building Character in the American Boy: The Boy Scouts, YMCA, and Their Forerunners, 1870–1920.* Madison: University of Wisconsin Press, 1983.

Majors, R. "Cool Pose: The Proud Signature of Black Survival." *Changing Men: Issues in Gender, Sex, and Politics* 17 (1986): 5–6.

————. "Cool Pose: Black Masculinity and Sports." In M. A. Messner and D. F. Sabo, *Sport, Men, and the Gender Order: Critical Feminist Perspectives*, pp. 109–14. Champaign, Ill.: Human Kinetics Publishers, 1990.

Mangan, J. A. *The Games Ethic and Imperialism: Aspects of the Diffusion of an Ideal.* New York: Viking Penguin, 1986.

Martin, P. Y., and R. A. Hummer. "Fraternities and Rape on Campus." *Gender and Society* 3 (1989): 457–73.

McCormack, T. "Hollywood's Prizefight Films: Violence or 'Jock Appeal'?" *Journal of Sport and Social Issues* 8 (1984): 19–29.

McHugh, M. C., M. E. Duquin, and I. H. Frieze. "Beliefs about Success and Failure: Attribution and the Female Athlete." In C. A. Oglesby, ed., *Women and Sport: From Myth to Reality*, pp. 173–91. Philadelphia: Lea and Farber, 1978.

McPherson, B. D. "Former Professional Athletes' Adjustment to Retirement." *The Physician and Sports Medicine* (August 1978): pp. 52–58.

Meggyesy, D. *Out of Their League.* Berkeley: Ramparts Press, 1970.

Messner, M. A. "Gay Athletes and the Gay Games: An Interview with Tom Waddell." *M: Gentle Men for Gender Justice* 13 (1984): 13–14.

————. "The Life of a Man's Seasons: Male Identity in the Lifecourse of the Athlete." In M. S. Kimmel, ed., *Changing Men: New Directions in Research on Men and Masculinity*, pp. 53–67. Beverly Hills: Sage, 1987.

————. "The Meaning of Success: The Athletic Experience and the Development of Male Identity." In H. Brod, ed., *The Making of Masculinities: The New Men's Studies*, pp. 193–209. Winchester, Mass.: Allen and Unwin, 1987.

————. "Sports and Male Domination: The Female Athlete as Contested Ideological Terrain." *Sociology of Sport Journal* 5 (1988): 197–211.

————. "Men Studying Masculinity: Some Epistemological Questions in Sport Sociology." *Sociology of Sport Journal* 7: (1990): 136–53.

Messner, M. A., M. C. Duncan, and K. Jensen. "Separating the Men from the Girls: The Gendered Language of Televised Sports." *Gender and Society* (forthcoming).

Messner, M. A., and D. F. Sabo. "Toward a Critical Feminist Reappraisal of Sport, Men, and the Gender Order." In M. A. Messner and D. F. Sabo, eds., *Sport, Men, and the Gender Order: Critical Feminist Perspectives*, pp. 1–18. Champaign, Ill.: Human Kinetics Publishers, 1990.

Michelson, H. *Almost a Famous Person.* New York: Harcourt Brace Jovanovich, 1980.

Mills, C. W. *The Sociological Imagination.* London: Oxford University Press, 1959.

Mishkind, M. E., J. Rodin, L. R., Silberstein, and R. H. Streigel-Moore. "The Embodiment of Masculinity: Cultural, Psychological, and Behavioral Dimensions." *American Behavioral Scientist* 29 (1986): 545–62.

Moore, R. A. *Sports and Mental Health*. Springfield, Ill.: Charles C. Thomas, 1966.

Morin, S. F. and E. M. Garfinkel. "Male Homophobia." *Journal of Social Issues* 34 (1978): 29–47.

Morse, M. "Sport on Television: Replay and Display." In E. A. Kaplan, ed., *Regarding Television: Critical Approaches*, pp. 44–66. Los Angeles: University Publications of America, 1983.

Mrozek, D. J. *Sport and the American Mentality, 1880–1910*. Knoxville: University of Tennessee Press, 1983.

Mugno, D. A., and D. L. Felz. "The Social Learning of Aggression in Youth Football in the United States." *Canadian Journal of Applied Sport Sciences* 10 (1985): 26–35.

Mummendey, A., and H. D. Mummendey. "Aggressive Behavior of Soccer Players as Social Interaction." In J. H. Goldstein, ed., *Sports Violence*, pp. 111–28. New York: Springer-Verlag, 1983.

Naison, P. "Sports, Women, and the Ideology of Domination." *Radical America*, July-August 1972, p. 95.

Nash, J. E., and E. Lerner. "Learning from the Pros: Violence in Youth Hockey." *Youth and Society* 13 (1981): 112–23.

Neff, C. "Return of the Hero." *Sports Illustrated*, October 10, 1988, pp. 62–63.

Nichols, J. *Men's Liberation: A New Definition of Masculinity*. New York: Penguin Books, 1975.

Oakley, A. "Interviewing Women: A Contradiction in Terms." In H. Roberts, ed., *Doing Feminist Research*. London: Routledge and Kegan and Paul, 1981.

Oglesby, C. A. *Women and Sport: From Myth to Reality*. Philadelphia: Lea and Farber, 1978.

Oliver, C. *High for the Game*. New York: Morrow, 1971.

Osherson, S. *Finding Our Fathers: How a Man's Life Is Shaped by His Relationship with His Father*. New York: Fawcett Columbine, 1986.

Parke, R. D., and B. R. Tinsley, "The Father's Role in Infancy: Determinants of Involvement in Caregiving and Play." In M. E. Lamb, ed., *The Role of the Father in Child Development*, 2d ed. New York: John Wiley, 1981.

Phillips, J. C. "Toward an Explanation of Racial Variations in Top Level Sports Participation." *International Review of Sport Sociology* 11 (1976): 39–55.

Petersen, F. A. and K. S. Robson. "Father Participation in Infancy." *American Journal of Orthopsychiatry* 39 (1969): 466–72.

Piaget, J. H. *The Moral Judgment of the Child*. New York: Free Press, 1965.

Pleck, J. H. "Men's Power with Women, Other Men, and in Society." In E. H. Pleck and J. H. Pleck, eds., *The American Man*, pp. 417–33. Englewood Cliffs, N.J.: Prentice-Hall, 1980.

———. *The Myth of Masculinity.* Cambridge: MIT Press, 1982.

Pleck, J. H., and J. Sawyer, eds. *Men and Masculinity.* Englewood Cliffs, N.J.: Prentice-Hall, 1974.

Pollack, S., and C. Gilligan. "Images of Violence in Thematic Apperception Test Stories." *Journal of Personality and Social Psychology* 42 (1982): 159–67.

Pronger, B. *The Arena of Masculinity: Sports, Homosexuality, and the Meaning of Sex.* New York: St. Martin's Press, 1990.

———. "Gay Jocks: A Phenomenology of Gay Men in Athletics." In M. A. Messner and D. F. Sabo, eds., *Sport, Men and the Gender Order: Critical Feminist Perspectives*, pp. 141–52. Champaign, Ill.: Human Kinetics Publishers, 1990.

Purdy, D. A., D. S. Eitzen and R. Hufnagel. "Are Athletes Also Students? The Educational Attainment of College Athletes." *Social Problems* 29 (1984): 439–448.

Rainville, R. E., and E. McCormick, "Extent of Covert Prejudice in Pro Football Announcers' Speech." *Journalism Quarterly* 54 (1977): 20–26.

Ransford, E. H. *Race and Class in American Society: Black, Chicano, Anglo.* Cambridge: Schenkman, 1977.

Ransford, E. H., and J. Miller. "Race, Sex, and Feminist Outlooks." *American Sociological Review* 48 (1983): 46–59.

Raphael, R. *The Men from the Boys: Rites of Passage in Male America.* Lincoln: University of Nebraska Press, 1988.

Rebelsky, F. and C. Hanks. "Fathers' Verbal Interaction with Infants in the First Three Months of Life." *Child Development* 42 (1971): 63–68.

Rigauer, B. *Sport and Work.* New York: Columbia University Press, 1981.

Riesman, D. *The Lonely Crowd: A Study of the Changing American Character.* New Haven: Yale University Press, 1953.

Rintala, J., and S. Birrell, "Fair Treatment for the Active Female: A Content Analysis of *Young Athlete* Magazine." *Sociology of Sport Journal* 1 (1984): 231–50.

Rosaldo, M. Z. "Woman, Culture, and Society: A Theoretical Overview." In M. Z. Rosaldo and L. Lamphere, eds., *Woman, Culture, and Society*, pp. 17–42. Stanford: Stanford University Press, 1974.

Rotundo, E. A. "Body and Soul: Changing Ideals of American Middle Class Manhood, 1770–1920." *Journal of Social History* 16 (1983): 23–38.

Rubin, L. B. *Worlds of Pain: Life in the Working Class Family.* New York: Basic Books, 1976.

———. *Intimate Strangers: Men and Women Together.* New York: Harper and Row, 1983.

———. *Just Friends: The Role of Friendship in Our Lives.* New York: Harper and Row, 1985.

Rubin, Z. "Fathers and Sons: The Search for Reunion." *Psychology Today,* June 1982, p. 23.

Rudman, L. B. "The Sport Mystique in Black Culture." *Sociology of Sport Journal* 3 (1986): 305–319.

Sabo, D. F. "Sport, Patriarchy, and Male Identity: New Questions about Men and Sport." *Arena Review* 9 (1985): 1–30.

———. "Pigskin, Patriarchy and Pain." *Changing Men: Issues in Gender, Sex, and Politics* 16 (1986): 24–25.

———. "Title IX and Athletics: Sex Equity in Schools." *Updating School Board Policies* 19 (1988): 1–3.

———. "The Myth of the Sexual Athlete." *Changing Men: Issues in Gender, Sex, and Politics* 20 (1989): 38–39.

Sabo, D. F., and J. Panepinto. "Football Ritual and the Social Production of Masculinity." In M. A. Messner and D. F. Sabo, eds., *Sport, Men, and the Gender Order: Critical Feminist Perspectives,* pp. 115–26. Champaign, Ill.: Human Kinetics Publishers, 1990.

Sabo, D. F., and R. Runfola. *Jock: Sports and Male Identity.* Englewood Cliffs, N.J.: Prentice-Hall, 1980.

Sabo, D. F., and the Women's Sports Foundation. *The Women's Sports Foundation Report: Minorities in Sports.* New York: Women's Sports Foundation, August 15, 1989.

Sage, G. H. *Power and Ideology in American Sport: A Critical Perspective.* Champaign, Ill.: Human Kinetics Publishers, 1990.

Schafer, W. E. "Sport and Male Sex Role Socialization." *Sport Sociology Bulletin* 4 (1975): 47–54.

Scher, M., and M. Stevens. "Men and Violence." *Journal of Counseling and Development* 65 (1987): 351–355.

Schneider, J., and D. S. Eitzen. "The Structure of Sport and Participant Violence." *Arena Review* 7 (1983): 1–16.

Scott, J. *The Athletic Revolution.* London: Free Press, 1971.

———. "A Radical Ethic for Sports." *Intellectual Digest,* 2 (1972.)

Segal, L. *Slow Motion: Changing Masculinities, Changing Men.* New Brunswick, N.J.: Rutgers University Press, 1990.

Sennett, R., and J. Cobb. *The Hidden Injuries of Class.* New York: Random House, 1973.

Sewart, J. J. "The Commodification of Sport." *International Journal for Sociology of Sport* 22 (1987): 171–91.

Sharistanian, J., ed. *Beyond the Public/Domestic Dichotomy: Contemporary Perspectives on Women's Public Lives.* New York: Greenwood Press, 1987.

Shear, M. D. "Pro Football Players Testify against Steroid Use." *Los Angeles Times*, May 10, 1989, sec. 3, p. 3.

Sidel, R. *Women and Children Last: The Plight of Poor Women in Affluent America.* New York: Viking Penguin, 1986.

Smith, M. D. "Significant Others Influence on the Assaultive Behavior of Young Hockey Players." *International Review of Sport Sociology* 3/4 (1974): 217–27.

Smith, R. A. "The Rise of Basketball for Women in College." *Canadian Journal of History of Sport and Physical Education* 1 (1970): 21–23.

Smith-Rosenberg, C. *Disorderly Conduct: Visions of Gender in Victorian America.* New York: Oxford University Press, 1985.

Spender, D., ed. *Men's Studies Modified: The Impact of Feminism on the Academic Disciplines.* Oxford: Pergamon Press, 1981.

Stacey, J. "Can There Be a Feminist Ethnography?" *Women's Studies International Forum* 11 (1988): 21–27.

Stacey, J., and B. Thorne. "The Missing Feminist Revolution in Sociology." *Social Problems* 32 (1985): 301–16.

Staples, R. *Black Masculinity.* San Francisco: Black Scholar Press, 1982.

Stuck, M. F., ed., "Drugs and Sport." A special issue of *Arena Review* 12, no. 1, 1988.

Summerfield, D., and A. White. "Korfball: A Model of Egalitarianism?" *Sociology of Sport Journal* 6 (1989): 144–51.

Swain, S. "Covert Intimacy: Closeness in Men's Friendships." In B. J. Risman and P. Schwartz, eds., *Gender in Intimate Relationships: A Microstructural Approach*, pp. 71–86. Belmont, Cal.: Wadsworth, 1989.

Tatum, J. *They Call Me Assassin.* New York: Doubleday, 1972.

Taylor, I. "On the Sports Violence Question: Soccer Hooliganism Revisited." In Je. Hargreaves, ed., *Sport, Culture, and Ideology*, pp. 152–96. London: Routledge and Kegan Paul, 1982.

Terkel, S. *Working.* New York: Avon Books, 1975.

Tevlin, J. "Of Hawks and Men: A Weekend in the Male Wilderness." In *Utne Reader*, November/December 1989, pp. 50–59.

Theberge, N. "A Critique of Critiques: Radical and Feminist Writings on Sport." *Social Forces* 60 (1981): 341–53.

———. "Sport and Women's Empowerment." *Women's Studies International Forum* 10 (1987): 387–94.

———. "Women's Athletics and the Myth of Female Frailty." In J. Freeman, ed., *Women: A Feminist Perspective*, pp. 507–22. Mountain View, Cal.: Mayfield, 1989.

————. "Gender, Work, and Power: The Case of Women in Coaching." *Canadian Journal of Sociology* 15 (1990): 59–75.

Theberge, N., and A. Cronk. "Work Routines in Newspaper Sports Departments and the Coverage of Women's Sports." *Sociology of Sport Journal* 3 (1986): 195–203.

Thirer, J., and S. D. Wright. "Sport and Social Status for Adolescent Males and Females." *Sociology of Sport Journal* 2 (1985): 164–71.

Thorne, B. "Girls and Boys Together . . . But Mostly Apart: Gender Arrangements in Elementary Schools." In W. W. Hartup and Z. Rubin, eds., *Relationships and Development*, pp. 167–84. Hillsdale, N.J.: Lawrence Earlbaum, 1986.

————. "Children and Gender: Constructions of Difference." In D. L. Rhode, ed., *Theoretical Perspectives on Sexual Difference*, pp. 100–113. New Haven: Yale University Press, 1990.

Thorne, B., and Z. Luria "Sexuality and Gender in Children's Daily Worlds." *Social Problems* 33 (1986): 176–90.

Tolson, A. *The Limits of Masculinity: Male Identity and Women's Liberation.* New York: Harper and Row, 1977.

Tosches, R. "Steroid Report a Revelation to CIF Hierarchy." *Los Angeles Times,* January 1, 1989, p. 18.

Townsend, R. C. "The Competitive Male as Loser." In D. F. Sabo and R. Runfola, eds., *Jock: Sports and Male Identity,* pp. 266–79. Englewood Cliffs, N.J.: Prentice-Hall, 1980.

Tutko, T., and W. Bruns. *Winning Is Everything and Other American Myths.* New York: Macmillan, 1976.

Twin, S. L., ed. *Out of the Bleachers: Writings on Women and Sport.* Old Westbury, N.Y.: Feminist Press, 1979.

Tygiel, J. *Baseball's Great Experiment: Jackie Robinson and His Legacy.* New York: Vintage Books, 1984.

Uhler, G. A. "Athletics and the University: The Post-Woman's Era." *Adademe* 73 (1987): 25–29.

Unbecoming Men. Washington, N.J.: Times Change Press, 1971.

Underwood, J. *The Death of an American Game.* Boston: Little, Brown, 1979.

Updike, J. *Rabbit Run.* New York: Fawcett Crest, 1970.

Vaz, E. W. "The Culture of Young Hockey Players: Some Initial Observations." In D. F. Sabo and R. Runfola, eds., *Jock: Sports and Male Identity,* pp. 142–57. Englewood Cliffs, N.J.: Prentice-Hall, 1980.

Warshaw, R. *I Never Called It Rape.* New York: Harper and Row, 1988.

Weeks, J. *Sexuality and Its Discontents: Meanings, Myths, and Modern Sexualities.* London: Routledge and Kegan Paul, 1985.

White, P. G., and A. B. Vagi. "Rugby in the Nineteenth Century British Boarding School System: A Feminist Psychoanalytic Perspective." In M. A. Messner and D. F. Sabo, eds., *Sport, Men, and the Gender Order: Critical Feminist Perspectives.* Champaign, Ill.: Human Kinetics Publishers, 1990.

Whitson, D. "Sport and the Social Construction of Masculinity," In M. A. Messner and D. F. Sabo, eds., *Sport, Men, and the Gender Order: Critical Feminist Perspectives.* Champaign, Ill.: Human Kinetics Publishers, 1990.

Whitson, D., and D. Macintosh. "Gender and Power: Explanations of Gender Inequalities in Canadian National Sport Organizations." *International Review for the Sociology of Sport* 24 (1989): 137–50.

Wiggins, D. K. "Great Speed But Little Stamina: The Historical Debate Over Black Athletic Superiority." *Journal of Sport History* 16 (1989): 158–85.

Williams, C. L. *Gender Differences at Work: Women and Men in Nontraditional Occupations.* Berkeley: University of California Press, 1989.

Williams, W. L. *The Spirit and the Flesh: Sexual Diversity in American Indian Culture.* Boston: Beacon Press, 1986.

Willis, P. *Learning to Labor: How Working Class Kids Get Working Class Jobs.* New York: Columbia University Press, 1977.

———. "Women in Sport in Ideology." In Je. Hargreaves, ed., *Sport, Culture, and Ideology,* pp. 117–35. London: Routledge and Kegan Paul, 1982.

Wilson, W. J. *The Declining Significance of Race: Blacks and Changing American Institutions.* Chicago: University of Chicago Press, 1978.

Wilson, W. J., and K. M. Neckerman. "Poverty and Family Structure: The Widening Gap between Evidence and Public Policy Issues." In S. H. Danzinger and D. H. Weinberg, eds., *Fighting Poverty,* pp. 232–59. Cambridge: Harvard University Press, 1986.

Wilson Sporting Goods Co. and the Women's Sports Foundation. *The Wilson Report: Moms, Dads, Daughters and Sports.* New York, 1988.

Winter, M. F., and E. R. Robert. "Male Dominance, Late Capitalism, and the Growth of Instrumental Reason." *Berkeley Journal of Sociology* 25 (1980): 249–80.

Wojciechowski, G., and C. Dufresne. "Football Career Is Taking Its Toll on NFL's Players." *Los Angeles Times,* June 26, 1988, sec. 3, p. 1.

Young, I. M. "Is Male Gender Identity the Cause of Male Domination?" In J. Trebilcot. ed., *Mothering: Essays in Feminist Theory,* pp. 129–46. Roman and Allanheld, 1983.

Zaretsky. E. *Capitalism, the Family, and Personal Life.* New York: Harper Colophon, 1973.

Zussman, R. "Work and Family in the New Middle Class." In N. Gerstel and H. Gross, eds., *Family and Work,* pp. 338–46. Philadelphia: Temple University Press, 1987.

Index

Adam A., 31, 49, 160–61
Adler, Patricia, 50–51, 54
Adler, Peter, 50–51, 54
Aggression, *see* Violence
Alcohol, 80–81; abuse of, 124–25
Altman, Dennis, 154
American Medical Association, 16
Amphetamines, 77–78
Antagonistic cooperation, 88–91, 106
Athletic embodiments, and race and
    social class, 81–84
Atlanta Falcons, 86
Atyeo, Don, 80

Barry B., 61–62, 71, 73, 75, 125, 127–
    28
Baseball: serious injuries in, 75–76;
    violence in, 70
Bill S., 26, 83, 96–97, 162, 163; knee
    injury of, 72–73
Bissinger, H. G., *Friday Night Lights*,
    108
Blacks, 11–12, 34, 82; and class differ-
    ences and early commitments to
    sport, 37–38; "cool pose" of, 57,
    83–84, 154; and interracial sexual-
    ity, 98–99; intimidation by, 83; re-
    spect for, achieved in sport, 56; and
    team friendships, 90–91. *See also*
    Race
Bob G., 97, 98
Body: and identity, 121–25; as instru-
    ment, 62, 77; and mind, 62–64; as
    weapon, 64–71, 81, 152
Bodybuilding, gay, 157–58
Bonding: dominance, 137; male, 91–
    92, 95, 96, 107
Boston Globe, 170
Boston Herald, 85
Bouton, Jim, 126
Boy Scouts of America, 14, 18

Bradley, Bill, 91; *Life on the Run*, 85
Breadwinner ethic, and success and
    care, 137–42
Bredemeier, Brenda, 68, 70
Brent F., 29–30, 59, 74, 87, 100–101,
    141
Brittan, Arthur, 100
Brown, Jim, *Out of Bounds*, 97–98
Brownmiller, Susan, 15
Bryant, Ron, 124
Bryson, Lois, 15

Calvin H., 24–25, 52, 54, 56, 94–95,
    134
Campbell, Scott, 86
Cancian, Francesca, 92
Care: for children, 137–42; and suc-
    cess and breadwinner ethic, 137–42
Career, end of athletic, 111–14; class
    differences in, 114–18; as crisis of
    masculine identity, 118–28
Carrigan, Tim, 156
Carroll, John, 149–50
Chaikin, Tommy, 78
Children, men's attitudes toward, 143–
    45
Chodorow, Nancy, 20
Chris H., 25, 46, 90, 93, 128, 137; end
    of career of, 112, 113–14; his life
    after sport, 129–31, 132, 133, 134,
    142; and work and family at mid-
    life, 146, 148
Cincinnati Bengals, 85
Clarence T., 58, 59, 94, 103, 123–24;
    and feminism, 161–62, 163
Class differences: and early commit-
    ments to sport, 37–41; and public
    success, 133–37; in retirement and
    disengagement, 114–18; and
    schools and peers, 52–60. *See also*
    Social class

235